PENGUIN BOOKS

# See Me Rolling

Lottie Jackson is a writer, editor and disability activist. Featured in the *Sunday Times Style*'s Women of the Year 2020 as 'an important emerging voice', her work offers a vital dissection of the myths that beset disability. She has written for British *Vogue*, *Elle*, the *Guardian*, *Sunday Times* and *Telegraph*, bringing her fresh perspective to the most urgent conversations of today that strike at the heart of identity, social progress and diversity. In 2020 she was selected for Penguin Random House's award-winning WriteNow programme.

T0358800

# See Me Rolling

*On Disability, Equality and*
*Ten-Point Turns*

## LOTTIE JACKSON

PENGUIN BOOKS

PENGUIN BOOKS

UK | USA | Canada | Ireland | Australia
India | New Zealand | South Africa

Penguin Books is part of the Penguin Random House group of companies
whose addresses can be found at global.penguinrandomhouse.com

Penguin
Random House
UK

First published by Hutchinson Heinemann in 2023
Published in Penguin Books 2024
001

Copyright © Lottie Jackson, 2023

The moral right of the author has been asserted

Epigraph from *Being Heumann* by Judith Heumann and Kristen Joiner published
by WH Allen. Copyright © Judith Heumann and Kristen Joiner 2021.
Reprinted by permission of Penguin Books Limited.

Epigraph from *The Mysterious Stranger* by Mark Twain (1916).

Epigraph from 'Not Dark Yet'. Words and Music by Bob Dylan.
Copyright © 1997 UNIVERSAL TUNES. All Rights Reserved. Used by Permission.
Reprinted by Permission of Hal Leonard Europe Ltd.

Typeset in 12.16/14.3 pt Garamond MT Std by Integra Software
Services Pvt. Ltd, Pondicherry
Printed and bound in Great Britain by Clays Ltd, Elcograf S.p.A.

The authorised representative in the EEA is Penguin Random House Ireland,
Morrison Chambers, 32 Nassau Street, Dublin D02 YH68

A CIP catalogue record for this book is available from the British Library

ISBN: 978–1–529–15605–8

www.greenpenguin.co.uk

MIX
Paper | Supporting
responsible forestry
FSC
www.fsc.org    FSC® C018179

Penguin Random House is committed to a
sustainable future for our business, our readers
and our planet. This book is made from Forest
Stewardship Council® certified paper.

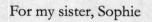
For my sister, Sophie

Change never happens at the pace we think it should. It happens over years of people joining together, strategizing, sharing, and pulling all the levers they possibly can. Gradually, excruciatingly slowly, things start to happen, and then suddenly, seemingly out of the blue, something will tip.

— Judith Heumann

[Humanity] has unquestionably one really effective weapon — laughter. Power, money, persuasion, supplication, persecution — these can lift at a colossal humbug — push it a little — weaken it a little, century by century; but only laughter can blow it to rags and atoms at a blast. Against the assault of laughter nothing can stand.

— Mark Twain

Behind every beautiful thing there's been some kind of pain.

— Bob Dylan

# Contents

# Introduction

*Disability n. / ˌdis-ə-ˈbi-lə-tē / (pl. disabilities)*

1. an illness, injury, or condition that makes it difficult for someone to do the things that other people do
2. a disadvantage

I'm going to level with you. Forget everything you've been led to believe about disability. You've been sold a lie. Disability is not a laminated blue badge nor an accessibility-themed emoji. And it's certainly not a members-only club where the cognoscenti are granted VIP status, amid the chintz walls, shadow-strewn mahogany and heady flow of negronis.

But it's quite simple actually. Disability is the resistance to let your body define you, it's the everyday and it's the future of missed opportunity. It's also the uproarious triumphs and quirky adaptations that make life that little bit smoother. Have *you* tried a one-touch tin opener? But most of all, it's a steely grip on optimism – the sheer refusal to give up when everything, for a while, feels bleak.

I've spent the past several years trying to negotiate a new relationship to my physical abilities, fighting the internal, unceasing frustration that I can no longer nip to the shops just for the hell of it, or ramble through the city placing one foot in front of the other. To zip, dash, dart and dive are deleted from my lexicon. But their trace remains – the feeling of striding along rain-dashed, glistening streets. Drippy street lamps swallowed up by the evening vibrations of the city; the metallic thrum of traffic bouncing down cobbled alleys, as the waggling tongues of strangers suck you in. All those magical, spontaneous freedoms that can now feel out of reach.

Since birth I've had a generalised muscle-weakness disability, a rare, non-progressive condition affecting my physical strength. For a long time, this condition didn't pose many constraints on my day-to-day life. I grew up with the belief that most things were achievable and nothing insurmountable. Then, plot twist: just as I was approaching adulthood, I faced several years of intermittent, yet severe illness (such as serious pneumonia), which entailed long spells in intensive care. This has significantly impacted my mobility and stamina – just getting around has become more challenging, so I'm dependent on places being easy to access. It has also affected the physical strength of my voice and, due to factors like noisy environments, it is sometimes hard to make myself heard or speak at length.

Now, there's an infinite vulnerability that comes with knowing that my experience in the world is shaped by elements out of my control. Being heavily reliant on external circumstances, like the accessibility of buildings or tolerant attitudes, is daunting – at times, nails-on-chalkboard excruciating. I have been forced to accept unwanted limits on my independence.

In my head, I wade and paddle through the currents of the past, of adventure and blissful possibility. I try to immerse myself in the ripples of normality. To forget this can no longer be actioned through my body and hold on to the vestiges of my past self. But for every reverie, there comes that crest of breathless realisation. Naturally, it's easy to feel both furious and fatalistic about this. To tell myself that all these limits placed on my power makes it hardly worth utilising at all. But a new reality has given me something I never expected – something that has struck my soul, defining my perspective in ways that I am only beginning to unravel.

Disruption has been the trigger for an invigorating purpose, creativity and ambition in my life. What was once dismantling, is now anchoring. I'll admit it has taken time to unearth this personal truth. To discard the exhausting stigmas and enraging delusions about disability that have tried to engulf me. And accept that my disability is a source of inner strength and vitality, not weakness.

As I scrawled and furiously typed, this book presented itself as a chance to make sense of what I have gained and, in turn, who I have become. It has reminded me that, no matter how challenging it feels to be restricted, I now have something hard-won and irreplaceable: the way I connect with the world. On every page, I saw my ability to extract humour, compassion, truth and beauty, even from the most unexpected places. This hasn't come about by chance. It has come about through struggle, defiance and unfaltering love – the sum of my experiences. So whether it's the tale of my narcoleptic driving instructor (humour), a timely mug of NHS tea (compassion) or my sister's unsolicited mullet (beauty?), there is meaning and action to be found far beyond the material constraints of the body.

But do not mistake this as Pollyannaism, or a fool's paradise. Inside this book lies a different kind of freedom – one that I believe is politically and philosophically important. As I push against a culture that demands physical perfection, I want to show what can be achieved when we rewrite the rules of a 'meaningful' existence, and expand our ideas of what constitutes a 'normal' body.

'Disability is not a brave struggle,' as the playwright Neil Marcus attests, 'it's an ingenious way to live.' This is perhaps the most intriguing and incisive statement that has been written on disability. But, right now, our culture refuses to accept its truth. Instead, everything about disability is grotesquely warped and twisted. Too often the perception of being disabled is locked into an archaic stereotype, where someone's body immediately defines whether they're to be pitied or feared. Our collective stance on disability holds about as much nuance as a pantomime dame. Like Widow Twankey's failure to convincingly portray the emotional landscape of a beleaguered housewife, we have squashed down the disabled experience into simplistic, reductive and often farcical terms. Disability stereotypes are illusions – no more real than the Missus Twankey's sock-stuffed bust, polyester tresses and melting beauty spot.

There's no denying that disability is still configured through a distorted lens. Research by the charity Scope reveals a staggering two-thirds of the public feel uneasy talking to disabled people, simply through fear of coming across as patronising or not knowing how to act. However, when it comes to millennials – a subgroup defined by progressive politics and liberal ideologies – the outlook is particularly alarming. For all our loud declarations of allyship, millennials are twice as likely as boomers to feel awkward around people with disabilities, while a fifth of 18 to

34-year-olds admit to avoiding interactions entirely because they're unsure how to communicate. If the next generation perceives disability as something problematic, or unreadable, are we going backwards?

Our social angst is underpinned by the fact that we live in a world that idolises able-bodiedness and catastrophises any sign of physical imperfection. While I might use a mobility scooter to help me travel around outdoors, it should not be a mark of defeat, embarrassment nor anything that should change how I am perceived. A scooter has given me an independence I otherwise couldn't imagine. But, regardless of the reality, lazy narratives will be deployed to make sense of what is seen as 'abnormal' or strange – partly because we lack the language and confidence to interpret such a diverse category of identity.

This exact ideal was blown apart in the public consciousness in the spring of 2019. During a midweek trip to Disneyland, the actor Selma Blair was photographed in a wheelchair following her MS diagnosis, spawning news headlines across the globe. This was more than your typical celebrity sighting. The media, hungry for clickbait, tried to rewrite the narrative of Blair's body. The presence of four chrome wheels was surely an indication that her condition had deteriorated? What else? Under the flash of the paparazzo's lens, Blair was portrayed as 'confined' to the wheelchair – or in her words, she was sloppily recast as 'one foot in the grave'. The incident laid bare the paradox of hyper-visibility and invisibility which is central to the disabled experience. Blair was stared and gawked at, yet her status as a human being and speaking subject was rendered almost invisible, just like one of those elusive Hidden Mickeys. Eager to regain control of her self-image, she spoke out on Instagram to almost

2 million followers: 'I can walk. Don't worry folks. But that uses up the whole day of energy . . . there is no shame in using whatever you can to get around.' Her post became a reminder of our impulse to ascribe false meanings upon the disabled body, inflicting sensationalist agendas without really 'seeing' the person.

As a society, we are criminally obsessed with outward appearances. From the tabloids to the streets, pinpointing the 'perfect' body has become a national spectator sport. The shame that surrounds illness or so-called deformity is devastating; oppressive even. Just a glance can spark that probing question, *'What's wrong with her?'* The very existence of this dichotomy of 'wrong' or 'right' exposes the stigma attached to disability – we must fit the mould or be seen as aesthetically flawed. Then, if you don't look disabled 'enough', it's quite the reversal of fortunes, as those with invisible disabilities still beg for the right to be seen and heard.

So, why do these deep-rooted misconceptions matter so much? Or, to phrase it rather crudely – why should you care? It is this lack of awareness that creates harmful everyday inequalities. Painful myths do not only exist in the mind, in print or as spoken words; they are fuelling disabled people's exclusion across all arenas of life: education, work, travel, relationships and love. Each false image, every whispered anxiety, translates into the discriminatory conditions of the physical world.

Take for instance, a standard shopping excursion. Let's be real – someone riding in on a mobility scooter is not currently construed as your archetypal fashion consumer. But this false assumption has tangible consequences when businesses often fail to consider diverse abilities in retail spaces. On a shopping trip, I'll likely encounter all manner of *It's a Knockout*-style obstacles. Retailers are, by law, required to make their shops accessible but a few rounds in the wringer and I can confirm, reader: they are not. After being 'regrettably' turned away from several shop buildings, due to stepped entrances and no portable access ramps to escort my Pride Go Go (the no-frills Škoda hatchback of the mobility scooter trade), I refuse to surrender. Finally, I zoom into a shop with a level threshold. But, with display counters packed in from hither to nither and a thoroughfare tighter than a gnat's chuff, I don't much fancy my chances here either. Performing what you would probably classify as a ten-point turn, I find myself slammed against a stack of rhinestone cowboy boots and some kooky porkpie hats. In a bid to manoeuvre back to the entrance, I slip the speed down from 'hare' to 'turtle' mode and galumph into a trunk of vintage hosiery as I go. Leaving the shop, I brace myself for the inevitable whiplash as I career over a Persian rug – endeavouring to avoid the tasselled fringing getting caught in my wheels. Not today, Satan. To say this particular trip had been smoother than my first fateful outing on the mobility scooter would be a wild understatement. That day I careered off a path and found myself wedged midway onto a grass verge, narrowly missing a honeysuckle bush. It was deeply uncool. A wheel spin later, and it was impossible to reverse off. Fortunately, some passers-by witnessed my sudden off-roading and, to much amusement, we successfully heaved it off the grass.

Fixing social inequality starts with a new willingness to really 'see' disability for what it is – an identity defined by innovation and resilience, not failure. Until we stop the dangerous fallacies that swarm around disability, how can we truly accept or accommodate anyone who strays outside of able-bodied norms?

It is easy to forget that disability is a socially constructed phenomenon. By which I mean, it is not just someone's biological make-up that classifies them as 'disabled'. Rather, disability is defined by our hostile built and cultural environments that stipulate what a 'normal' body should be able to accomplish. In my case, disability does not only live within my body; it lurks within stairwells, behind heavy doors, and even the cramped aisles of that quaint little vintage store. In Sara Hendren's *What Can a Body Do?*, she explores the spatial politics of the world we live in, who it's built for and where disability is located within this framework. 'Ability and disability may be in part about the physical state of the body,' Hendren confirms, 'but they are also produced by the relative flexibility or rigidity of the built world, its capacity to bend or adapt in a dance with bodies in a range of states.' Limitations emerge when society operates with a monolithic sense of human ability, when a fixed level of strength, mobility and social conduct is the gatekeeper to success. By failing to address everyday barriers that exist for all people with disabilities, exclusion is written in the world around us.

Right now, ableism is systemic. It's an insidious force that infects yet remains invisible to the naked eye. The presumption, if you're disabled, is that you lack the required elements for full participation in society. You are condemned to exist in the margins. And from there, you must seek a cure for your misfortune. Without even realising it, disabilities are seen in terms of deficit and loss. The academic Dr Sami Schalk identifies this as the 'common-sense nature of ableism in our culture', noting how 'the belief that a disabled life is inherently a lesser life and that non-disabled people represent the ideal' often goes 'unnoticed' and 'unquestioned'.

The act of sifting out this prejudice is impossible when we are failing to identify it in the first place.

As I sat down to begin writing this book in the spring of 2020, the world stood united against another indiscriminate contagion: Covid-19. Strict travel bans, quarantine orders, hand sanitiser with a price per ml to rival Crème de la Mer, and Captain Tom's inexplicably agile hips, shook the nation. It was terrifying. The manager of my local post office was even sleeping with a metal colander atop her head to arm against Covid transmission in 4G (the logic was shaky, yet her conviction unwavering). I, like many other people with disabilities, started shielding at home, due to being at high risk of getting extremely ill. Time coalesced into a singular, incomprehensible moment as entire cities fell silent, abandoned and then embalmed as concrete monuments of a past life, much like an urban Atlantis. But this state of apocalyptic uncertainty gave rise to new introspections.

For me, the pandemic illustrated the possibilities of transformation. It was no longer inconceivable that our society can be radically disrupted, or reformed, overnight. In that Damascene moment, I saw that we possess the necessary force to redefine our value systems, that we are sitting on the precipice of the greatest opportunity to seize change. Now is the time to facilitate deep, profound shifts in perspective.

Across the coming essays, I will sculpt a new space to address the depth of stigmas and share my empowering vision for disability – one that is unclouded by historic oppressions, sentimentalism or masked agendas. At the core of each essay, I pose overarching philosophical questions: what does it mean to 'recover' in the aftershocks of life-altering illness? Can we reframe our sexual desires to eliminate ableism in the bedroom? Where can we find freedom without the ability to seamlessly move through the world? What will it take for classrooms to become crucibles of change, teaching us to see beyond stigmatising labels? Is it possible to expand beauty ideals and finally liberate the disabled body? Do technology and the internet promise a radical, inclusive reality for disabled people? And can we redefine our ableist ideas of productivity in an age of non-stop, anonymous labour?

I have settled on these questions because, to me, their answers hold the key to obliterating disability inequality – purging society of that long-standing myth that 'a disabled life is inherently a lesser life'. They represent the puzzle pieces which, slotted together, might achieve something coherent and beautiful. As I sift through, I'll hit stumbling blocks, make errors, discover many lost pieces, and surrender to the possibility that the answers aren't always waiting. But, regardless, I am writing the future on my own terms, refusing to allow the indefensible exclusions of the past to continue and constructing a portal to a new era.

At times, I grow conscious of how I am fighting to change a world I am not currently a part of – can I accurately judge the state of it when it's captured and distilled through my television screen, or refracted on social media? I feel breathless at injustice yet equally so by my limited capacity to change it. In these moments of questioning, I glance over to a quote scribbled in purple ink on a Post-it, which is lying, tea-splashed, beside my laptop. 'Changing the story isn't enough in itself, but it has often been foundational to real changes. Making an injury visible and public is often the first step to remedying it, and political change often follows culture, as what was long tolerated is seen to be intolerable.' These words, extracted from Rebecca Solnit's essay collection, *Hope in the Dark*, hit me with renewed vigour. Real change, as Solnit describes, takes place not in the halls of power but in the minds of those who are discounted as mere spectators. This speaks profoundly to me, and the disabled experience in general, as physical limitations may preclude any real-world political action or protest. Sometimes it doesn't matter where you are positioned, the shadows or the spotlight; the revolution that counts is conceived in the imagination – so long as you have hope.

Today I have that ingredient to change – hope. And urgency. Disability is part of the human condition. But still, for the 13.9 million disabled people in the UK (over one-fifth of the population), inequalities are widening. If you're disabled, you are more than twice as likely to be unemployed, living in food poverty or experiencing domestic abuse than your non-disabled counterpart. These inequalities will breed in silence unless we strive for change. The moment we speak out and tackle the negative perceptions that beset disability, we can begin to eradicate these social barriers and reimagine a different future. A future where disability doesn't limit your chances and adopting an inclusive attitude is the most radical thing you can do.

Over the course of writing this book, I have made life-affirming, often hilarious and joyful revelations about myself at every turn – seeking out hundreds of enriching insights from writers, philosophers, activists and film-makers throughout history. I want to give you a window into my reality and inspire you to see new ways of existence. So in every aspect of life, I will redefine what it means to be disabled.

# The Art of Recovery

Growing up, the term 'life-changing' appeared devastatingly glamorous. Imagine one greedy bite of the life-changing tagliolini all'arrabbiata, at the kind of Tuscan trattoria you'll only find scribbled in the margin of a century-old travel guide. Or a life-changing expedition to chase the aurora borealis, where a moment of euphoria is awoken by the dancing symphony of emerald light – the horizon aglow with another plane of existence. Or even that carefully constructed illusion of the life-changing 'gap yah'. The idea of submitting to a new reality once seemed aspirational; sacred even. But now it's irreversibly tainted. A life changed is no longer a rapturous celebration or a flamboyant boast. It's the devastation that strikes when your body writes its own rules.

In time, life changed. At my wrist, the fettered pinch of a hospital ID band became the fulcrum of my existence. My strength and stamina were diminished by an endless succession of illness, requiring long stints in intensive care. While I've had a muscle weakness condition since birth, my childhood passed by without substantial need for medical intervention. I was lulled into a false belief that this steady flow of life was to be my reality, I suppose. But illness strikes like a rupture in the dark. I ricocheted from a world where everything seemed possible, expectant and open – to a realm where almost everything came with caveat, curtailment and rice pudding. As the writer Susan Sontag puts it, 'Illness is the night-side of life, a more onerous citizenship.' We all hold dual citizenship to the kingdom of the well and the kingdom of the sick, but sooner or later, Sontag concedes, 'each of us is obliged, at least for a spell, to identify ourselves as citizens of that other place'. Like a clerical slip-up, my voyage to 'that other place' was fast-tracked.

While my peers were out discovering independence by way of 4am taxi rides, forensically tagged Facebook albums and a roster of going-out tops – the sartorial signifier of someone who is becoming the person they once hoped to be – I was left frustrated as my body pulled me back. The tonnage of an NHS blanket was a constant. The punishing aftertaste of liquid Voltarol was persistent (what promised the flavour profile of tutti-frutti, delivered a casket of pot-pourri. God, I can still taste it.) And the low vibrations of machines working to keep people alive were, almost, uninterrupted. It was impossible to forget that the life I was supposed to be living was out there, waiting, breathing. To ignore the disorientating truth that who I ended up becoming could be so polluted by the unforeseen. The series of admissions to intensive care affected my mobility and the strength of my voice. Every missed eighteenth birthday party or cancelled plan became reminders of the splinters in my life, of how I was failing to recover. I desperately needed to find a way back to my true self. But for this to happen I had to make sense of this turbulent journey and forge a new path for myself.

So, how do you reconcile the process of recovery with life-changing illness? If recovery demands a return to your previous state of health, are the two fundamentally incompatible? A punishing oxymoron, if there ever was. Can we resign ourselves to the impossibility of wholeness without self-destruction?

In reality, recovery is more than a physical phenomenon. It's not the first unassisted step, the removal of stitches – a slip, pull and a tug – nor the vanishing act of a storied scar. It's a state of returning to the essence of who you are, rediscovering yourself in the face of a terrifying betrayal of the body.

I am a testament to the possibility of transformation, of unity after dislocation. When the constraints placed on my body felt suffocating, there was lightness and humour waiting, even when I failed to see it. Whether it was a patient's rib-tickling, Shakespearean-esque monologue from behind the drawn hospital curtain. The molten apple pie that, nearly, gave rise to a dozen critical incident forms. Or a nurse's contretemps with a DIY eyebrow tint. These were the pockets of light – fluttering in, as reminders of all that existed beyond the bounds of illness. Reader, things get pretty dark for a while, but beneath these fragments is everything that made me.

I've never translated or condensed these experiences into words. In an act of self-preservation, I've refused to give my trauma the narrative shape it demands, to pick what adjectives, metaphors to use – until now. Is it even possible to impose coherence on something so disordered? To capture the inchoate in lined sentences, boxed paragraphs. Tempering it into words feels like a betrayal of the actual experience. Nothing could render it in linear, or three dimensions. The visceral reality. And I don't want it to. I cannot offer a facsimile – my thoughts are so full of contradictions that narration is almost an impossibility. I find that I hardly know what I think. But whatever form it takes, the story-telling process offers a healing effect. 'The need to narrate the strange experience of illness,' writes the medical and psychological anthropologist Cheryl Mattingly, 'is part of the very human need to be understood by others, to be in communication even if from the margins.' Illness and dis-ability can unsettle core aspects of identity, including social roles and relationships, and so narratives help us make sense of these disruptions. To tell a story is to slather oneself in a psychological salve.

After month-long stints in intensive care, I felt alienated from myself – I was institutionalised and little more than a ten-digit NHS number. I became painfully acclimatised to the clanging trolley wheels, perturbed voices behind curtains and unremitting screeches of infusion pumps, ventilators and bedside monitors. If a whiff of alcohol gel cut through the static air, I knew this heralded the clumsy wallop of pneumatic doors. The jolt of adrenaline as you realise those heavy footsteps are coming towards your bed-space to announce some new findings and, perhaps, a path forward.

Then after-hours when the lights are dimmed, the scene transforms into a chiaroscuro. A nurses' station is the central illumination, while a triptych of LED panels – the digital intimations of life – cast their blue aura into the darkness. Later, the scene is disrupted. A patient next door receives a visit from the junior doctor, and the strip lights are switched on, 3M sterile plastic packets torn open in preparation. Next, the on-call registrar, and then the consultant, arrives. A gathering, mounting tension. Decisions that cannot be delayed. I became attuned to these diligent rhythms. The act of sustaining life – how its kinetic and emotional cadences rise and fall like the trace of an erratic electrocardiogram.

The gritty realities and theatrics of the hospital environment are examined in Lucia Berlin's short story collection, *A Manual for Cleaning Women*. With piercing accuracy, she dissects the sensory overload. The story 'Emergency Room Notebook, 1977' takes the form of an auto-fiction – weaving Berlin's own experiences working as a nurse with that of her namesake narrator, Lucia. From the patient's dull skin to the coarse blankets, her surroundings are rendered in greyscale, yet there is still much to be observed, to take fascination in: 'I like the fact that, in emergency, everything is reparable or not. The pace and excitement of ten or fifteen people, performers . . . it's like opening night at the theatre. The patients, if they are conscious, take part too, if just by looking interested in all the goings on. They never look afraid.' Here lies the bizarre otherworldliness of the hospital ward. Like Beckett's Theatre of the Absurd, it is a realm where time is disordered, it hangs on action, and the mysterious facts of the human condition are laid bare. The shedding of life's comforting illusions is borne nobly, as aches and despair become entwined with a sense of resolve.

As someone who dealt with severe health problems, requiring her to carry an oxygen tank for a decade, Lucia Berlin understood the need to cut through the pain, and focus on that intransigent glimmer of hope. I, too, have observed this coexistence of horror and raw determination. In the moments where everything quickens – hurried footsteps, chaotic hands and the rustling of plastic aprons – life slows to a point where you are met with a simple binary existence. The liminality of living or dying. In its most perverse moments, recovery is about release. There is something freeing about everything fading to meaninglessness apart from one solitary task. Just to survive.

Illness holds a curious power. I felt isolated from myself, yet in some strange way, I've also never been compelled to show so much of who I am. Hospitalisation forced me to access my inner strength. The fight to survive is what makes us human. It lays dormant within all of us, as the vestiges of our ancestry. Once unleashed, this state of being is hard to move away from; it's a skin you wear and cannot shed even as the years place distance between you.

It strikes me, however, that the majority of recovery narratives centre on stripped identities and stolen agency. In *Constellations: Reflections from Life*, Sinéad Gleeson articulates the strange phenomenology of illness, and the shocking, self-effacing reality of existing within the confines of hospital walls. For her, entering into the medical sphere involves a transference of power. At once her body is placed into the hands of doctors. She must bequeath the crimson liquid in her veins, abdicate control and surrender herself to all the associated risks of infection, of not waking up. 'To become a patient is an act of transmutation, from well to sick, liberated citizen to confined inpatient,' she writes. Her concept of 'a hospital body' reflects how our identity is radically rewritten under the absence of free will and free movement. Unmoored from family, careers, everyday lives, a patient is 'not a person' but a 'medicalised version of the self'.

Gleeson's account of self-erasure recalls one of the most famous texts in this canon, Oliver Sacks' *A Leg to Stand On*, where he declares that patienthood is a state of dehumanisation. 'It is strictly analogous to becoming a prisoner, and humiliatingly reminiscent of one's first day at school. One is no longer a person – one is now an inmate.' But Gleeson goes a step further, conveying the feminist roots and gender politics of her pain, how her experience as a patient is entangled with an inheritance of female bodily shame. As she finds herself trapped in a panopticon-like hospital, her body is under constant surveillance, always visible in some way, if not always seen. With a roster of male doctors delivering her care, she cannot detach the 'overwhelming embarrassment' she feels as a patient from her experience as a woman coming of age in Ireland, circumscribed by laws that refuse to recognise her bodily autonomy. 'I wanted to make myself smaller, to minimise the space I took up ... I knew from pop culture that I should *want* to be looked at, but when regarded I didn't know how to feel.'

When a body is placed under a microscopic gaze – examined under anaesthetic, heartbeats tallied, swab samples taken – I agree, this is a terrifying existence. But under a total, and what felt like irrevocable, loss of control, I simply did not care. In those hours and days, I was in my own head. Self-consciousness was a luxury. More than anything I wanted the solution, the key that could unlock me from that desperate reality and push me towards normality, whatever that may look like. Self-perception and the ability to conceive myself in the eyes of others would come later, perhaps as an early intimation of my recovery.

Waking up on an intensive care ward is like realising you've dozed off mid-performance at the theatre. Lights up, you could find an entirely new cast of patients, medical staff, masked faces – all with designated roles to play. A revolving stage rearranged between sets. In the same way that props are wheeled out from the wings, previously unseen machines emerge onto the scene, their irregular, syncopated rhythms falling between existing beats.

On one particular morning I awoke to a new arrival on the ward. As a mark of initiation, the middle-aged patient was given his obligatory 'obs' before close family members were allowed to visit – 'real-world' figures breaking down the fourth wall. I was sleuthing this from behind a curtain, mind. My account here could be wildly inaccurate. Whether an air flow mattress was being pumped up through an inserted tube, or the man was being delivered a thermometer up the jacksie, I was potentially (and mercifully) none the wiser. Once charts had been marked up and four-way colour biros retracted, his wife pushed her way through the double doors. Dressed in a crimson eighties power suit with bolshie shoulder pads, this woman was on a mission – and that mission was to aggressively plump her husband's pillows. The pummelling! Was it Mike Tyson behind the curtain? Trailing behind her was a teenage girl in school uniform and duffle coat (assumed progeny). Just as her squeaky footsteps approached my bedspace, we exchanged glances. In that moment, I saw myself through her eyes. I was not dissimilar to her in many ways, yet I was a person who belonged to this unnerving environment. I had crossed over into another dimension. I thought about what my friends were up to right then, and experienced the full, devastating weight of just how far I had to go before I could get back to anything like normality, to the other side.

The hospital is a place so alien to ordinary existence that even as patients we assume ourselves to be the anomaly. I felt like a stranded visitor, at odds with the grim paraphernalia of sickness. In a *New Yorker* piece, the humourist David Sedaris raises a critical point about self-perception in the clinical space. While undergoing a bladder biopsy, or what he calls the thrusting of 'a Golden Globe Award up my ass', he wants to be the exception. 'I'd hoped to stick out in the radiology wing, to be too youthful or hale to fit in,' Sedaris writes. But then, a point of anagnorisis is reached – he is like any other patient. 'Looking around the waiting area, I saw that everyone was roughly my age, and either was bald or had gray hair. If anybody belonged here, it was me.' As someone full of individuality, he didn't see himself reflected in the stale, soulless medical space. This is an important concept for illness, and disability at large. Too often we see disability as something that is trapped in this unfamiliar, clinical world. I quickly reminded myself that illness and any new physical limitations would never define me. This wasn't all I was. I was just out of context.

Existential crisis averted, I turned back to the flickering TV screen in front of me. For a few days of my hospital admission, I'd commandeered a television unit on wheels. You wish you were me. Terrestrial channels were the sum of its offering, and I think it had a slit for VHS tapes. This was around the time of an election, so it was a Channel 4 political debate on the viewing agenda for me. 'You sure you're up to this, chick?' said a nurse with a knowing glance, after overhearing some performative ramblings of an MP while she tucked in the hospital corners on my bed, with the nimble pinch of a Japanese origamist. I threw a convincing smile back. Curiously, she appeared to be monitoring my blood pressure more attentively that evening – perhaps wise?

One morning you are suddenly able to see the life that was ripped from you, is waiting. My ability to find hilarity in even the most hellish scenarios is always the first indication that I am coming back to myself. The last time I was in hospital, it was the week-long saga about a patient's motionless bowels that provided the necessary levity among the traumatic rounds of blood-taking and frank exchanges over the bed-side. Just as a hospital porter was summoned to take the poor chap for an investigatory scan, the urgent rush of a brigade of nurses to his bedside indicated a Vesuvian eruption. The whiff around the papery curtain told me that the enema had done what the laxatives could not. While it was too exhaust-ing to let out a laugh, I couldn't help but give a cheeky snig-ger from the other side of the cerulean curtain – a mixture of pure horror and relief that I could once again find mirth.

The following day, I awoke to the sight of a nurse frantic-ally darting across the ward (ever a cause for alarm). But curiously there were no emergency sirens, crash teams or glaring red lights, just farcical cries of 'Please! Derek! Put your clothes back on! There are ladies present.' After five minutes of trying to coax him back into a standard-issue hospital gown, the elderly gentleman admitted defeat. But as he reluctantly turned back to his sparse white bed space, the futile rag was gaping in all the wrong places, leaving his backside hanging out as brazen as a baboon. This was drap-ing indeed, but not as Donatella foretold on the Versace catwalks circa '98.

I tore my eyes away from the marauding nudist, pressing feverishly at the bed controls in a bid to lower myself out of his eyeline. The bed mechanics were unresponsive; they had stalled. I'd had enough drama for one day. Then, as if the bed had pent up all its energy, I was sent crashing down in one cacophonous blow, garnering concerned looks from visiting families.

Privacy, on a hospital ward, is as tenuous as the slip knot on Derek's gown. Dirty laundry is aired, gazes are averted, and silhouettes of bodies persist through the wisp-like curtains. Over the course of a day, private lives unfold like the plot of a Noël Coward original — frankly, it's a task to keep up. Door slamming was simply replaced by a sassy zipping of the bedside curtain, which naturally got jammed on its runners, sabotaging any dramatic effect. I was privy to curious goings-on, marital bust-ups and sometimes graphic, scatological details that had me retching into my bowl of soggy Frosties. Feigning ignorance at some scandalous tidbit that was thrown over the curtained threshold was a skill I quickly picked up.

Hospital lifts, in particular, are like confession booths. No topic is off limits, no gory detail is spared — something to do with lost inhibitions and vertigo, I guess. What goes down between the red floor and the yellow floor remains under the Hippocratic oath. Overheard conversations could spark endless intrigue: the growth that was prised from a woman's left nostril and, mysteriously, had to be shipped off to Brazil. Why?? The cold case post-mortem where all the bone samples — femur, tibia, ulna — transpired to be from a KFC family bucket. How?? The Polish teen who awoke from anaesthesia with a thick Liverpudlian accent, requesting the Scouse delicacy of Wet Nelly pudding. What the actual fuck??

In those lifts, you were guaranteed to live a thousand lives — Scheherazade could never. After four weeks stuck in a 2-metre-squared bedspace, I was venturing out on an excursion (physio's orders) to the main foyer. As I headed into a packed lift, a thirty-something man with a foot-long baguette under his arm was discussing a medical matter with his friend. 'It was awful,' he whispered. 'Martin had to hide it before anyone could see.' As is the way with the lift confessional, the noun in the tale is often unidentified; particulars are sketchy. I, and the rest of the lift occupants, were nevertheless engrossed. 'Unfortunately, it got tangled in the bedsheets,' he continued. 'Then overnight it grew *this* long.' Without thinking we all looked up at once, desperate to get a profile on what 'it' could be and to what magnitudes it had grown – even a moribund woman strapped onto a gurney heaved herself around to get a look. The man had gestured the length of the cheese and pickle baguette. But with seven prying eyes now locked on him, he immediately fell silent, threw the baguette under his coat and absconded out the lift doors, his friend scuttling behind. We had been caught!

After a conspiratorial wink from a cleaner, I rattled down the corridors atop a hospital wheelchair – terrified to be out of the ward, and exhausted from trying to cling onto something that had as much gear control as a supermarket trolley plucked from a skip. My destination was the StockShop, the self-proclaimed 'home of retail therapy'. A beacon of mindless consumerism in humanity's hour of need. The customer journey, however, was chaotic. At the entrance aisle, I found everything from the eclectic to the damn right bewildering: buddha head planters stacked beside ginormous polka-dot knickers and kingfisher wind chimes. What horrors lay in the clearance aisle were not for the convalescent, nor anyone undergoing investigations for angina. I was just trundling past a lavender tea light set and gnome weather forecaster (apparently, two items deemed essential for a hospital admission) when it suddenly dawned on me what this place offered. The StockShop was the distraction we all seeked. From the family members anxiously awaiting news from post-op recovery, to the work experience students with blue lanyards and borrowed suits, it was our sanctuary. Items could be picked up and examined without really being seen – conversations, that once faltered, now scripted by these insane knick-knacks. For the first time, gazing at a *Live Laugh Love* door plaque, I almost forgot about the fluorescent-lit room, the empty bed upstairs, awaiting my return. Just to chance upon something so ridiculous and funny – something that took me outside of myself – was more revitalising than I had envisaged.

Finding laughter in the bleakest of moments is a gift, and a lifeblood. As the poet Martin Armstrong puts it, 'Under the spell of laughter, the whole man is completely and gloriously alive: body, mind and soul vibrate in unison . . . the mind flings open its doors and windows . . . its foul and secret places are ventilated.' Laughter is figured as an act of resuscitation – mental *and* physical. Scientific research has corroborated its therapeutic value, with humour proven to relieve symptoms of pain and enhance immunity. In one study, 85 per cent of patients felt that humour helped them to foster positive emotions and deal with the present by empowering hope. For me, humour can hide fractures and fault lines, collapsing the boundaries between the claustrophobic domain of recovery, and the inherent joy of the world outside. It moves us at a cellular level.

This connection between illness and humour has been a matter of philosophical intrigue. First articulated by the German philosopher Kant, the incongruity theory states that laughter arises when an experience breaks expected or typical patterns: 'In everything that is to excite a lively laugh there must be something absurd (in which the understanding, therefore, can find no satisfaction). Laughter is an affection arising from the sudden transformation of a strained expectation into nothing.' This is clearly ripe for the hospital setting where little goes to plan, bodies are perpetually off-script and absurdity is pumped out like gas and air.

There are numerous cultural examples of humour being used to grapple with the unexpected nature of illness or injury. After an accident resulted in the amputation of their lower legs, the writer Willem Helf began using social media to inject humour into their rehabilitation story – in their words, they do not have amputated legs, merely 'a minimalist body'. Named by *Vogue* as one of 'the sharpest wits on Twitter', the 29-year-old can turn 280 characters into a hilarious, compulsive work of unrelenting genius. 'The fact that I'm literally missing half my legs after a horrible accident and still am pissing myself abt [*sic*] whether I need to use retinol on my one tiny eye wrinkle', a typical late afternoon musing reads. Interspersed with mirror selfies flashing their rose gold prosthetic legs, Helf uses their seditious wit to deliver sobering messages on anything from the desexualisation of disabled people to why they'd like to abolish that intrusive question: 'What happened?' In an interview with the magazine, they spoke candidly about the need for humour among the frustration and boredom that comes with recovery: 'It can be hard to find the beauty in life when your body hurts.'

In a similar vein, the bestselling author and comedian Samantha Irby encapsulates the mutinies of chronic illness, filtering it through her self-deprecating and deliciously irreverent humour. A typical account will detail the countless indignities of a hospital stay: 'i [*sic*] spent five days on my back in the least sexy way imaginable, hooked up to monitors and machines with tubes going every which way, at the mercy of a huge group of very nice people who seemed to never *really* understand that forty-five minutes is not a very long time to let a bitch "sleep."' See, Irby is the kind of funny that is raw and spontaneous, never forced. However, she reminds us to tread carefully: 'People find their empathy center better when they're laughing,' she said in an interview with *The Nation*, but 'I never want anyone to think it doesn't hurt or that it's not inconvenient or I'm not struggling.' Dark humour has become a coping mechanism to shield her from the uncertainties of her arthritis, Crohn's disease and depression. It's about shifting the balance. If there's one hilarious aspect in a dire situation, she will play on this, tease it out and allow it to subsume the whole. 'My knee-jerk response to everything is to find the nugget of humour, because when shit is so terrible, I need to know can I laugh at that?' she said. 'If you can find the one absurd piece, it's like, "OK, this is ridiculous – I can deal with this."'

Gallows humour is also a pressure release valve for the medical staff who take on the minute-by-minute task of sustaining life. Adam Kay, former junior doctor and author of *This Is Going to Hurt*, appreciates the therapeutic potential of a good laugh – how it can act as a bungee cord, pulling you back from dark, craggy edges. 'It was going up to my hospital on-call room and writing down silly things, the disgusting things, the funny things,' Kay recalled in an interview with the *Observer*. 'I didn't really know this was why I was doing it, but in retrospect it's totally clear: I was looking for the shards of light among the dark.' Whether it's a sarcastic one-liner from the ward sister or an elderly patient savagely rejecting her prescription nightcap as 'cat piss', comedy offers resistance to the tug of despair.

I realise now that humour is more than a fleeting diversion, or a helium *Get Well Soon* balloon destined to slowly sink, pucker and pop. To suggest that laughter propels you from the tremendous confines of the body by means of distraction, gimmick or escapism is to underestimate its power. I want to say it helps you access a deeper understanding of yourself, or that it's some profound act of self-discovery, but I'm hardly sure that's true. In reality, humour serves as a reframing device that allows you to regain control of the narrative. To transform your darkness into something that one day might be easier to process. While the trauma does not fully dissipate, in some amorphous way, over time, humour will mattify and soften its iron fist. And potentially, construct new meaning, where the open promise of the future is there to claim.

Aside from regaining my sense of humour, the greatest leap towards recovery is the milestone of leaving hospital and returning home. I was still bruised from the drip lines and patched together with adhesive bandages. But instead of the 24/7 fluorescent glare of overhead strip lights, I was soaking up the warm sunlight of a springtime day. And in place of the cold, slip-resistant rubber flooring, I could sink my toes into plush carpet. It was healing. A placebo more potent than any pill you could swallow. That stillness of home holds instant restorative power.

However, there's a moment before discharge when the prospect of existing without a finger pulse oximeter becomes terrifying. With nothing to appraise your every breath and heartbeat, the fear of being left unplugged, floundering, is crippling. As I waited nervously to be picked up later that morning, a tea trolley lady sensed my sudden unease. 'Alright me babber?' she lovingly enquired as she readjusted the creases in her blue plastic apron. Vowing to bring over a 'nice cuppa' before the next drug round, an NHS tea sounded like nectar. Wasn't it the playwright Arthur Wing Pinero who said the humble teabag was the essence of hope? Well then, a pensive gaze into the sad grey dishwater before me was enough to bring on an existential crisis. The gesture, however, was everything.

I endeavoured to sip this cup of boiled despair as a nurse fashioned a chic updo for my imminent homecoming. After combing it through, spritzing on a can's-worth of dry shampoo, and twisting it up into a chignon, other nurses started to gather around the bedside and exclaim how amazing it looked. I think a nineties Angelina Jolie was referenced at one point. Curious to see how she had pulled off this wizardry, I caught sight of myself in the sink mirror as I was wheeled out. It was pure horror. But more than that, it's an emotional thing to catch yourself in a mirror after a month of hospitalisation. The act of reacquaintance with what you look like, and seeing the physical toll of the trauma, is a vital moment in recovery.

The following week, I sat down for an at-home appointment with an overenthusiastic occupational therapist named Sally-Ann. Her curly, bobbed hair was swinging wildly as she marvelled over an enormous brick of a brochure (this thing had a girth to rival the pre-Christmas Argos catalogue). Where I saw scary orthopaedic contraptions, this lady saw powerchair ponchos de rigueur, sultry easy-access bras, and 'boho' non-slip suede moccasin slippers with tassels. In her eyes, there was nothing a diamanté-encrusted Zimmer frame couldn't fix. After politely declining her offers, I felt obliged to try an easy-pull tights aid. I mean who doesn't find hosiery a faff? Its claim to 'restore dignity by allowing independence when putting on socks or hosiery' was intriguing. Could it be, as Sally-Ann so boldly claimed, 'revolutionary'? After one failed attempt to use the apparatus – getting in a red-faced tussle and snagging my tights in the process – I can confirm there was little dignity about it. But what are temporary and (well, allegedly) labour-saving adjustments mask a complex psychological recovery taking hold.

Just when the initial shock of illness dissipates and the needle punctures, scalpel incisions begin to heal over . . . bam! The ever-shifting yardstick of recovery hits you in the face. In a twisted paradox, recovery becomes more complicated, and potentially more devastating, when the physical trauma becomes entangled with all its social implications. Now comes the challenge of shoehorning myself back into my old life, of reinhabiting the space I once took up, of finding out whether I would slot into place. It was no longer a distant prospect, but an imminent reality creating constant internal friction.

Small, tentative steps into the outside world are unremittingly daunting – an instant where everything you've lost flickers into agonising focus, and the weight of having to recapture the scattered fragments of yourself is suffocating. It's like buckling on an old pair of patent Mary Janes, the stiffness of the leather squeaking and contorting your feet in a way that feels familiar, but foreign. Habituation seems impossible at first, but something you must dare to endure.

During these first few weeks, I'd describe a ten-minute trip for coffee down the road as intrepid. On one occasion, I ventured out with my parents to a quiet neighbourhood café – this was a kind of litmus test where failure is exhaustion. While I managed to remain cautiously optimistic and avoid feeling demoralised, the trip wasn't without a hitch. We mistimed it by mere minutes, finding ourselves wedged two tables away from an ex-hairdresser who we'd been surreptitiously avoiding since she gave my sister a mullet cut in 2004 (it took a year to grow out, but its vestigial stain lives on in the family photo album). The spectre of that cruel cut hung between the empty tables, as we avoided eye contact, grabbed the bill and then flounced out with all the subtlety of a spurned lover.

Until that point, the outside world had been transmitted through the 3-inch screen on my relic of a flip-top phone. I'd lived vicariously through quotidian text messages from friends. Their updates about a teacher who had gone off the rails, or the tale about a fluorescent acrylic nail found languishing in a bowl of carrot shavings in the canteen, were thrilling. Those questions of 'how are you?' or 'feeling any better?' would hang in the air. 'Better' was a mythical, ever-shifting concept – moving towards better was a Sisyphean task. I hardly knew how to articulate a reality that I still couldn't understand, not least in the perilous terrain of predictive text. It was like Sinéad Gleeson said: 'Illness is an outpost: lunar, Arctic, difficult to reach. The location of an unrelatable experience never fully understood by those lucky enough to avoid it.'

I began to resent my inability to detach myself from the identity of someone who'd been ill, to escape from the margins. The cadence of pity, prefixed by a knitted brow, became constant reminders of everything I wanted to push away from. I needed to desperately, and quickly, move on. I was flooded with an intense pressure to recover, and the inevitable dread that I was failing.

As anyone who has experienced serious illness will know, recovery isn't a linear process, and often it can be plagued by intense feelings of guilt and frustration. 'No one could tell me why I wasn't recovering, so I couldn't explain it to friends,' reveals 27-year-old Mimi Butlin who, after contracting viral meningitis in 2013, developed a pain condition called fibromyalgia. 'I honestly didn't even really know chronic illness existed. I didn't know there was a limbo where you were alive but you couldn't be fixed. I think the hardest part has been the constant grief – imagining what life would be like without pain, where I would be and what I would have accomplished.' For Mimi, recovery is now about acceptance but it took many years to find peace with her newly disabled self. Social media communities were pivotal to her healing, after creating the popular Instagram platform @cantgoout__imsick for people to share their experiences of disability and highlight unrepresented issues like the silencing of those with invisible illness. 'The community completely changed me and now I realise that just my existence makes me worthy of love, friendship and respect. I now battle a lot less with feeling like a burden.'

In the face of extreme health uncertainty, the power to remain resilient and keep going can be an overwhelming emotional strain. Five years ago, Charlotte Amor was bitten by a tick which caused neurological Lyme disease. This sparked a litany of symptoms like severe allergies, migraines and dizziness. But after months of being misdiagnosed with everything from anxiety to vomiting syndrome, it was hard to stay optimistic that recovery was possible. 'Living with uncertainty and a lack of hope is so difficult to come to terms with,' says the 29-year-old. 'I found it meant that I just couldn't relate to others, particularly friends and people my age. I have lost over half of my twenties to serious illness; it feels like grief.' For her, the disappointment and fear of failed treatments is a constant juggling act. Recently, she underwent a stem cell transplant in California which involved an entire year of feeling significantly worse before seeing improvements that saved her life. 'Count your successes and celebrate them; don't wait until being recovered to do this because it's not guaranteed. There is a life to be lived between illness and recovery.' When we are taught to desire perfection and completeness, it is counter-intuitive to feel contentment among the rubble. It takes courage to shake off that yearning for a legible existence and, instead, unearth new routes to pleasure.

Regaining any semblance of 'normal life' after severe illness is far from seamless. But, for young women who are already navigating a culture of strict expectations – dictating how they must behave and when they should reach set milestones in their career and personal lives – it's a fraught endeavour. While my friends and classmates were planning wild, parental-free getaways to the mythical strips of Ayia Napa, meeting life partners and ultimately plotting their futures in a way that was expected, if not prescribed, I was continually playing catch-up. If life was a dot-to-dot, I was under the care of a hyped-up, Crayola-wielding toddler, scribbling back and forth so the complete picture was failing to emerge. I had lost a sense of belonging without knowing how to articulate it. I am not sure I have ever reclaimed it, or if I should even want to.

Health issues amplify many of the life stresses that all millennial women confront. The strain runs even deeper when you're trapped in the slow cycle of recovery. In recent years, the concept of self-optimisation has been adopted by women, as an obsession and raison d'être. To be the opti-mised self, we must chase a kaleidoscope of social obliga-tions set forth by society. Here the dot-to-dot looks like: instant career success, a posse of selfie-ready friends, an intimate knowledge of reformer Pilates, and a boyfriend who can recite Ngozi Adichie's *We Should All Be Feminists*. We must also be fully versed in the incumbent practices of wellness, enthusiastically engaged in the monopoly of self-care. All to create the illusion that we are living our most shiny lives, that we are, above all, succeeding. Whether we're faking it or not is immaterial, because we're rewarded with the sweet, self-satisfying glow that we are doing what's expected of us. In a world where success is now measurable via social media, we exist under a rating system or barometer where *anyone* can level up. As Pandora Sykes, journalist and author of *How Do We Know We Are Doing It Right?*, explains, 'Self-optimisation challenges the idea that we are trapped in our own bodies – instead, our bodies can be upgraded like smartphones if we just commit to the change . . . [it's] about tweaking yourself so that you can operate harder or faster.'

But hang on, what does this mean for the women grap-pling with illness who cannot simply 'upgrade' their body to fulfil these scripted roles? Are those who are 'trapped' by physical constraints still held up to the same standards? In a game where it's all about getting better and becoming the superlative version of yourself, for me this is an exhausting, if not unwinnable, quest. I am a rule breaker, whether I like it or not. My body becomes a silent protest to the mores of womanhood. Choice is removed from the equation, and this can be painful to accept.

In Michele Lent Hirsch's book, *Invisible: How Young Women With Serious Health Issues Navigate Work, Relationships and the*

*Pressure to Seem Just Fine*, she uncovers a surprisingly large, yet hidden demographic of disabled and chronically ill women like herself, for whom this pressure to 'get better' and 'self-optimise' is magnified. As someone recovering from multiple health crises, including cancer and near-fatal anaphylaxis, the unfulfilled need to achieve perfection, not least normality, creates a heavy burden. Refusing to stick out, Lent Hirsch continually tried to minimise her difference, to convince others she was 'totally fine'. But this façade became impossible to sustain after her hospitalisation. As much as she wanted to be upbeat, join in at parties and meet new people, she was constantly thinking about where to find the nearest emergency room, the spectral fear of relapse. 'Back into the world of regular post-college life – or what we think that's supposed to be – it was impossible to be the person that my friends expected . . . I am the weirdo here', she writes. In a striking image, she compares herself to scagliola, a form of fake stone, where what appears like natural, solid marble is really a painstakingly made veneer patched together from a mix of plaster, glue and dye. 'Because I am young, and because I do want to seem buoyant when I can, I'm constantly masked. Sometimes by choice, other times by default because of how my body appears, I'm painted over to look like something solid. And so people find it hard to believe that underneath I am crumbling plaster.'

To appear as 'buoyant' as possible when recovering from illness, we must put on a credible front and construct a veneer of vitality. Here, the desire to appear competent outweighs the need for illness to be understood by others. But this is a double-edged sword – one that can pierce your self-worth and disrupt the healing process. When health is judged on the basis of exterior appearances, the true narrative of our bodies becomes harder to believe. It creates an inevitable sticking point when people cannot accept anything that contradicts the illusion. Frustratingly, you're punished for a stoical attitude, for trying to keep up, for trying to just be normal.

'What if our bodies were transparent, like a washing machine window?' wrote Lucia Berlin. 'How wondrous to watch ourselves.' As eccentric as it sounds, her idea of being able to objectively see what a person is grappling with may solve a problem. It would facilitate greater understanding and cut through the opacity of pretences. But the body conceals its secret workings, it isn't transparent – as evidenced in that familiar, everyday greeting, 'You look so well!' It would seem like the perfect compliment, yet I recall many times when this has been said to me and I've thought, 'Wow, really? 'Cause I feel rougher than a badger's backside.' I've also encountered the reverse. The casual savagery of 'Gosh, you look really tired': a universally loathed remark that elicits a surge of resentment towards your detractor.

However, the failure to read illness properly is by no means confined to small talk. For some young women – who appear too youthful or beautiful to be struck down by severe illness – it has resulted in dangerous diagnostic assumptions. In certain cases, women are not seen as stereotypical candidates for particular diseases, which creates gender-based disparity in our medical system. As Michele Lent Hirsch confirms, young women have become one of the most overlooked groups in the healthcare sector. 'We want people – we need people – to recognize that our bodies are doing some difficult things beneath our youthful exterior.'

'Life isn't always what it looks like from the outside and the hardest part of the journey is to be judged by the way you look instead of the way you feel,' said Bella Hadid during a speech at the Global Lyme Alliance gala in New York. One tumble down the supermodel's Instagram grid, you'll snoop everything from barefaced beauty campaigns to self-ies en déshabillé and a fleet of Gulfstream jets on demand. It's the aesthetic language of a woman who supposedly 'has it all'. Many refuse to accept that beneath this exterior she is grappling with aggressive symptoms of Lyme disease, including joint pain, nausea, headaches and inflammation. 'She's spoiled and rich, and she's looking for attention all the time,' wrote one social media troll, out for blood. 'Oh god. You're fine. Get over it,' typed a second. While another piled on with a faux expression of concern: 'We are just wondering if she actually even has it. I know someone with Lyme and it's debilitating, it doesn't seem like Bella has this.' If sickness has a 'look', apparently, this wasn't it. As Hadid has shown, it seems there is a hierarchy of illness, where health is ranked and determined on the sole basis of out-ward appearances. This creates a competitive dynamic – it's the very question of who is deemed ill *enough* by society, of who gets that last seat on the bus.

But perhaps more dangerous is the contest we face within ourselves, the struggle to match one's exterior and interior. As the actor and singer Selena Gomez revealed to *Harper's Bazaar* after her kidney transplant due to complications related to the auto-immune disorder Lupus: 'It's not some-thing I feel I'll ever overcome. There won't be a day when I'm like "Here I am in a pretty dress – I won!" I think it's a battle I'm gonna have to face for the rest of my life.' Health is a private, intimate journey that should never be qualified by the unsolicited interpretations of others. To be framed as an unreliable narrator of your own story is an injustice.

Paternalistic views leave no room for understanding the very personal experience of illness and its unique trajectories. The pressure to simplify, abridge, or paint one's recovery in black and white, will interrupt the sprawling processes of emotional healing.

So, what does successful recovery look like, if such an abstract thing exists? Firstly, it's about demythologising and reclaiming your body – refusing to see its new physical condition as a form of punishment or something laden with fatalistic implications. It's not a trial of moral character, a militaristic battle to be won or lost, nor a divine act of retribution. But societal perceptions of illness and recovery have been constructed on these myths. There is a desperate need to deprive illness of all its false and elaborate connotations. To liberate patients from a long history of being burdened by stigma, pity, dread and wild misinterpretations. To carve out space to express, hear and understand the truth about these universal human experiences.

In Susan Sontag's seminal book, *Illness as Metaphor*, she dissects the 'lurid' metaphors and 'punitive' fantasies that have afflicted illness for centuries. Here Sontag is found, as fellow writer Olivia Laing evocatively puts it, 'tear[ing] away at stigma like a person stripping ivy from a wall'. Written during her recovery from chemotherapy treatment for breast cancer, Sontag saw first-hand how people were failing to read her illness as simply a mechanical fault, or a shift in her physical reality. Instead, she was hit by an avalanche of unsolicited psychological and spiritual explanations for the disease, which almost became as disruptive as the cancer itself. 'The metaphors and myths, I was convinced, kill,' Sontag exclaims, while describing how fellow patients evinced disgust at their disease. They were stuck in a spiral of all-consuming shame and had bought into the fantasies about their illness of which Sontag remained 'unseduced'. Just the word 'cancer' rouses such horrifying visions, that in some instances, naming a diagnosis to patients has the power to kill, almost instantly. 'As long as a particular disease or disability is treated as an evil, invincible predator, not just a disease, most people will be demoralized,' Sontag writes, refusing to see the sick body as anything other than itself. 'The solution is hardly to stop diagnosis, but to rectify the conception of the disease, to de-mythicize it.'

Ableist myths surrounding illness are fuelled by cultural narratives that present themselves in diverse, and sometimes cunning, ways. Consider the artistic tendency to fetishise illness and present it as a desirable state – from Edvard Munch's paintings of the *femme fragile* where his tubercular girls manifest erotic, sensual undertones, to Romantic poetry's belief that consumption was synonymous with euphoria, sublime beauty and high aesthetic merit. This feverish validation of sickness is just as harmful as the overtly sinister portrayals, because it denies the material reality of disease. In our Instagram era, there have been parallel attempts to metaphorise illness as glamorous, sexy and attention-grabbing. The mind boggles. In 2020, a Paris-based fashion label called Kimhēkim used faux medical paraphernalia during a high-profile fashion show. Models emerged onto the catwalk with veins hooked up to drips, bandaged and trailing mock-IV bags (the latest It bag?). Another model teetered in stilettos, naked apart from oversized sunglasses and a white T-shirt with the slogan 'SICK'. According to Kimhēkim, who spoke out in defence of this ill-advised pageantry, it was a commentary on how society has begun 'seeking attention by any means possible, including faking illness'. There is evident danger in diminishing illness to the status of a provocative Instagram post, where it's figured as a weapon, and something that can be manipulated for narcissistic motive.

Kimhēkim's show came only a few years after Kylie Jenner's controversial cover photo shoot for *Interview* magazine, which saw her posing atop a gilded wheelchair, styled with a deathly gaze and a black latex, bondage-esque bodysuit. The coverline read 'The Surreal Life'. In the accompanying images, Jenner is clad in skintight assless chaps and lies in a wooden, coffin-like box. I mean, firstly, what were they thinking? Her mannequin-like figure veers into the realm of the uncanny valley, the creeping sense of unease we feel at encountering an entity that is almost, but not quite, human. By playing with positions of power and control, the portraits aimed to explore Jenner's status as an object of vast media attention, how she can exploit and engineer her image at will. But it was lost in translation. Instead, physical disablement and patienthood came to symbolise image manipulation for personal gain. Illness was rendered as nothing more than a publicity stunt capable of exerting power over gullible spectators, reinstating the most oppressive versions of ableism through the backdoor.

Audiences relish the nightmarish fictions and fairy tales that surround illness and disability. As a gauge of cultural taste for almost a century, the Oscars have thrown up some illuminating data. Since 1947, out of fifty-nine nominations for disabled characters, twenty-seven won an Academy Award. That's almost a 50 per cent win rate. These hyper-sentimental narratives, which often fit into the 'inspiration porn' genre, clearly have the power to elicit an unrivalled emotive response. But, given our historic aversion to disablement, why is this? In the cinematic world, illness and disability function as 'delivery vehicles' that transfer extreme emotions into audiences. From tragedy and humour to pity and disgust, sick bodies are vessels that offer psychological possibility. Think Hilary Swank's star turn as a boxer who is left quadriplegic in *Million Dollar Baby*; Eddie Redmayne's acclaimed portrayal of Stephen Hawking in *The Theory of Everything*; Daniel Day-Lewis's interpretation of an artist with cerebral palsy in *My Left Foot*; or John Mills playing the ableist archetype of a mute 'village idiot' in *Ryan's Daughter*. What we are seeing is 'narrative prosthesis' in action. This is a term coined by the academics David Mitchell and Sharon Snyder to articulate the ways in which disability helps to prop up a narrative and drive its key objectives.

The same trend can be observed in popular television soaps. Countless times you'll see an adored character facing a life of disablement, then ultimately their condition is overcome in a few episodes and never mentioned again. Here, illness is a sloppy plot device that widens a character's internal arc yet generates little genuine understanding about the reality of such experiences. Instead, these characters become saccharine objects of catharsis for the able-bodied gaze. Often, recovery is figured as a narrative prerequisite for happiness, belonging and positive social connection – the happily ever after must be achieved at all costs, no matter how fantastical or unrealistic the plot twist may be to get there.

The 'magical cure' or 'fixing' narrative, where a disabled character is eventually healed as a reward for their virtue, finds its origins in childhood classics and moralistic

Victorian narratives. Take the Brothers Grimm tale 'The Maiden Without Hands', where the female protagonist has her hands chopped off and is forced to survive on the charity of others. Her luck ultimately turns around when she meets and marries a king, at which point her hands miraculously grow back as a reward for her faith. It's the outcome we crave – unruliness is tamed and a painless future secured. But, as cockle-warming as this trope may be, it perpetuates the false belief that individuals can overcome their physical constraints and disabilities through virtuousness or sheer force of will. It may well defy the laws of science, but recovery is so expected that we fail to question it. The alternative, of course, is unthinkable. Consider the novel *Me Before You*, in which a quadriplegic man ends his life through assisted suicide, or the aforementioned *Million Dollar Baby* where the resilient fighter Maggie Fitzgerald cannot compute her new physical reality and takes a fatal injection of adrenaline. When a cure cannot be located it prefigures a narrative death. Disability is represented as an alien, pitiful state – it's a difference that must be erased in order for us to conceive a prosperous and effective place in society.

These myths about illness and recovery are so strongly entrenched in the public psyche, they have the power to win elections. In 2016, Donald Trump's successful presidential campaign put its faith in the metaphor of a 'crippled America'. As a rousing manifesto slogan it conveyed to the electorate that illness and disability were symbols of everything that was wrong with the nation. If a 'crippled' state symbolised inertia and impotence, the only way to fix their country was to cut out the disease and regain power. This invocation of full recovery as an obligation for survival is sinister, threatening and outrageously ableist. As political cannon fodder, the ill subject is figured as invisible and dis-qualified from expression, and so these myths perpetuate in the hands of those who cannot understand.

As a society, we make it impossible to forget the limitations of one's body. Robust health, strength and physicality are global currencies right now. They're the linchpins that hold our lives in respectable shape. When stripped away, their absence denotes utter devastation and collapse – a violent coming apart. Whether it's the hostility of the built sur-roundings, a lack of accessible opportunities or a pernicious stare, at every turn, you're left painfully aware of your weak-ness and barred from moving on. A life without full health isn't perceived as a viable or desirable option, and so when illness strikes a person, we are blindsided and consumed by fear. I admit I was once guilty of this mindset. We've hardly dared to consider what potential it could hold if our culture made physical ability matter less, demolishing this ableist value system where sickness is seen as the coda to life.

Life itself is an act of infinite shapeshifting. So why should we continue to perceive illness, an intrinsic aspect of the human condition, as a concrete state of exile? From success to failure, autonomy to dependency, triumph to catastrophe; it's nonsensical and runs counter to everything we know about living. In reality, there is immense strength in weakness, moments of joy amid sorrow, and often resolve to be found in the most confounding of moments. Illness is full of these ever-shifting nuances and contradictions that reach to the very core of what it means to be alive. It's what

Rebecca Solnit would call the 'faraway nearby'. In her memoiristic essay collection of the same name she explores how experiences of illness can nourish us in new, entirely unexpected ways. As she navigates her own breast cancer scare, alongside her mother's cognitive decline due to Alzheimer's disease, Solnit begins to decrypt the code of illness. To take this uncertain, shrouded existence and examine what it might teach both society and the individual. A major illness, she reassures, 'invites you to rethink, to restart, to review what matters. It's a reminder that your time is finite and not to be wasted, and in breaking you from the past it offers the possibility of starting fresh.' Instead of signifying expiration, illness offers expansiveness – it requires you 'to stitch back a storyline of where you're heading and what it all means'.

As I sit here with a balmy Sunday afternoon stretched out in front of me, gazing out onto the scorched grass and thick movements of laden branches, the heat pressing down on me, I can feel a rising pressure to reach some conclusion. I want to access that cathartic, lyrical end. To roll over into the past tense, recovered. To find a purpose in the faraway nearby – don't I owe it to myself? At times, I've felt the keen weight of it through my fingertips as I write. A vengeful impatience. A slightly sick, yet hopeful sensation where I can sense something momentous is coming like lightning's silver impulse from a charged thundercloud. For years I've desired the transcendent dimensions of this breakthrough, but to offer it now would be an act. It would falsify a sense of clarity, a neatness that is still missing. I want to say it's on its way, but I can hardly promise that with any certainty, and I'm not waiting any longer.

It's the idea of recovery as an art form that I keep returning to. Both recovery and art raise ontological questions about who we are, where we find ourselves and the very nature of our existence. In the sprint to locate a singular, conclusive meaning, you are confronted with the mystifying truth that there is no finite interpretation. Liable to change meanings in different contexts, recovery and art are living entities that evolve, expand and shrink like the oscillations of an amoeba. Their true meaning will only ever become known to their creator, and even that is not guaranteed.

In recognising this, I feel something shift. There's a freedom and, perhaps, the verge of a new beginning. To experience the rupture of illness on the cusp of adulthood forces you to divert the course of your life even before knowing with any certainty what it may look like. It requires you to accept that you may never have the life you choose; to soothe that faint thrum of grief, the chasm between the person you would have been and who you have become. The hardest internal battle is translating my determination into tangible recovery – because sometimes progress isn't possible no matter how hard you will it. Part of the cycle of recovery is recognising this distinction, and then letting go. While I'll never truly accept the new physical limitations I face, my spirit is stronger and more powerful than ever. Looking down to locate the scars where needles once met my skin, tiny luminous daubs of white, almost iridescent in the sunlight, I see with resolution and fortitude the depths of where my body has been, and where it may go from here. This, to me, is my recovery.

# Love, Regardless

It was late November, and I could already see my breath. Like wisps of candy floss stuck to my lips, it spiralled out in front of me before dissolving into the black, wet air. I leaned back into my seat, closing my eyes to feel every texture of the rough asphalt transcribed through the car wheels. Sitting beside me, squiggling furiously into the condensation that covered the windows, was my sister. 'I'm not giving you any more clues,' she protested as the condemned man awaited his hanging. The drippy sun began to glisten through the holes, framing her blonde bob, as she sighed in frustration. My failure to guess the blank letters (our usual telepathy had momentarily glitched) would not do; and I overheard her making formal arrangements with the cockpit to have her booster seat moved to the passenger seat for the return ride home. Devastated by her desire to be apart, I turned away, gazing into the water-dappled window with a melancholy that quite surpassed my eight years of age. My Sony Walkman, locked and loaded with a cassette tape of B*Witched, was playing to the point – 'C'est La Vie'.

Hatchets, though, would always be buried faster than vendettas ignited. The car, swerving sharply as it entered the final roundabout approaching the flyover, sent our booster seats flying into zero gravity. Together, without thinking, my sister and I reached out to grab hands, as an *AA Road Atlas* was propelled like a shot-put over our heads into the wind-screen. In that white-knuckle instant, ricocheting back and forth in unison, we turned to each other. Eyes sparkling with hysterical joy, hair wildly uprooted: we were flying. Hand in hand, she is my double and my pole star.

After reaching our destination, we walked towards the Victorian red-brick hospital, with its white windows and a verdigris clock tower. I was relieved to have my sister beside me to shutter its gaze, to dull the frustration of feeling like a medical specimen. Apprehension hung between us, a haunting uncertainty about what a day inside the hospital walls might bring. Not a game of Nintendo Mario Kart, it would seem, which was being monopolised in the waiting room by a Glaswegian family. A local kid, with a bandaged head and saintly patience, was showing them the ropes, his pedagogy hindered by their pronunciation of Yoshi, Luigi and Koopa Troopa. Not long after casting a discerning eye over the buckets of books and bedraggled Barbies, we were plucked from the ring of wipe-clean chairs and herded off to the gymnasium by two physiotherapists. The first, a delightful Swedish woman with a syrupy voice, pixie-like hands and a fondness for ginger tabby cats. The second, a bison-like woman with angry eyebrows and a swinging truncheon (what I was later reassured was a tendon hammer, though I still had no doubt she could bend iron bars).

After stripping down to our white cotton vests and knickers, for 'heights and weights', I fashioned my hair up into an onion top pony; this, I sneakily thought, would add another 1 or 2 inches to my height, by design. But my wiles and my trickery would not fly with this Trunchbullian figure (a woman who had conceivably done service as a Soviet jail warden). She scowled at me until I repositioned my hair into its regulation style. The lure of the trampoline I spied in the corner of the room was too strong – if I was going to get my turn, I needed to keep her sweet, play the game and buy some time.

Measurements charted, the physiotherapists sat us down on squishy gym mats, going through the motions, manipulating our hammies, quads and glutes. I looked over enviously at the Swede's lightness of touch on my sister's limbs, as the bison's pumice-like palms slapped and kneaded me vigorously like an overworked, glutinous sourdough. She'd had enough already. My sister, who has a natural warmth and sensitivity that people are drawn to, listened intently to their spiel about how the site was converted into a makeshift orthopaedic hospital for soldiers in the First World War. I, displaying remarkable sangfroid in the face of some intense muscle stretches, only tuned in at the revelation that Roger Daltrey was delivered in the wing next door.

The session was given a competitive frisson as we entered the strength-testing segment. 'Squeeze my finger,' the bison bellowed to me. My time had come for revenge – for did she not say, 'as hard as you can'? The trampoline, I sensed, was already a lost cause. Disappointingly, she did not blink and charged off to get a stopwatch for the next test: a race to stand up from the floor. As we dabbled in trash talk and fisti-cuffs, I vowed not to let my sister outplay me. We crouched in position as the bison, who was now beat-boxing the riff to 'Eye of the Tiger' (a move that took us all by surprise), roared out, 'Ready, set, GO!' She abruptly stopped me for not one but two false starts. On the restart, I refused to let her slanderous allegations drag me down. I scuffled hard. And I scuffled good, scrabbling my way to the top. It was neck and neck. But my masterstroke of a final pirouette shaved a second off my time. And despite my sister's pro-testations – reader, I won.

I suspected that the bison took sick pleasure in announcing that an MRI scan had been booked for me, as she suddenly banished me to the radiological underbelly of the hospital. My sister, meanwhile, was told to stay behind – she was convinced she was being put onto the junior watchlist for MI5 (based on little but a sixth sense and an apparent sighting of the curly, ginger-haired boy from *Spy Kids* back in the waiting room). I assured her they'd never want her, much less be recruiting children from a physiotherapy department in an inner-city hospital. My pragmatism always jarring with her gullible, fanciful ways. As I was sent deep into the scanner tunnel, watching my mum's reassuring face get smaller and smaller from the control room window, I shut my eyes. It was only when loud banging and sawing noises rumbled through the machine that my eyes shot open. I was not smizing for a Kodak moment, though. Claustrophobic, hyper-observed and unauthorised to even scratch my nose, I was but a prisoner, handcuffed to a bottom bunk, at the nearby Wormwood Scrubs.

The day struck another downbeat when our medical histories were probed, repetitively, inside a box-sized clinic room with a cold examination couch. My parents patiently providing the scoops and headlines in the face of a serpentine interrogation. The floor was packed out with anonymous medical students, junior doctors and their superiors, all looking at our bodies, some bored and disinterested, others a little too curiously. Not knowing where to look, I stared down at my feet, promising myself it would be over soon. It was then I caught sight of my sister and her lilac Skechers. Their glitter-daubed soles lit up, flashing uncontrollable rainbows, as she got wedged between a corner desk and a yellow sharps bin. Right there, I was hit by a sense of our togetherness. In spite of our condition and its preconceived limitations, she is at once a silent assurance of my normalcy and a reminder of everything I strive to be. In her reflection, I can always find who I am.

It is my sister and I who share an inexplicable bond. Not a bond we ever wanted or asked for, but one that's foretold by our DNA. Having an older sibling with the same muscle weakness condition, our bodies inscribed with this prophesy, meant she led the way. She showed me what was possible and what was expected. At times, we've shown each other how to live. Since my birth, it has given us a parallel under-standing of existence, from its cruelties and absurdities to its beauties and victories. It is a tacit understanding, a molecular attachment, that I will never share with anyone but her.

Throughout my life, whatever I have faced, the strength of my family and close friends has held me up. Their energy, optimism and unconditional love always unfurls my sense of possibility, putting its arms around me – sometimes, wrench-ing me away from the path of despair. Like in that panicked instant, terrified and shaking with frustration, when I was struck by the reality of getting a mobility scooter for uni-versity. What would it mean? What would it say about me? It was my parents who kept a cool head, reminding me that this was my means to greater freedom. It did not change the fact of who I was. It was a reality check that pulled me from the riptide, giving me the necessary courage to persevere, to see past the material.

To suggest these are mere gestures of support would be a fallacy. They have been the scaffolding that I rest my life upon. My mother's relentless enthusiasm and warmth is felt by anyone she meets – her capacity to give praise and offer encouragement being a particular kind of wonderment.

My friend, despite the passing of twenty-something years, still comes over in a warm glow when she recalls how my mum once complimented her beautiful knack of colouring inside the lines. And, when my sister mistakenly slapped a whole garlic bulb on her homemade mini pizza, my mum munched through a slice and, quite miraculously, was still able to utter some complimentary words about its moreishness, its sweet aromas and piquancy. Though two bites and ten garlic cloves down, I'll admit the response was not entirely cogent. My dad, on the other hand, is the person I turn to in a crisis (more than just inveterate troubleshooting for Wi-Fi issues). In hospital, I've looked to him for composure and stability in the most shattering of moments – the person I could trust to find urgent solutions, delivered with optimism and, often, a punchline. Together, they have supported me through past health challenges that seemed insurmountable. Sacrifices have been made, countless and without question, to ensure my physical protection and the essential fact of my survival – I guess it has got me to where I am today.

For many people with disabilities, this feeling is mutual. Our immediate families – the people who truly know us – afford a safe space which is free from discrimination and devoid of the othering gaze. This is by no means a conscious or calculated endeavour. It is instinctive, the most natural thing, illustrating how love will always bypass the fear and discomfort that surrounds disability in the public sphere. To find total acceptance and understanding at home is a privilege I do not take for granted; it would be disingenuous to say I've got here without it. The same can also be said for my abiding friendships: they have implanted the solid roots of belonging, an affirmation of my identity, that runs beneath everything I do.

Whether it's familial love, friendships or deep romantic partnerships, these intimate bonds require us to connect with a person beyond their exterior. To love means making someone knowable and understood – to a point where even the unbridgeable stigma and antipathy surrounding disability cannot disrupt its magnetic pull.

I have experienced love's life-sustaining intensity. I know how it can be harnessed to transform the way disabilities are perceived by others; and how it may engender tolerance in the most challenging circumstances. It is self-love, meanwhile, that holds yet more remedial power. The moment we dial into this internal energy source – embracing our desirability and true worth – the more instinctive it becomes to reject any role society has laid out for us, as dependents or outsiders. Love, in all its guises, is the emotive force field that unites us. It will pull us together into a more potent and unbreakable collective.

It was easy. Friendship, a fluffy locked diary of a thing. What began as a vast spread of blank pages to pour out our every frustration, secret confession and most side-splitting observations has slowly evolved. Today, it's a binder of knowledge, composed of a thousand compelling details, all the memories from lives that once scribbled along in tangent. It remains something unputdownable, something that only we share the padlock combination to. Inside, I'll find the time my best friend insisted on wearing her new Tammy Girl wedges, with lattice straps and 4-inch cork-effect heels, to our birthday disco – how she shuffled, how she crawled, how she was nearly put on bed rest (she did look enviably cool arriving at the village hall though. Peaks and troughs, we agreed). Or, the time she panicked in an interview and ended up claiming that the greatest film she had ever seen was the 2005 cult classic *Monster-in-Law*, starring J.Lo and Jane Fonda. And, not forgetting the time we spent an entire Sunday waxing our legs, laughing hysterically, unable to muster the courage to rip off a mosaic of ambitiously laid Veet strips. Eventually, we devised a plan to bite down on a screwed-up towel in the same way that a soldier, writhing from battle-inflicted trauma, would historically undergo surgery. Terrycloth being our chloroform-soaked rag.

With another of my closest friends – the only person who detests Parma Violets and peanut butter more than me – I can flick back to the time we attended a regional casting call for *Harry Potter and the Chamber of Secrets*. She pitched her performance of Ginny Weasley, in extremis, screeching out to be saved from the basilisk (me), with such ferocity that the casting agent grew visibly concerned. 'Take a breather,' the woman mouthed as she dashed through several groups of performing students to tap my friend on the shoulder, miming something about fruit squash in the green room. And then there was the time she helped me, arm-in-arm, ascend to the gods of the theatre to watch Roald Dahl's *The BFG* (the flights of stairs comically endless). The climb was ultimately pointless, for we could neither see, nor hear a thing from our celestial vantage point – quite something given the protagonist's Brobdingnagian proportions. Or the time we, randomly, took her British Shorthair cat to a national cat show which was in town. We were floored when little Daisy was awarded Best of Breed and we leapt up to smother her pudgy, powdery grey fur in kisses. Her first-place rosette hung proudly from her collar, gleaming in royal blue sateen. A sight that attracted thinly veiled displeasure from the veterans of the circuit – the Miss Tallulah Tinkerbells, Topaz Liberace VIIs and Angeline Sofias of the whiskered elite.

Flicking back, I will never lose all these many versions of myself. I am an accumulation of these intersecting, shifting moments – years of experience that cannot be erased. The friendships sealed during my university years, while different, have been similarly formative. I found acceptance and respect at a time when I was still figuring everything out; and, though I never showed it, I was desperately trying to reach steady ground after intense spells of illness. In their wittiness, brilliance and alertness to the power of their voice, I saw a new reality – one that I had felt agonisingly detached from for so long. Finding my way out of the depths, it was both a vision of what life should be and the invitation to a new chapter.

My friendships have become an essential, affirming part of me. And yet, as health challenges sent my life into a tailspin, their aftermath imposing new limits on my participation, I have had to accept that a certain physical distance is now placed between us. That however strong these bonds may be, I will often be situated as an outsider, a second-hand observer of the action. The sticky floors of experience, shared privacies and rapid conversations, all those immediacies, are mostly patched together in rumour and retrospect. What started as an unfamiliar, bruising feeling, when all I wanted to do was seamlessly slip in and assume my empty place, is something I have grown to live with.

The knowledge that a more active, social version of my life is available, and that I am the only impediment to living it, is tough. At times, it's lacerating. It is like being hemmed in by an invisible force: a restraint, enforced by nothing apart from my own body. This sometimes requires a resignation to pockets of loneliness and isolation – a level of restlessness, I suppose. Sustaining these bonds, in every way I can, is a commitment borne not just by myself, but also my friends, when I'm not always a physical presence in their lives. I am, however, consoled by the fact that it has, at times, taken us into deeper levels of wisdom and attachment. I have found the warmest, most genuine and enduring form of friendship.

I was fortunate to have forged these strong bonds throughout my childhood and early adulthood. But, growing older, as long-established relationships become more satellite, there comes a time where you must move away from this ready-made network and venture outwards to construct an entirely new one from scratch. Finding a social world beyond the family and established friendships is essential – though not always seamless when you have a disability or a visual difference. The act of building new connections requires you to confront head-on – and without choice – the stigma that besieges disability. Upon meeting new people, the lack of awareness about what it means to be disabled is writ large. The worst-case scenario is that it will generate awkwardness and timidity in others. It is a reticence that lines every word, every glance. A quizzical, angular look, much like someone is trying to solve a Rubik's cube, mentally unscrambling, sifting through limitless possibilities and configurations to figure out what's gone 'wrong'. I appreciate this is a natural human instinct, rather than a negative reflection of someone's character. However, it is still a torturous routine; one that is underpinned by the terrifying statistic I highlighted earlier, that two-thirds of the British public feel uncomfortable talking to people with disabilities for fear of seeming patronising or saying the wrong thing.

Often all it takes is a conversation or a shared experience to witness a sudden shift, a warming in that person's demeanour. But I think we can all agree that for a disabled person to be placed on the receiving end of this initial treatment each time they encounter new people is exhausting, and frankly needless. For someone like myself, who doesn't have an instantly identifiable disability that you can click into place or slap a diagnostic label on, what I've learned is that people will be led by me. As useful as this knowledge may be, put simply, it is not always easy to lead. As much as I have grown to love meeting new people, there are multiple influencing factors that determine whether I can take control in a social situation. I do not have a strong voice physically, so a conversation requires effort on the part of the listener and can be misread as quietness. The combination of loud environments and poor accessibility means there are limited opportunities where these new encounters can take place. Sometimes, when you have a disability, establishing connections can make you reliant on the thoughtfulness and open-mindedness of others – and that is a frustrating fact.

For every destabilising first encounter, there is a kind of euphoria that lies in meeting someone who doesn't subscribe to this routine, someone who can see past it all. You never know who it's going to be, but when it happens there is instant chemistry, like you share a secret about life. It has been my experience that these people have both a cool confidence and a deep sensitivity which has often arisen from first-hand awareness of illness and disability, mental or physical, either in themselves or in their family. For them, it is part of the normal order of experience. They get it. They are unfazed. It doesn't matter. This, in my view, proves what is possible for the future. It is my hope that everyone can develop this tolerant mindset, where awareness of disability becomes so engrained in the psyche that this laidback approach is replicated across society.

When I set out to write this book, I knew that – besides laughter and blunt statistics – my most effective weapon would be a loving compassion. That by persuading you, the reader to really feel something, meeting me at a place of understanding, it could move us closer to a culture where people of all abilities are valued. This is critical to my project. When disabled individuals are accepted into every aspect of life (education, media, politics, the workplace), our daily interactions with disability will become second nature; normal even. This is a world where there is no need for awkwardness, discomfort, or heartbreaking seclusion. Disabled people will now have freedom to form new friendships, seek out roommates, meet colleagues and spark romance without fear of exclusion or intimidation.

Discovering a community – a place where you feel seen, and ultimately have the chance to create your own desired version of a family, whatever that may look like – is a cornerstone of the human experience. But building intimacy remains one of the trickiest challenges facing people with disabilities. When enraging misconceptions are waiting to cut in and disrupt this quest, it's vital that we plumb down into the depths of these stigmas, with the intention of expanding our philosophies of love and desire.

Since an early age, I've had an awareness of the importance placed on romantic relationships as a source of security, completion and self-fulfilment. It all started one morning when a close friend brought a ring into school, claiming that Bradley McIntosh, star of S Club 7, had proposed overnight. They were engaged to be married. Our Year 5 classroom was ablaze. We cooed as she fluttered her left hand around, chattering about their impending nuptials in Bora Bora – an exquisite, rose-petalled fantasy plucked from a Sandals brochure. Scepticism only crept in when someone, with a face like they'd just licked piss off a nettle, hissed that the red plastic 'engagement' ring bore an uncanny resemblance to last term's Christmas cracker gifts. Ouch.

Like everyone, I began to take fascination in the tales of blossoming teenage love that surrounded us. The story of Quentin – a bespectacled redhead and first boyfriend of a classmate – carried far more excitement than the liaison of Marianne Dashwood and Willoughby in our crispy, yellowed copies of *Sense and Sensibility*, open on the desk in front of us. Theirs was a meet-cute for the ages: my classmate described how Quentin was astonished, knocked for six, by her ability to recite the whole alphabet in Elvish. Moving on from those days, my friends could discuss what their future wedding dresses might look like, ideal partners and family plans. It wasn't a conditional fact. It was going to happen. There was an assurance that they would be desired, and I had no doubts for them either.

I was growing up in a culture where our stories are told through relationships – romance being the only valid narrative arc. We are tied to a 'punitive vision' that our life will be miserable unless we 'date in our twenties, find the ideal partner by twenty-eight, and have our first child at thirty-one', as Ayisha Malik explains in *Conversations on Love*. But I felt slightly anomalous. This arose not from a lack of want or self-confidence, but a flicker of uncertainty about my romantic prospects. It's possible that this was just my personality – a desire to base decisions on feeling, never on convention. Or a knowledge that any vision of who I was going to be, years down the line, was tentative. But in retrospect, it feels like something else was at play. Perhaps I held an unconscious awareness that my disability was always going to be a complicating factor?

While I believe that emotional connection, platonic or romantic, can transcend the stigma that surrounds disability, it would be naïve to think that my physical condition would have no bearing on my relationships. When there are plenty of fish in the sea, why would someone angle for me? This is an incredibly destructive line of thought, which I know to be untrue, yet it doesn't stop myself and others from buying into that mindset. It takes serious confidence to believe that you could be fundamentally yourself, that you don't have to cover yourself or bring better qualities than anyone else to 'offset' your limitations. For many people with disabilities – and this does *not* represent everyone's experience – it's only the prospect of romance that makes them consider themselves disabled. Why is there a sense that relationships for disabled people are a result of great fortune? A feeling of gratitude that someone has been able to see past their condition or impairment? It's hard for me to accept that my disability limits my ability to make connections with new people. And that how someone sees and responds to disability is one of the factors that will shape who I can be with. In that sense, this is probably where disability will have the most tremendous impact on my life, my options. Employment matters, education matters, access matters. But these are all a means to live. Love is the reason to be alive.

The internalised pressure to find love in early adulthood multiplies when you have a disability or health condition that throws your life out of sync and steals experience. Single-dom already dispenses a dump of unflattering connotations for women, but disabled people are hit with yet more damning stereotypes about what they should expect, or rather, not expect, in their private lives. If you're not in a relationship, it is interpreted as a sign that no one is interested due to your physical imperfections, never a personal decision. It should not be necessary, but a healthy relationship is a stamp of normality – it's a mark of legitimacy, a means to gain connection and credibility in the withering gaze of a society that denigrates disabled lives. 'For some disabled people, the ultimate goal is to be in a relationship with a non-disabled person,' according to a landmark book, *The Sexual Politics of Disability*, 'because this represents total acceptance, total validation as a human being.' But even that isn't foolproof. Relationships between disabled and non-disabled individuals are consistently held under suspicion or seen as imbalanced. It is salacious how the default assumption is of an ulterior motive (now, I ain't saying she's a gold digger but . . . or is that their carer, a sibling perhaps?). When society tells us that disabled people aren't worthy partners, conspiracy theories are created to reconcile someone's relationship with what we've been taught. Single or coupled up, there is no escape from false judgements.

But here lies the truth: genuine acceptance, trust and commitment – the ability to really *see* someone, not just want them – are not easy to find. The presence of disability in any relationship can create an unconditional bond between two people that others may dream of. While this is something I am yet to experience, I know it to be true. In an op-ed for *Vogue* magazine, Lena Dunham writes her own version of this 'happily ever after' following her marriage to the musician, Luis Felber. During the early months of their relationship in 2021, living together during the pandemic in a sunny garden house in England, Dunham – who has Ehlers-Danlos syndrome, a connective tissue disorder – fell ill with a severe bladder infection. 'It seemed to me like the death knell of this magical period,' she writes candidly. 'He would realize, finally and forever, that someone like him . . . could not make a life with someone like me.' She felt like the parts of herself she had been desperately trying to tuck away were spilling out – her weakened, non-compliant body becoming untameable when she was finally admitted to hospital. It was make or break, and what emerged was something better than she could have imagined. 'He visited faithfully, wearing sunglasses at night to make me laugh and chatting up the nurses like he was Sinatra working Vegas. He was somehow making this place of disappointment and pain feel almost . . . fun. To him, it wasn't much, but to me it was everything.' When we open up the possibilities of what relationships can be, not forcing ourselves to live up to society's expectations about what 'normal' looks like, love comes alive. Life doesn't always turn out the way we expect, so having a solid connection to weather the turbulent times, to make even scary experiences 'fun', can be redemptive. And the magical part of it? 'I didn't do anything special to get there – besides a little therapy – except just continue being myself,' chimes Dunham.

Dunham's experience is proof that romance can be an unexpected source of healing. This notion that our relationships may cast light into the terrifying fringes of ill health, is also explored by the author Barbara Webster. Her work strikes a more pragmatic and realist note, informing us that emotional ties are not impervious, nor unshakable – how it would be an illusion to suggest so. In her book *All of a Piece*, Webster shares how her marriage received a hard blow when she developed multiple sclerosis, how it 'took time to learn the new parameters of normality'. It seems the power of romantic bonds manifests differently when a life-changing disability unexpectedly strikes a long-term partner-ship. It may require a couple to restructure their bond. To creatively reimagine everything they once knew about each other. For Webster, there was a torrent of misplaced anger from her husband Nick, an 'exceptionally good-humored' and 'easygoing man', when he realised that her MS wasn't something he could fix. Of course, this was true in a literal sense, but the bond they shared held its own curative power. 'I was reminded of how rare and wonderful it is to be uncon-ditionally loved and accepted,' she concludes. 'There were many times during this process when I was not particularly lovable and yet I was loved and accepted by those closest to me . . . Those were the people who enabled me to find and use my own strength.' True love is pliable; it adapts and grows to meet new, extremely testing circumstances, binding us tighter and tighter.

In *Modern Love,* a television series based on real-life stories from the eponymous *New York Times* column, we see how the instabilities of the body can expedite a relationship from the very first date. One tumble off the sofa, a broken glass, a severed bicep nerve and a six-hour stint in the hospital, Yasmine and Rob's romantic evening is a certified disaster. But despite this derailing, the events all collude as a fast-track to closeness. 'It's like we've fast-forwarded years somehow', remarks Rob, as Yasmine wheels him around the hospital in a wheelchair and helps him to undress. At one point, the romantic trope of the male suitor giving his jacket to his beloved is humorously inverted: Rob fails spectacularly, given that he can no longer lift his arms and Yasmine must take matters into her own hands. Moments like this show how disability can instantly disrupt and shift the dynamic between a couple – even between two typically fit, healthy and young individuals. 'People are so concerned to put on this big front normally, but now you've seen me at my most vulnerable, frightened, bleeding,' says Rob. 'It's my worst fear realised.' If you can push past the 'big front', embrace a raw vulnerability and stare the fear of rejection in the face, you may find a more intense connection than you could think possible.

The quest for a secure and loving relationship requires an investment of courage. While most millennials can empathise with the cruel realities of rejection, ghosting and 'swipe right' culture, disabled people experience another layer of vulnerability in the dating game – more than just the knife edges of tortuous small talk and awkward, stilted exchanges. Consider the limited opportunity to meet people in accessible places, for example, or knowing the 'right' way to open up about the sensitive topic of disability. These challenges have conspired to create a dating culture where only 5 per cent of able-bodied people have actually been on a date with a disabled person.

The impetus to change this statistic, to tackle the obstacles facing disabled individuals who want to fall in love,
has been severely wanting. Think of the horrific ableism
served to 27-year-old journalist, Lucy Webster, after she
made a simple enquiry to a 'professional' dating agency – a
story that made global news headlines. 'Regretfully', wrote
Matchmakers Dating in reply to her interest, 'achieving
good outcomes for full-time wheelchair user clients can be
quite challenging. You should consider this before looking
to take out a membership with us.' The agency's erroneous
attempt to be 'open and honest', as they put it, drew her
to tears. If the company was aware of the disparity experienced by its disabled service users, why was this blindly
accepted? And beyond that, why was there no attempt to
investigate these inequalities or commit to change? There
are few scenarios where this under-the-counter discrimination – packaged up as considerate, gentle discouragement –
would be acceptable. The subtext of this appalling saga is
that disabled people's pursuit of love is less valid, and more
niche, than their non-disabled counterparts – the company
was not, in their words, a 'specialist agency'. It brings the
language of special schools, special care, special needs into
play, creating potentially unhelpful divisions in the emotional landscape of dating. This habitual ghettoisation of
disability means that the company's legal duty, to make their
advertised matchmaking services accessible to all, was easily
glossed over.

Lucy Webster's experience reveals just how high the
stakes are for disabled people throwing their hearts on the
line – the pain and trauma you might unwittingly expose
yourself to. It strikes me that her treatment is symptomatic
of a new businesslike detachment that has been normalised

by dating app culture, where something that was once ser-endipitous and intimate, the search for love, can turn cold and mechanical in the refracted realities of a pocket-sized phone screen. Essentially, the way a Tinder user navigates the app mimics a marketplace. 'Transactions' are made like a wild trolley dash. Split-second decisions are driven by sexual desires. And a superficial once-over of face, body size, age and race is used to determine a punter's needs and attraction. There is little requirement to slow down, to really get to know someone, read the small print and accept their imperfections. Why would you bother when a much hotter candidate is just a tap, tap and a finger swipe away? This volatile mindset has not only bred an ethos of disposability, but it has given us carte blanche to discriminate. As much as the app user's decisions seem autonomous, they are not. Dating apps are controlled by algorithms. But what is an attempt to squeeze connection out of soulless mathematical equations carries hugely problematic implications.

In the same way that Netflix will base television recommendations on what you've just binge-watched, online dating algorithms learn from user's previous matches and present similar profiles back to them. In the dating app context, this filtering process is more sinister, opening a door to unconscious – and conscious – bias against those with minority identities. Users can become trapped in a kind of epistemic bubble, where their hook-up opportunities are insular and lacking in diversity, likely pulling them away from people they would otherwise pair well with. The main objective for any dating service is, quite clearly, not social progress. Their concern is achieving successful matches based on rudimentary markers of identity. If that reproduces societal biases, so be it. Without an ethical obligation, these closely guarded systems often reinforce the closed ways we think about attractiveness.

For all its negatives, I cannot deny that online dating brings a panoply of benefits for people with disabilities. Although wooing opportunities may be thwarted by our artificial measures of dateability, it has at least provided *some* social interaction, where before lay a void. Tinder, Bumble, Hinge et al. are seemingly imperfect conduits, bringing romantic possibilities to our fingertips that would otherwise be non-existent. For a generation that has grown up with the internet, spontaneous real-world encounters – where love is kindled in coffee shop queues or on train station platforms – seem like a quixotic fantasy peddled by the rom-com industrial complex. There is a growing sense of incredulity, perhaps cynicism, that accompanies such fanciful images. But this hopelessness magnifies tenfold when you bring the logistics of disability into the equation, where the probability of meeting a partner among everyday life feels much like stumbling across an Old Master in a dust-lined Volvo station wagon at a car boot sale – not likely. Virtual dating has undeniably opened up the dating landscape. Research found that 32 per cent of relationships started between 2015 and 2019 began online, a figure that will increase to 50 per cent by 2035, according to Imperial College Business School and eHarmony. It has given long-awaited access, an entry point, for disabled daters in ways that were previously unimaginable.

Dating apps, if used right, can allow users to sidestep initial awkwardness, break down barriers, and even deal with rejection before meeting face to face. When I last explored this topic of disability and dating for the *Sunday Times Style* magazine, I remember one incredible woman, Sophie

Bradbury-Cox, explaining how online dating offered her an element of self-protection. As a wheelchair user, she made a point of flagging her disability on her profile to act as an unofficial vetting process: 'It weeds out people who aren't worth wasting your time on,' she told me, matter-of-factly. 'A good test of character from the outset.' I can't say I disagree with Sophie's logic; she has found most of her relationships, including her husband Nathan, via online dating. It's clearly a successful strategy. Ultimately if someone cannot see beyond disability, it's not going to work. This assertive mindset was shared by another interviewee, Jessica Kellgren-Fozard, who met her wife through a women-only dating app. Like Sophie, she was open about her invisible disabilities from the outset. 'The right person for you will not be scared,' Jessica said. 'It won't even matter.' And it didn't; the couple had moved in together after two weeks and were engaged within five months.

But there's still a part of me that wonders: is it better to avoid broadcasting your health status when dating apps encourage such normative, surface-level assessments of attraction? When society is programmed to view disability in blinkered terms, it takes a lot for anyone to strip themself of these basic human impulses, to make the first move. By highlighting your disability, there's a fear that you will close yourself off from finding that one elusive 'soulmate' – someone who may need more than a visual prompt to start thinking more expansively, and inclusively, about disability. 'Unsurprisingly, a couple of guys did unmatch with me when I told them,' revealed Meelina Isayas, another interviewee who has cerebral palsy. 'I had one guy just say: "You're really pretty . . . wait, are you disabled lol?" Still to this day I don't know exactly what was so funny.' It's a shameful yet unassailable fact that disabled people who can minimise their impairment, or 'pass' for normal, have more success in meeting romantic partners.

The question of whether to 'disclose' your disability from the outset is played out in *4 Feet High*, a boundary-smashing Argentinian miniseries, screened at the Sundance Film Festival in 2021. For the seventeen-year-old, blue-haired protagonist, Juana, who uses a wheelchair, the prospect of male attention is intoxicating; the dating app she has downloaded pulls at her fingertips. When Juana selects a profile photo from her camera roll, she strategically scissors away all signs of her disability, leaving her wheelchair out of frame in a dark abyss, cutting at her body, changing its story. Her phone's melodic trills – the zips! and pings! of Cupid's bow – begin swirling across the scenes with news of her latest matches. '*Es un supermarcado de gente*' (it's a supermarket of people), Juana explains to her family, who are curious about where all the new noises are coming from. But will the switch from screen to real world be frictionless? Juana agrees to meet her first match, a tall man called Thiago, in a nightclub. As Thiago turns around, gazing down at her body bathed in ultra-violet light, there is a moment of visual buffering as he recalibrates his expectations. At this point, I think I am more nervous than Juana, who asks, undaunted: 'Do I look pretty to you – as in, just like the photos?' (*¿te parezco linda? O sea, como en las fotos*). The scene that ensues flouts our natural instincts to catastrophise and exaggerate Juana's difference. 'Yes, much prettier than in the photos' (*Sí, sos mas linda que en las fotos*), Thiago responds before they sidle over to the dancefloor. Both fearless and persistent in her hunger for romantic liaisons, Juana is emboldened by her sexuality, rarely diminishing her desires under the pressure of society.

Where *4 Feet High* excels in pushing a cultural narrative that de-dramatises disability, the reality isn't always as radically inclusive. Against the threat of ghosting, breadcrumbing, caspering and the like, enormous self-possession is required when disclosing a disability to your potential date. I am sure that most of us harbour a withering suspicion that we possess some innate quality that makes us unlovable. When connection lies at the very core of human experience, this is a somewhat universal anxiety. Are we too needy, outspoken, eccentric or flaky? For disabled people, it's alarmingly easy to believe this 'innate quality' is a set of physical limitations. Rejection can happen for any reason, because of your disability or not, but often it's impossible to distinguish.

To counter this negative thinking, we must engage in a delicate alchemy – mining our true selves for the purpose of accepting who we are and believing that we are, of course, worthy of someone's affection. While self-interrogation is essential prep work in anyone's love story, it's arguably more complex, more ungovernable, when you factor in a disability. Much of our understanding around relationships, what it means to love and be loved, is shaped through the prisms of culture. But cinema, art, music and literature have historically failed to give a narrative echo to the romantic lives of people with disabilities. Without a guiding constellation to map out your reality, you are untethered, condemned to spend a lifetime searching and roaming unchartered territory.

In a bid to consult an expert, I flip open my laptop and sleuth around online for a disability dating guru. I am just recovering from a stumble down an eye-popping Quora thread – a shuttle train to insanity, as ever – when my cursor lands on Dr Danielle Sheypuk, an exceedingly glamorous-looking 'sexpert', based in Manhattan, NYC. As the 'leading commentator' on dating and relationships for disabled people, she is screaming Carrie Bradshaw to me – only, mercifully, with some scientific nous (Sheypuk holds a PhD in Clinical Psychology). As I scroll up to her contact page, I am struck by an image of Sheypuk, blonde hair cascading down her nude body, as she straddles a horse, Godiva-style, in what looks to be a pair of gold Louboutin stilettos. I must say, I'm intrigued. And, just slightly, wondering how life got me to this point.

While I await a reply, I settle in to watch her TEDx talk from 2015 – suspending my usual scepticism over this cult-like circus where 'powerful ideas' seem to be juggled around theatrically but left somehow intangible. As a wheelchair user, Sheypuk opens with an anecdote about a 'fantastic' Match.com date she recently went on. Under the electrifying gaze of a moonlit city, their chemistry, she says, was 'flying all over the place'. When the third date came around – an intimate dinner in the Lower East Side – there was an unexplained chasm between the pair. Until he blurted out: 'How are you going to be a mother? How are you going to do the duties that are going to be required of you? And even as a wife, how . . . I'm not sure how that's going to work.' Sheypuk was rendered to little more than a service provider – to me, that is the antithesis of romance. Putting the blatant sexism to one side, these questions illustrate the kind of logistical thought processes people with disabilities run through almost every day. Nothing is ever insurmountable; with creativity and willpower, practical challenges can always be met with solutions. And yet, she never heard from him again.

People searching for a romantic partner seem beholden to a set of concrete, tick-box 'wants' and requirements that a disabled person is automatically assumed not to fulfil.

What's worse is that these assumptions are often baseless and unfounded. Take motherhood and parenting, for example: this can be an incredibly natural, enriching role for someone with a disability – 21 per cent of family households have one disabled parent. But, due to our near-total cultural erasure of disabled parenthood, it still seems like an alien concept.

Everyone claims to be looking for a love connection, something soul-stirring and otherworldly. But, when it comes to disability, there are caveats. We are fettered by the social constructions of the physical world – unable to move beyond the bodily logistics of dating someone with a disability or disobey the rules about what a partnership should look like. It is profoundly odd.

So, in the face of these painful assumptions and hang-ups, how should disabled people break into the dating arena? When I hear back from Sheypuk later, she is jet-bound, en route to Mexico. After a few emails I've gathered a wealth of advice on how to turn inwards and hashtag 'do the work'. The critical thing, she explains warmly, is not to let the fear of rejection take over, but to claim agency over your destiny by building up a 'dateable self-esteem'. This is a term that Sheypuk coined in her therapy practice, to separate someone's general self-esteem from how they rate themselves as a romantic partner. 'Often, people with disabilities have high self-esteem when it comes to our friends, families, and careers,' she says. 'But, when it comes to seeing ourselves as viable, desirable dating partners, our dateable self-esteem is in the gutter.'

Healing starts with hurling ableism out the window and viewing your differences as 'normal'. Puff yourself up with a sense of bravado, act with conviction and throw your heart into the ring. 'So what?' Sheypuk will always tell her clients.

'So what if you use a wheelchair? So what if you can't stand or walk? So what if you have difficulties with speech? You have amazing things to offer as a romantic partner, both emotionally and in the bedroom. Once you truly believe this and internalize it, you will find that you have that swag . . . There's nothing to lose and so much to gain.' I instantly admire Sheypuk's straight-talking gusto. By avoiding the act of becoming truly known and understood, you embark on a self-fulfilling prophesy. How can you expect anyone else to see you when you are consumed by a dread of exposure? But, when we exist in a social climate where women are hypersexualised and disabled sexuality is scorned, it is invariably easier said than done – pushing the curative powers of romance further and further out of reach.

'To be desired is perhaps the closest anybody in this life can reach to feeling immortal,' wrote the novelist and cultural thinker John Berger. His remark – made in response to a seventeenth-century sketch of a woman, immortalised in ink, with an open pout and long, deliberate eyes – hits a raw nerve for my generation of millennial women who were tutored to be looked at. When the female existence rests on a flawed idea that being desired is synonymous with power, life becomes a push and pull: seeking and deflecting men's aesthetic appraisal. Girls must strive to belong to a pedigree of bodies that have successfully, and publicly, earned their desirable status under the male gaze.

This culture was endemic while I was growing up, the male gaze consecrated in television shows like *The Inbetweeners*.

I remember one episode, where a blind date rocks up to a shopping mall and is branded 'a freak', 'a giant', 'King Kong', 'an immense, cock-sucking American landmark', all for her tall stature. Here, girls who didn't measure up to 'fuckable' standards were readily discarded, humiliated even. It was embalmed in our school yearbook – girls ranked on 'best body'. But, like the journalist Sirin Kale, I almost accepted these verdicts, falling dangerously close to treating them as objective truths. Reflecting on the toxic noughties climate for women, Kale recalls her first day as a university fresher. Pictures of every girl were pinned to a bulletin board in her halls and scrawled over by older male students with an 'attractiveness' rating. 'None of this seemed particularly objectionable to me, an eighteen-year-old girl. This was just the way things were,' Kale writes. 'Hell, I was just happy I got a high score on my photograph.'

As Berger says, external validation can offer a slippery sense of immortality, the feeling of being invincible. It's clung onto as if it were a wayward chicken fillet threatening to jump out of a push-up bra, desperately and frantically, with an awareness of how much is at stake. But when bodily 'perfection' offers protection, and endorsement of one's sexuality, what does it mean for the young woman undressing in front of a man, her scars now visible for the first time? The female Tinder user who got a 'swipe right' but suddenly discloses a serious health condition? Or the teenage girl who arrives on a date to find she cannot independently climb upstairs to use the restaurant toilets? And where do I fit within this punishing scenario?

I was very much aware of this social backdrop, but my place in it, as someone with a disability, was unclear. Personally, I can't deny that I felt partly exempt and distanced from it. In this, there is a freedom. Without the pressure to mould myself for the male gaze, to survey my actions for the purpose of asserting my desirability, I never felt the need to make choices based on social expectation. Now, I question whether this independent mindset was, in fact, liberation or rather a loss of some powerful, essential part of my own sexuality. Perhaps, my feeling of exemption was an internalisation of social prejudices, a sign of how my own validation felt out of reach.

I've discovered there is a certain level of confidence that comes with being desired. I would like to think that it would never change my self-perception, that I am entirely responsible for my empowerment. But the reality is, this sense of one's own desirability adds another layer of self-assurance – a fearlessness and a security in the context of a society that judges people on their sex appeal. It is bizarre how the knowledge that I was desired may boost someone's perception of me. Though this is inevitable when we live in world that constantly questions the sexuality of people with disabilities.

I recently learned of a wheelchair user who was accosted in a supermarket by another grocery shopper: 'Can you have sex?' the woman asked, thirstily. I gasped at this opener, a mixture of outrage and mortification coursing through me. This, coming from a stranger, in a supermarket, quite splendidly bestowed with a straight face. How was she expecting it to land? A blow-by-blow account of her last intimate encounter, a softcore re-enactment with the aubergines piled in her trolley, maybe incorporating a peach or two? While curiosity is not always negative and pernicious, this breach of privacy was unmistakably degrading. The power dynamics of the encounter suggest a threatening sense of ownership, an entitlement to know everything, all the most private intimacies of the disabled body. I thought a lot about her story while writing this essay. Admittedly, it is a rare, hyperbolic scenario, a rubbernecker who has grossly overstepped the bounds of what is socially acceptable. But still, I think it speaks to an unhealthy and hurtful preoccupation with the sexual politics of disability. Even those who would never articulate it out loud secretly question how disabled people can possibly navigate sex and relationships. There remains an underlying suspicion of asexuality, of inadequacy. Do people with disabilities possess bodies with sexual desires? Can they even have orgasms or erections? Could they ever be held up as objects of desire?

And yet, despite all this voyeuristic curiosity and hysteria, the matter has often slinked away from in-depth cultural analysis. This leaves the emotional landscape surrounding disability and sexuality inscrutably messy and misunderstood. Think about it: sexual agency is synonymous with thrill, risk, independence, liberation, pleasure and release. It is everything we are told disability is not. With such narrow assumptions about sexuality, people with disabilities (who are cast as infantile, passive, dependent subjects) are often disbarred from this arena. 'Pity or fear, in other words, are the sensations most often associated with disabilities,' the scholars Anna Mollow and Robert McRuer explain. 'More pleasurable sexual sensations are generally dissociated from disabled bodies and lives.' That, we are told, is all part of the existential sorrow of being disabled.

This view that sexuality is irrelevant, or even contrary, to the disabled experience is partly instigated by a lack of progressive, sex-positive education. As part of the taboo-breaking podcast series *Doing it!*, the self-styled millennial sex influencer Hannah Witton – who lives with ulcerative colitis – held an incisive roundtable discussion that veered into the topic of sex education in schools. One participant, Nima Misra, who has partial paralysis of her legs after having spinal cancer as a baby, spoke of the 'odd' assumption from her teachers that disabled students would not want to learn about relationships and sex. 'I went to a mainstream school with a unit attached where, if you had an impairment, you'd go and get your treatment, your physio,' she explained. The minute they were embarking on sex education the majority of these kids were 'removed' from the sessions. Cue gasps from the assembled roundtable. But Nima refused to leave, deciding it was important to stay: 'I wanted to have these experiences in life, but I think they just assumed that the other guys didn't . . . Despite having the unit which was supposed to be empowering in enabling us to study alongside able-bodied students, it was really strange.' The humiliating act of removal, a symbolic closing of the door, wasn't only about being deprived of an essential life lesson. Inside that classroom lay an invitation to claim their defining freedoms as human beings. To be casually denied this right would surely have a subliminal effect on one's future self, limiting people with disabilities in ways that are cruelly imperceptible at first.

It is unsurprising, then, that disabled people see sex and relationships as one of the most isolating, taboo and psychologically distressing issues. I can't help but agree with the disability activist Anne Finger, who writes that sexuality is 'the source of our deepest oppression' and 'our deepest pain'. As she casts light on the soreness, the erasure, Finger makes the valid point that it is far 'easier to talk about and formulate strategies for changing discrimination in employment, education, and housing than it is to talk about our exclusion from sexuality and reproduction'. She's right – I feel despondency, embarrassment even, at this exclusion but this is not the same sense of injustice I feel towards poor accessibility. Or the fury I feel towards the perilous state of disability employment. It cuts deeper, as something even more personal, more uncomfortable. Any society that is unable to see disabled people as desirable, or desiring, is one that rejects their humanness and concretises their difference. The emotional, sexual rights of disabled people are often overlooked and seen as trivial in the context of other basic, more pressing human needs. To demand them requires another level of courage. A courage I'm not sure how to navigate or explain.

I'm beginning to realise that resolving these matters could hold greater liberatory potential than I first imagined. Sexual rights extend far beyond the bedroom, their expression being a necessary means to not only connection, love and intimacy, but large-scale emancipation and political agency. Denying disabled people access to a foundational principle of our existence is inexcusable – it reifies society's lowly expectations for disabled people, damages self-image and, quite literally, strips away any promise of futurity. So, it is essential that we begin to undress the exclusion of disability in the tangled domain of sex and relationships.

As with a growing number of societal woes, it seems one cause of this exclusion can be located inside Goop HQ, the now-infamous wellness and lifestyle empire founded by Gwyneth Paltrow – where the monetisation of Californian suave becomes silliness on steroids. (And a $75 vagina-scented candle can inspire a degree of fervour that anthropologists will likely be studying for centuries.) Back in

January 2015, a new article went live on the Goop website. The content was a little different to their usual beat, which is to shovel recipes for banana nut muffins and proclaim pea milk to be the panacea (yes, even the humble pea has been subject to a milking). The well-being agenda was no longer hellbent on nutrition and beauty, it was stretching its slurpy tentacles onto sex – or, to be specific, the recommendation that women 'steam clean' their vaginas, thereby cleansing the uterus and reviving energy levels. 'The real golden ticket here is the Mugwort V-Steam,' the post read. 'You sit on what is essentially a mini-throne, and a combination of infrared and mugwort steam cleanses your uterus, et al.' How regal. Then came the Yoni Egg furore of 2017. Grandiose claims that hoarding jade crystals up your vagina was a medical cure-all for everything from uterine prolapse to incontinence – through a process of non-stop vaginal weightlifting, *quelle horreur* – finally precipitated the hire of a full-time fact checker. Next a Netflix docuseries hit our screens: a curious show where people's sexual disorders were prodded and probed during a couple's retreat hosted by Gwyneth herself. Sex had been goopified, locked in a realm where everything is made competitive, optimised and wildly unattainable.

While I'm hardly suggesting that incubating a rose quartz Yoni Egg is an imperative or a concern for most, it speaks to the wider cultural imagination. The ideology of sex has become entangled with a lexicon of fixing, healing, curing – all intrinsic parts of the wellness shibboleth which demand our allegiance to physical and mental self-improvement, creating yearnings that will never be satiated by anyone, not least someone with a disability. All these dizzying requirements, which idolise bodily perfection and abhor physical impairment or malfunction, threaten to blow up in our face like a Goop™ exploding vagina candle. What was founded as a platform to 'crack open taboos' is now multiplying them – rising to an inferno where 'sex positivity' clouds the disablist thinking beneath.

But the more I delve into the subject, I realise the notion of self-optimisation in the bedroom is nothing new. The thirteenth-century friar Albertus Magnus, for instance, provided some exotic remedies for achieving 'immediate yen for sexual intercourse'. His recipe, laid down in Aristotle's *De Animalibus*, advises that 'a wolf's penis is roasted in an oven, cut into small pieces, and a small portion of this is chewed' by the man. An image that screams 'come hither'. It appears the link between one's sex life and ability is a cliché, perhaps primitive. Goop is merely commodifying the dogmas that have always governed sex, where the body must be compliant and primed for bio-hacking. Here, able-bodiedness is non-negotiable.

Sex is 'almost always' described in the context of health and well-being, according to disability scholar Tobin Siebers. 'A sex life must be, first and foremost, a healthy sex life, and the more healthy a person is, the better the sex life is supposed to be'. This core assumption results in an oppressive need to work on one's body and fitness, 'to do special exercises or adopt a particular diet for it, to spice it up all for the purpose of discovering the ultimate pleasure'. Take the words of Lotte Berk, the German-born ballet dancer who created the barre method in the 1960s, 'upskilling' a generation of women, including Joan Collins and Bond girl Britt Ekland from her Marylebone dance studio. 'If you can't tuck, you can't fuck,' Berk said, referring to one of her trademark pelvic gyrations. While ableism still polices our understanding of what's sexy, desirable and virile, the sexuality of disabled people will forever be painted in terms of failure and deficiency. These mandates around sex are yet another sign of our compulsive desire for able-bodiedness, which invades and occupies every aspect of our lives.

Within our cultural history we have seen radical attempts to jump in and intercept – to stop and say, able-bodiedness is *not* a necessary component of sex appeal. And disabled people are *not* exempt from being desirable, or desiring. Such protests, however, have been far from unproblematic. In June 1985, an army of freshly printed *Playboys* shot through white picket fences, landing on suburban lawns across America, and marched onto the dusty top shelves of newsagents across the globe. Readers were unaware of the revolution that lay under its cover, beneath the titillations of its white typeface and blown-up image of a pert, swimsuit clad-arse. For the first time in its history, a disabled woman – a 23-year-old student with paraplegia from California State University, Fullerton – had been photographed for an eight-page editorial. But would her image represent a jailbreak? Or prove to be yet another occasion for what academics Robert McRuer and Anna Mollow call 'marginalisation or marvelling', where the sexuality of disabled people is depicted as 'tragic deficiency or freakish excess'?

Two years after sustaining a spinal cord injury in a car accident, Ellen Stohl wrote to the editor-in-chief of *Playboy* magazine, Hugh Hefner – a man culturally synonymous with nude centrefolds, louche smoking jackets and a sleazy den of corseted bunny girls. 'Sexuality is the hardest thing for disabled persons to hold onto,' her impassioned letter read. 'Not to say that they are not capable, but rather that society's emphasis on perfection puts this definitive damper on self-esteem. Well, I believe it is time to show society the real story. Anyone can be sexy.' Intent on taking her message public, Stohl floated the idea that Hefner's horny magazine showcased a woman with a disability. This radical exposure, she believed, would prove that sexiness is not defined by the gaze of another, but a matter of how an individual feels from within. A belief that to many feminists, then and now, is somewhat paradoxical: *Playboy* being a publication where sex appeal is very much defined by a male readership. Desire is rendered entirely ocularcentric, packaged up and traded in a series of erotic snapshots, sexualised bodies splayed out for the anonymous spectator.

Hefner was so compelled by her story, her mission, that he wanted her to star in an upcoming issue – but only in 'a really classy way' (no comment). The *Playboy* editorial team, however, had serious reservations: was the potential fallout worth it? Would the magazine be held in disrepute or considered, as they put it so crassly, 'bad taste' for fetishising a 'cripple'? Even as the issue was going to print, associate editor Barbara Nellis was anxious that it teetered on the edge of 'real scuzz exploitation'.

Stohl herself was aware of being misread as 'just a sex object' and angering women's libbers. But the current role she was assigned was just as distressing: 'I was a child again, and people treated me as such.' With so few positions available to women at that time, and a cultural tendency to typecast, Stohl was faced with an either/or scenario. It was Hobson's choice – would she subscribe to a hypersexualised feminine ideal or remain infantilised with no sexuality at all? 'I wasn't taking off my clothes for men. I posed for *Playboy* to discover my own sexuality, to celebrate that part of me that was stripped away by a disability,' she said. 'Would you want that taken away from you?' As a disabled woman, the decision to ally herself with *Playboy*, to submit to the male gaze, is not a moral failing or a lapse in her feminist principles. Rather, it indicates an oppressive reality: she had to fight to declare her sexuality in the first place, before she could go about exerting agency over it.

The issue created a media frenzy, the *New York Times* leading with the headline 'Disabled Model Defies Sexual Stereotypes'. As I flick through the spread now, witnessing this mainstream inclusion of disability, it does feel revolutionary. In fact, I think it would incite a similar reaction if the magazine were published today – an indication of just how excruciatingly slow progress has been nearly half a century on. But is it, in fact, 'revolutionary'? Stohl's disability is visible in the clothed photos, as she socialises in her wheelchair on a university campus, but in the sexualised images all signs of her physical impairment are erased. Her figure – blonde, bosomy, blue-eyed and blemish-free – fills the pro forma of the *Playboy* pin-up. One image shows her in a revealing wedding gown. In another, her nude body is decorously exposed between the bed sheets. She slips into Hefner's cotton-tailed coterie unnoticed, appearing no different to the nude bodies splashed across the other 178 pages. In the eyes of Irving Zola, a sociologist and past editor at the *Disability Studies Quarterly* journal, the photographs cemented precisely what Stohl criticised: 'society's emphasis on perfection'. Would the publication be so receptive to a woman with more obvious deformities? One who couldn't pass as able-bodied or subscribe to patriarchy's palatable beauty ideals? Well, the answer was a decisive 'no'.

Hefner maintained that the nude images should not flaunt Stohl's disability. His argument being that the iconography of a wheelchair would not only veer into S&M territory, an 'exploitative kinky type of thing', but it would invalidate Stohl's mission: to separate her disability and sexuality. Here's where the logic becomes warped – if validating disabled people's sexuality can only be achieved by creating an illusion of able-bodied perfection, it does not solve the problem. The airbrushed *Playboy* feature was therefore a superficial fix that had limited effect on tackling deep-rooted stigmas.

Ultimately, I believe that it is important to accept Stohl's verdict. For her, it was mission accomplished: she had reclaimed her sexuality. I want to say this is an act of 'choice feminism', the belief that no matter what a woman decides, it is inherently feminist – just as when Emily Ratajkowski poses nude on Instagram for the purpose of subverting toxic masculinity, we must accept her praxis. But in doing so, we fail to see that Stohl's 'choice' to play out this normative vision of desirability is a product of a system where ableism and misogyny intersect. When sex is so riven with politics, there is a layer of subliminal control that must be eliminated before any choices can be deemed entirely autonomous, or an act of free will.

It's important to note that this oppression is, by no means, exclusive to women; the dogmas governing male sexuality are arguably just as ferocious. To achieve ideal masculinity, you must expunge any trace of weakness or vulnerability, supplanting it with an impression of boundless strength and machismo. For men, disability acts as an impediment to this project. Male sexual prowess is cancelled out by bodily impairment, a myth that has been instilled by cultural tropes like 'Chatterley syndrome'. When D. H. Lawrence's character Sir Clifford is left paralysed by war, the long-term sequelae are somewhat punishing: his wife runs off with the virile gamekeeper, and to the assertion of his father-in-law, he is 'a lily-livered hound with never a fuck in him'. When you venture beyond heterosexual orientations and binary gender identities, the prejudices become even more knotted. To receive validation as a member of the LGBTQIA+ community, when disabled people are already fighting to assert any sexuality at all, may put you at risk of double discrimination. This results in some disabled people hiding their true sexuality or gender identity to avoid perceived hatred.

We cannot deny that in the realm of sex, ableism runs wild. But the task of wiping out this prejudice, society's abjection towards disabled people's sexuality, is extremely difficult – because, in the words of philosopher Amia Srinivasan, 'no one is obligated to desire anyone else' and 'no one has a right to be desired'. In her controversial essay 'Does Anyone Have the Right to Sex?', Srinivasan interrogates how sexual desire, who we are and are not attracted to, is shaped by societal injustices – and also relevant to their eradication. Here, the undesirability of disabled people is understood as an inevitable symptom of their marginalisation. 'Consider the supreme fuckability of "hot blonde sluts" and East Asian women, the comparative unfuckability of black women and Asian men . . . the sexual disgust expressed towards disabled, trans and fat bodies. These too are political facts,' she writes. To deny that power hierarchies infiltrate the bedroom, claiming that who we desire is just a matter of personal taste, is to conspire with ableism. That whispered confession of 'he's 100 per cent my type on paper' in the sun-drenched *Love Island* villa is *never* just personal. It is a highly charged political statement.

However, failing to be turned on by a disabled body or to find physical impairments sexually arousing, does not explicitly make someone an intolerant or 'muggy' person. In an ableist, appearance-orientated culture, where our assessment of a person's fuckability is overwhelmingly based on looks, how can we expect any different? Our desirability is dictated by the category of body we are assigned; just as our idea of what is desirable is mimetic of other people's. We're in a bind.

These discriminatory sexual preferences are inescapable – any assumption that visually impaired people are exempt is wrong. Not unlike sighted people, they still judge who is a desirable sexual object based on visual markers of identity. In the *New York Times*'s Modern Love column, the writer Leona Godin – who has been progressively losing her sight since the age of ten – proves that attractive looks still hold currency even when they are unseen. In the dating game, she describes seeking confirmation from her sighted friend, asking, 'Is he cute?' Later she also admits, 'I could tell from the way people treated him that he was good looking.' The same applies to straight men: in a BBC article, the journalist Damien Rose recalls the time a new girl arrived at his boarding school for blind children. She went unnoticed for weeks, 'until one lad said they'd heard she was blonde', then she was inundated with suitors. The oppressive value system used to classify bodies is contagious – no one can remain immune to the politics of sexual desirability.

Resolution is complex; clearly, any solution must push further than the visual surface. It is likely there is an element of evolutionary psychology that is stopping us from seeing disabled people as desirable sexual partners, a latent eugenicist impulse that compels us to seek a healthy companion.

In Srinivasan's view, combative action – like more diversity in advertising or disability-inclusive sex education – does not offer a cure-all: 'to think that such measures would be enough to alter our sexual desires, to free them entirely from the grooves of discrimination, is naïve . . . what works in one case will not work in the other'. The discriminatory grooves are terrifyingly deep, I agree, but they are not bottomless. Desirability is dictated by societal injustice, but we have the power to create these social conditions or step out of them. To fail to try is to concede at the fist of discrimination. Stories of desire and love between the disabled and able-bodied prove that this is possible: our sexual desires can be detached from prevalent inequalities. While we may not have the 'right' to sex, everyone, including disabled people, has the 'right' to exist in an inclusive society, one that doesn't instinctively brand them an unworthy sexual partner.

What I am touching on is the concept of 'sexual citizen-ship'. Championed by disability activists as a rallying cry for greater sexual access for disabled people, sexual citizenship is the theory that the act of sex blends the private and public; intimate experiences are always tied to the communities and prejudices from which they emerge. Consequently, it is our duty to create a social environment that respects disabled sexuality. For disabled people to be seen as full sexual citi-zens, we must understand that the obstacles have never been biological. However, it might mean envisioning new ways of thinking about sex, moving away from the phallo-centric, rigid idea of what constitutes normal sexuality towards something more flexible. As the artist Tracey Emin explained following her extensive cancer surgery in which she was fitted with a stoma bag: 'I might have had half of my vagina cut away, but I'm not dead. My sexual feelings come from my skin, all over my body, not just one part . . . [It's] about feeling love, about feeling want.'

In 1996, *The Sexual Politics of Disability* became the first text to place disabled sexuality within this context of political barriers, rather than individual defects. It encouraged the world to foster a radical sex culture, 'to think expansively and creatively about what defines sexual experience' for the purpose of opening it up to all disabled people. The authors believed that a continuum of sexual practices – 'a greater willingness to embrace diversity, experimentation and alternative sexual techniques' – would ultimately be beneficial to everyone who is sexually active.

Nearly thirty years on, this assignment remains incomplete. The status of disabled sexuality in our society is still problematic. I am optimistic, however, that for the next generation, some positive changes are afoot. In late 2021, a third series of the taboo-busting teen comedy, *Sex Education*, rocketed to the top of the Netflix charts. With 209 million subscribers worldwide, the streaming platform has become fertile ground for opening conversations that might, ultimately, engender social change. I, like many other viewers, was left speechless by one scene (this is no mean feat for a programme so deliciously awkward that it has made everything from strawberry condom-induced anaphylaxis, to a turd-in-a-sock being catapulted out of a coach window, seem de rigueur). Notable for its beauty, its intimacy, this particular sequence saw the lead character, Maeve, having sex with Isaac, a disabled character. With its light piano score and the sun's lustre penetrating the caravan windows, it was a drastic departure from the show's hectic, slapstick sex scenes. And nearly all television sex scenes that had come before, for that matter.

'You wanna know what I can feel?' asks Isaac, who uses a wheelchair due to his paralysis. 'Well, I can't feel anything below my level of injury. If you put your hand on my chest I'll show you.' As Maeve traces her fingers up his body, exploring, she asks sensitively: 'So, would you be able to come or . . .' To which he says 'Yeah', and explains, 'When I get touched in the places that I can feel it can get a little intense.' The intimate sequence that ensues – before it's interrupted by an oven timer – will not represent everyone's abilities or experiences, but it encourages us to expand our view of what sex could be, to create that 'continuum of sexual practices'. It's sex, on their own terms. Together, Isaac and Maeve open up a bespoke space – one of deep connection, total respect, communication and understanding that refuses to subscribe to society's rulebook or the unrealistic standards instilled by pornography. There is a natural intimacy that feels more powerful, and more vulnerable, than anything we had previously imagined. As the actor George Robinson, who plays Isaac and collaborated on the script, told the BBC, 'What makes that scene so beautifully crafted is the way it speaks to how sex isn't always about the physical stuff but the intimate act of opening yourself up to one another. That's really what sex is.'

It's a myth that the sexual experiences of disabled people are unsatisfying or a gross failure – in fact, they can take what is the very best about sexuality and institutionalise it in the bedroom. As a society, we haven't yet leaned into these possibilities, these individualised spaces. Instead, we have responded by disregarding them entirely, refusing to see that we have this strong incentive to take disabled sexuality seriously.

Although people with disabilities are widely thought to elicit sexual aversion, there are instances where they are subject to quite the opposite: extreme fetishisation. For individuals, known as devotees, disability is intensely sexy. Disabled bodies that have been derided by mainstream society becoming a source of erotic pleasure. This phenomenon begs the question: could devotees offer a clue to undoing the sexual exclusion of disabled people? Put simply, no. Devoteesim is not harmless appreciation, but an insidious form of ableism where physical impairment comes to define someone's personhood, transforming them into an object for sexual domination. It is yet another example of the discriminatory nature of human desire.

However, punitive assumptions will often be made in these scenarios: isn't being in receipt of *some* sexual contact better than nothing? Disabled people must simply take it or leave it. This is the kind of thinking that allows sexual predators to justify their abusive treatment of people with disabilities, making light of harassment as an act of flattery or favour. It is, in turn, why disabled women are often discounted as victims of sexual violence and remain invisible to the collective outcries of the #MeToo campaign.

What began as a viral hashtag in the autumn of 2017, following the revelation of multiple sexual abuse allegations against Harvey Weinstein, supposedly evolved into a universal movement. But, in the process of exposing the systemic rot of rape culture, the movement's blind spots were made clear: the realities of disabled women were excluded from what is now a global conversation. Perhaps it seems

inconceivable that disabled people should face a disproportionate threat of sexual assault, including physical invasion,
groping and rape. But the statistics show disabled women
are twice as likely as the general population to experience
gender-based violence. It is my view that while people with
disabilities are dehumanised and perceived as powerless,
they will remain prime targets.

The problem is not going away; in fact, it is worsening.
In 2021, rates of sexual violence against disabled women in
England and Wales had more than doubled to 5.7 per cent
in the past six years, compared to 3 per cent of non-disabled
women. In the US, 39 per cent of all female survivors of
rape had a disability at the time of the rape. Meanwhile,
hundreds of sexual violence allegations brought by disabled
women are 'not going to court', according to the campaign
group Disabled Survivors Unite. This is partly due to our
failure to label their claims as abuse – with a recent survey
by the group revealing how victims have been told they are
'not attractive enough' to be sexually assaulted.

There must be no blurred lines. When abuse occurs, it
is imperative that we treat it as such and offer due process.
And yet, as the disability rights activist Simi Linton points
out, these incidences can sometimes be interpreted under
'a different power relationship, a different set of rules'. In
her memoir *My Body Politic*, Linton recounts an incident that
occurred in the final minutes of a job interview. The man
interviewing her suddenly places his hand on the outside
of her thigh, informing her she is sitting in her wheelchair
incorrectly as if she was 'his patient'. When Linton tries to
move her chair back, her would-be employer draws closer
and persists in touching her leg. 'I was unable to summon
the words to describe his transgression . . . An authority that

gave him license to touch me,' she writes. 'His gesture would seem to the outside world a generous one, a selfless one, and no one would understand why I felt hurt and violated.'

Devotee desire is constructed on this imbalance of power. It's a fantasy where disabled lovers are wholly dependent on them. In their longing to assume a caretaker role, devotees may conceal exploitative behaviours under a veil of generosity and compassion. In extreme cases, the devotee quest to seek out a disabled lover is disturbingly sinister. Over-Ground, for example, is an online forum based in Belgium where devotees can immerse themselves in the murky sub-culture, detailing sightings and encounters with amputee women. Another publication, *Amputee Times*, encourages voyeuristic behaviours, urging readers to report the names and addresses of amputee women for a 'national (or international) register of attractive amputees'. One woman, Charlotte Fielder, featured in BBC3 documentary *Meet the Devotees*, once discovered that a photo, showing her missing hand, had been taken from Facebook and uploaded to a porn site, where it was receiving X-rated comments.

In an article for *VICE*, the writer Venessa Parekh, who is a wheelchair user, recalls her first interaction with a devotee on the dating app Tinder. It started with a DM slide: 'Have you always used a wheelchair? I find them very sexy.' For Parekh, the possibility of a man being sexually aroused by her disability was at once 'baffling' and 'distasteful'. But here is where the issues become complex. Her words betray a problematic impulse: why is any link between disability and sexiness automatically regarded with suspicion? If we are conditioned to view anyone who is attracted to disability as offensive, disturbed even, what does this imply about the sexuality of disabled people?

Desire towards disabled women is presented as 'a pathological trait requiring therapeutic intervention' according to
the academic Alison Kafer, as she points out that medical journals contain 'the only analyses of devoteeism'. As
a wheelchair user, Kafer describes how she falls into the
dangerous assumption that anyone who flirts with her must
be a devotee – aka 'pathological'. When she is hit on at the
airport by a well-dressed man in his thirties, she immediately fears he is a devotee and shuts down. His off-the-cuff
compliment about her smile, and invitation to get drinks
sometime, are interpreted as creepy. Sensing her discomfort,
the man apologises and quickly retreats. It's a heartbreaking
fact that scepticism is a natural reaction to these interactions.
Is it genuine attraction? Pity? Curiosity? Or something more
sinister?

Without an unshakable belief in your own desirability,
doubt and uncertainty come creeping in, obscuring any clear
interpretation of romantic intentions. 'How sad that I was
unable simply to feel flattered in his offer, to feel pleasure in
this man's desire,' she writes, in reflection. 'How disconcerting that I was so quick to buy into the ableist assumption that
my impairments eclipse all other aspects of my life. Do I
subscribe to the notion of devotee's exceptionalism, the idea
that only devotees can find bodies like mine desirable? I want
to say no, but my reaction to this man suggests otherwise.'
When we fail to question a culture that brands lust towards
disabled people as 'pathological' – a medical condition that
must be cured – how can we expect anyone with a disability
to feel worthy of desire? I want to feel attractive because of
my unique body, not in spite of it.

The solution, as Kafer hints, lies in self-possession – just
having the confidence and agency to say: anyone can 'find

bodies like mine desirable'. I suppose, at times in my life, I have lived with an awareness of my body as a place of terror and disorder. It's hard to ignore the fact that as my generation was coming of age, I was trying to silence my body's unpredictable workings, to accept that my medicalised self was no longer under my absolute control. In fact, when people begin to experience disability or illness for the first time, you can sense your body becoming more exposed; public even. Whether you're enduring medical treatments, receiving care or being visually dissected by the public, it amounts to a gradual loss of ownership and privacy. For survival, it's often necessary to temporarily disassociate and switch off. To sever the soul from what is happening to the flesh.

Making the transition back, casting off the medicalised self to find sexual expression, requires time and a leap of faith – to trust that this disobedient, chaotic force of energy could ultimately be a source of pleasure and desire, not betrayal. That process of seeking reconnection with the body is much like the Japanese art of *kintsugi* – desire being the liquid gold, molten and burning, that will repair the brokenness, the gaps, the severed edges.

While I don't claim to have it all figured out, I know this much: sexuality is a powerful source of self-worth that should not require you to wait for permission. It's an expression of who we are, what we feel, but also an emotional freedom that cannot be defined by another person. I'm confident that a generation of disabled people who are empowered by their sexuality will change the narrative of exclusion. As someone with a disability, this starts with me claiming authority over how I see myself and my own body.

It is matters such as these that are often trivialised and kept in the shadows – especially in the face of other shocking inequalities. But when they are so intimately connected to how society sees people with disabilities, and how we are conditioned to view ourselves, I would be remiss to discount their seriousness.

While laying bare the issues that underpin the sexual marginalisation of disabled people, I've sensed that the stigma is far more complex, and strikes harder, than any other issue I will tackle in this book. There is something ineffable about it – something that refuses to show its full dimensions clearly. It won't be illuminated by pulling out statistics or reducing it to mere facts. Perhaps because it puts us so close to finally liberating disability, to reimagining how we treat disabled people, far beyond the bedroom.

Just as I am about to suspend my desire for a seamless resolution, without realising it, I have found my own, more imperfect, one. Disability, it seems, is interpreted differently across the spectrum of our relationships. Familial ties, friendships and secure romantic partnerships can cement feelings of acceptance, showing us what it means to love someone without conditions. When it comes to sexual intimacy and dating, it's a battlefield for people with disabilities – able-bodiedness often being a prerequisite for successful interaction.

This distinction, I believe, is politically important. One basic reason concerns how we perceive love and desire as two separate, yet analogous forces. If love places value in a person, connecting two souls through reciprocal compassion and understanding, desire is unmistakably different. While it does not necessarily denote a lack of respect, desire assigns no real value to the desired one. To physically desire someone is to act based on need and satisfaction. It is an impulsive, self-centred action that requires little more than visual appeal, a seductive glance, to be awakened. True connection, which we all seek, goes beyond desire – stripping away superficial measures of attraction, our social conditioning and fixation on the body. It rests upon the ability to deeply engage with someone beyond their exterior, to see value in their being.

For this reason, I regard love as an indispensable tool in the fight for equality. Now I am not talking about gushing declarations of love, punctuated with heart emojis and Aerosmith lyrics, for your latest Tinder match. Rather it is about attributing genuine value to everybody, including value as a sexual partner. When we are inspired to see connection, never difference, and imaginative possibilities over constriction, that's when love becomes a political remedy – blowing apart the subordinating walls of bigotry.

People will often say, you only truly 'get' the issues facing disabled people when it affects someone you love. Being close to someone with a disability, humanising the barriers they face and taking on the frustrations as if they were your own, is kind of revolutionary. For love is not an individualistic act, it is a social force that can bring about real progress. This vision is what theorist bell hooks refers to as a 'love ethic'. Here, love is not merely a feeling, but a continuous, guiding practice where 'we see our lives and our fate as intimately connected to those of everyone else on the planet'.

Love, after all, is not a commodity nor a finite resource. It's gloriously free and transmissible, travelling from body to body, identity to identity, generation to generation, breaking across divisions and differences. Like a network of optic fibre, love is the connective tissue that tethers and binds us. Our existence is tied together by its invisible bonds, and I find hope in the possibility that somewhere, even though we may not always see it, there awaits this generative, yet quietly radical, power. At a time when our political systems are failing to secure meaningful change, I think it may be all we have. To live in a world where everyone knows what it means to love and be loved, regardless.

# True North

Their faces bespoke the apocalypse. The panic-stricken eyes, the heads hung back in anticipatory grief gave a wild, Munchian quality to the streetwalkers. Shopping bags tumbled to the ground, as muslin-wrapped babies were thrust back into Bugaboos. Every expression was now capsized by alarm. Two unsuspecting figures stroll into the scene, instantly becoming sucked into this collective outburst of tortured souls. It was just the typical, prosaic reaction that follows the sighting of a learner driver on the road, really.

For when those hysterical bystanders saw my Nissan Micra beginning to roll down the hill, jerk violently, tip back, then lurch forwards as I over-revved the engine, they assumed a motor collision was imminent. I had hoped the red 'L' plate, slapped to my car bonnet, would offer a kind of mea culpa – but that seemed to only inflame their anxiety, becoming an omen of deep suffering. They saw me rolling and, boy, they were hating. My hill-start manoeuvre had failed, ending in a sort of bathetic bunny hop that saw the heads of myself and my instructor, Terry, momentarily caress the internal car roof. I drove off, trying to regain some composure and focus. 'Hey! Is that Greg Wallace?!' I enquired, at the sight of a bald man driving up the road from the alternate direction. There was ringing silence. As we reached a set of traffic lights, I turned to look at Terry, expecting some sage words, a consolatory pep talk (confirmation that it was indeed the sweet-toothed *MasterChef* judge, maybe?), but I realised his white, bloodless palms were glued to the grab handle above his head. How long had they been like that? And when did he get that sickly pallor? Terry scooped up his Sudoku and lunchbox from the footwell, looking me pointedly in the eyes as he took a minute to rearrange them back inside the glovebox. He then fed me the inevitable conclusion: my initial attempt at a hill-start would constitute a 'failable offence' under the jurisdiction of the Highway Code. I sighed, as the lights turned to red again.

My boy racer beginnings belied a nimbler artiste lurking underneath. As the weeks progressed, I learned the concept of 'finesse' in the driver's seat. I would no longer slam the brake pedal with reckless abandon – Terry, who was customarily sat atop a cushion, had bad hips already. I was now wheedling my way through lines of traffic with a gentle fondling of the wheel and a tease on the accelerator. It was Terry's method of the 'peep 'n' creep' that marked the turning point, I think. What sounded alarming to the untrained ear, illegal even, was a simple technique to improve vehicle control. You would pull out slowly from a blind junction (the infamous 'creep'), looking both ways for updates on oncoming cars (the cheeky 'peep'). His repeated calls for me to do the 'peep 'n' creep' would take on different stresses, as an indication of his mental state. If his words had long, drawn out 'ee's, I could rest assured that I was doing fine – his calming assonances suggesting a cautious optimism in my driving. The plosive sound, however, was a precursor to mortal peril. It would cause him to almost spit out his chewing gum onto the windscreen before reaching over to yank the wheel, or worse still, make a frantic bid for those mortifying dual controls.

In fact, that chewing gum was another reliable marker of my progress. The instructor's mastication habits – the velocity and tempo – were almost a speech act, not just a measure of my success and failure, but a screaming declaration of when to get it together. Margaret Atwood once shared the same observation in a piece for *The New Yorker* about her own attempt at learning to drive. As a vindication of my bungled hill-start, the author's first experience on the road with her father in the sixties was similarly harrowing and ham-fisted. 'I'd mistaken the gas pedal for the brake and almost rammed his car into a stone wall,' she admits wryly. 'No tears shed by me: I had other things on my mind, such as existentialism, moon goddesses, and the writing of tortured poetry.' Consequently, Atwood hired in a professional instructor with 'nerves of steel'. When she was testing those nerves, 'he chewed gum very fast', and when she was doing well, 'the gum-chewing slowed'. Everything lied in those subtleties when you were behind the wheel.

I think my desperation to drive, however, was greater than many other seventeen-year-olds. Without even a mobility scooter at that point, independence was prescribed by how far I could walk. Driving offered me something that I couldn't have in my present: an animating principle. It was speed, extreme mobility and control – everything to do with moving forwards – when I was living an existence marred by standstill. That rush, the power of movement. The ability to blast myself, an otherwise motionless entity, through space and realise the euphoric thrills of kinesis. At a time when my life was full of false starts and constantly running on empty, I remember that first drive was revitalising. I could spend months regaining my strength from a hospital admission, only for progress to come to a screeching halt again. But, in those hour-long lessons, I was no longer stationary. I had the ability to self-navigate. To hold real, tangible control over my direction for what felt like the first time. In every acceleration the present was sent into fast forward, and in every deceleration lied a meditative pull back. I could escape my destiny, whatever was waiting, and that was revelatory.

But it was more than that. In every rotation of the wheel lay an urgent mission. I could see how these new abilities were becoming more and more imperative to my freedom and my future. A driver's licence signalled an unclipping of wings – a means to transgress the bounds of my reality and circumnavigate a world that was finally offering itself to me, yet was closing in.

Looking out at the street drifting and dismantling beneath my car wheels, the cityscape opened up in a way that I could never experience by foot. As I drove, I traced how the city fit together, its joints and expressions. The incantations of urban hieroglyphics – the stops, the starts – rang out through the smoke and lights of kerbside bars, sending drivers into a trance. Directions and possibilities etched onto street corners. Illuminated buildings were taken captive by the dark harbour waters – where, in its rippled reflections, I saw the raising of a replica city. And after congestion comes release. Cruising the eerie expanses of industrial parks at dusk – those minutes where the falling purple sky is held up only by the black struts of streetlights. Electrical pylons, stencilled across the horizon, stand as conductors in the gateway to another dimension. All those ripe, yet seemingly mundane details that I had been shut away from. To be out in the world, to assimilate its emotional topographies and feel that jolt of otherworldly connection, is something we easily overlook.

Planning the trips I might take, places I may discover, felt like adulthood. Everything was in reach. Throughout that year, driving was my rite of passage, something I could do and then afterwards exchange hilarious stories about it with my friends. With two small adaptations, a panoramic rear-view mirror and easy-release handbrake, I could roam free. Now, all I had to do was get rid of Terry.

So I was a-peeping and a-creeping one day when something bizarre struck. In a spine-tingling instant, out of nowhere, I found myself turning into a street which, I'd conjecture, was not dissimilar to the surface of the Sun. Searing rays of white light were bouncing off wet tarmac and eclipsing my view. Even the sun visor and my Ray-Ban Clubmasters were redundant. Eyes streaming, I threw a signature 'rescue me now' glance in my co-pilot's direction. No response. Terry, it seemed, was out cold. I honked the horn in desperation, a move that miraculously summoned the clouds, but not my 'charge-by-the-hour' instructor, into action. Then, a sheepish grin spread across Terry's face and he quickly roused himself, reaching to grab a limp banana from the dark depths of the side door compartment. He unpeeled, and then munched on that brown banana with an insouciance that was frankly distasteful given the events that had just unfolded. Throwing me a look that said, 'What's all this rumpus about now?'

Next lesson, it happened once again. But knowing his slumber would only be momentary, I decided to politely ignore it. I drove on with Terry's unconscious body laid out beside me. It bounced flaccidly as I mowed across a stretch of speed bumps, his head jiggling up and down to the rhythm of the road. I braced myself as I took a hard corner; Terry meanwhile – lacking any discernible body tone – was thrown, smack into the window. I was beginning to enjoy these peaceful moments to myself. If anything told me I was ready to take my test it was the sight of my driving instructor sleeping, like a log, in the passenger seat.

On test day, my palms were glued to the steering wheel, moving gingerly with an awareness of the freedoms that awaited me if I could just feign competency for the next forty minutes. I was also on constant lookout for roadkill. My friend, who having been castigated for running over a badger in a driving lesson, ultimately failed in her test for swerving a dead fox – the trauma, the injustice. I refused to be derailed by nature, unmistakably red in tooth and claw. But five minutes in, my own tragedy befell me.

I was zooming along a leafy residential road – fast enough for the examiner's toupée to exhibit a considerable flutter, but slow enough to not pose a threat to life – when it unexpectedly fed into a busy main road at an acute angle, aggressively so. I had to act quickly to avoid veering into traffic. But before I had a chance to decelerate and enact the slow, performative glances demanded of a peep 'n' creep, the toupéed thespian in the passenger seat roared out: 'BRAKE, BRAKE, BRAKE.' Each syllable was underscored by a punch into the dashboard, three hard blows that shook the entire bonnet. I could tell he was enjoying it. Terry, who had taken the back seat that day, was facepalming – an action that I could not see but felt in the core of my soul. The post-test debrief required untold composure and humility on my part. During the examiner's monologue, I felt like grabbing my jumbo-sized rear-view mirror and easy release handbrake and flouncing out of the vehicle.

In the months and years that followed, further illness meant I could not return behind the wheel or collect that licence to greater independence. The body, it seemed, played watchman – pulling me ever further from the domed metropolis, those spacious visions of tree-lined parks, and lamplit portals to sprawling underground networks. I was stuck, stricken by a reality I had no intention of accepting.

My mind, however, was in constant motion. Was health always going to be imperative to my freedom? Or could I have worldliness without wellness? Was one possible, without the other? These are questions I still ask myself, but the answers stretch far beyond the everyday experience of travel, of pottering and its practicalities. It is a deeply philosophical concern – one that spills over into ideas about how our identity is shaped by the spaces we are permitted to access, inhabit and unfold in. It's about discovering new horizons, all those unmapped places beyond our observable present. It's about community and interconnectedness. It's about living. And how can we exist without that boundless promise of exploration?

Writers have long been preoccupied by the study of consciousness and the built environment – the ways in which our embodied relationship to the city, urbanism and its topographies can reinvigorate the soul. For Virginia Woolf, especially, the experience of travelling around London was something of a psychological phenomenon. Her habit of wandering alone in the city where 'everything seems accidentally but miraculously sprinkled with beauty', offers endless pleasure and creative inspiration. In her essay 'Street Haunting', Woolf charts the radical process that unfolds when we step out of the front door and into the generative role of *flâneur* – that ambulatory, sauntering figure who flutters around 'like a butterfly', enthralled by the urban spectacle. Out in public, Woolf explains, 'the shell-like covering which our souls have excreted to house themselves . . . is broken'. The self now becomes porous, creating holes for new experiences and knowledge to seep in. This rhizomatic and interactive process – which is denied to many people with disabilities who cannot effortlessly navigate the world beyond their front door – is where freedom and adventure lies. 'To escape,' as Woolf attests, 'is the greatest of pleasures'.

In contrast, for many disabled people the prospect of travelling and traversing the city is not liberating, nor 'sprinkled with beauty'. Restricting and full of friction, more likely. Movement and fluidity are hindered at every corner: barriers like steep pavements and a lack of dropped kerbs can make the streets difficult to negotiate by foot, or with a mobility aid. Add to this a couple of bollards, some potholes and bulging tree roots – then you're in assault course territory. Public transport, meanwhile, can be equally fraught. Disabled travellers are often beleaguered by obstacles like jostling crowds, no step-free access and unreliable support from rail staff. Should you succeed in reaching your destination, public spaces like restaurants, banks, shops and theatres may be excruciatingly inaccessible due to anything from stepped entrances to a lack of hearing loops.

The impact is irrefutable: each year disabled adults travel just over half the distance covered by their non-disabled counterparts. On average, they make 26 per cent fewer trips. This inability to pootle out of the house, to glide through the world with ease, to feel free, is an issue that, I believe, lies at the root of disability inequality. Inaccessibility is curtailing lives and opportunities. It is the cause of limited social footprints, loneliness and meagre employment rates. But we must not see this as a moment for despair, rather a revolutionary opening. Tackling the systems that are excluding disability from the public sphere promises a domino effect. Inclusive infrastructure could topple prevalent injustices, enabling disabled people to enjoy these rightful liberties. And, fundamentally, to discover new, exhilarating horizons. In order to bring about this change, we must first interrogate the politics that pollute our everyday environments.

Spatiality, in the words of the radical geographer and social scientist Doreen Massey, is 'always and everywhere an expression and a medium of power'. Look around! Whether you're leaping onto the bus through a logjam of yo-pros, snaking across an airport terminal, teetering down a dimly lit stairway to a nightclub, a subterranean world emerging in the darkness, or contemplating the two steps up to 10 Downing Street, spaces are groaning with power relations. There are clues all around us, every angle endowed with the potential to exclude and include – telling us who is going to be at ease in the world, who is made to feel welcome and connected, and who is left alienated.

It is axiomatic that spaces establish a power hierarchy where disabled people are consigned to the bottom rung. Every day the supremacy of able-bodiedness is upheld by inaccessible environments. 'Closures' and barriers exist everywhere in the built world for disabled people, according to Sara Hendren, an artist and lecturer in architecture at Harvard Graduate School of Design. As exemplars of non-normativity, people with disabilities may contest the cult of purity, containment and self-reliance that dominates modern design. In practice, this means that a square-peg, round-hole conundrum takes hold when the disabled body clashes with its surroundings. Take, for instance, a wheelchair user who is blocked by the sleek, narrow architecture of a doorway. Or a visually impaired person who is foiled by the 'mood' lighting in a boutique. Or perhaps it's the spiral stairs into a mid-century apartment block, and then the Fort Knoxian mechanics of a front door lock . . . the barriers really are endless when you start looking.

Hendren's appreciation of how the disabled body is often mismatched with its man-made environment came about when her son was born with Down's syndrome. As he started to interact with his surroundings, Hendren saw, for the first time, the disabling barriers that revealed themselves when his body met an inflexible world. It posed a challenge: could our environments be given more elasticity, to flex around the unpredictable nature of human bodies? Hendren cites an example of disability activists in Denver, who during the late seventies, engaged in a guerrilla-style 'editing' of the city. Armed with hammers, they took to the streets and smashed away concrete kerbs, creating cuts that would allow wheelchair users to transition from pavement to road. They were left with no choice: the city had discontinued its kerb-reduction programme and disabled people were frequently being struck by motorists while trying to get up impassable kerbs. Today, the crumbled relics of their protest can be seen on display in the Smithsonian: the rubble stands as a potent reminder of how humanity has possessed, and always will possess, the ability to define the spatial conditions of the future. Even the most concrete, solid structures can be made putty-like, through sheer force of will. Often, it is only through activism that these radical victories can be realised; collective action to disrupt the historic power dynamics that endure in our built surroundings.

Transport networks are proof of the highly political nature of space, of how the places we inhabit have the power to reproduce or eradicate the divisions that govern our perception of disability. By design, transportation is a link that weaves together the comings and goings of city dwellers. It is a network that should connect us, accelerating flow and movement. When ableism rots the system, the network is broken and disabled individuals are thrust into a state of marginalisation. A marginalisation that is not only literal and geographic, in the way that those with disabilities are tethered to the home and stuck on the periphery, but also highly symbolic, as each broken link consolidates the social 'othering' of disabled minorities, pushing them further out of sight.

In February 1995, scores of disabled people came together to rage against this exclusion from public transport. Denied the right to move around their cities, they questioned how a whole segment of society could be left immobilised and exiled from daily life. This could not continue. It was a freezing cold morning that struck London like a blow to the chest. Undeterred, adrenaline-fueled protesters gathered on Westminster Bridge. There was fire raging in their bodies: wrists were handcuffed to red double-decker buses, bringing traffic to a standstill. Angrily painted placards were now fighting against the biting wind. Provocative chants, demanding accessible public transport for disabled people (now!), blare out from megaphones. 'They call us wheelchair warriors, we're kicking up some fuss. And we will keep on marching till you let us on the bus,' screamed one protester. Tensions mount and resolve deepens, as wheelchairs were lifted off the ground and shuttered away into police vans. No matter – prosecutions wouldn't happen. They couldn't when police cells and magistrates' courts were also inaccessible.

This high-profile stunt – masterminded by a group of disabled activists known as the Direct Action Network (DAN) – symbolised a turning point for the disability civil rights movement in Britain. In the early nineties, the 'Danners' triggered a surge of mass protests across the country, with more than 100,000 people uniting to call for change. Buses were hijacked, wheelchairs were used to block main roads like coronary arteries, and disabled protesters quite literally flung themselves under vehicles – all to campaign against the inaccessibility of public transport. It represented a new, unruly style of politics whereby disabled bodies, seen as weak and vulnerable, were thrown on the line for the creation of a more equal society. It shocked and appalled the nation. Legions of disabled people occupying contested space, vigorously demanding 'rights, not charity'. The Danner mission statement was, 'To boldly go where all others have gone before'. Perhaps then, hopping on the bus to the supermarket wouldn't feel like an intergalactic mission?

Rallies soon erupted outside of parliament, pressurising the government to ratify a groundbreaking anti-discrimination bill. Exclusion from public transport was one of the most pernicious acts of everyday discrimination, according to Alan Holdsworth, the charismatic leader of DAN. It was hoped that protective laws – like the race and sex discrimination acts which had been passed some twenty years earlier – would bring an end to the injustices felt by the disability community, but these protections never materialised. Without vital equality laws, bus doors were designed with steep, cumbersome steps. And wheelchair users were required to give several days' notice just to travel by train. Even then, they were segregated and poked away at the rear of the train in the guard's van, due to a lack of space in the main carriages.

The crucial point here is that our communal transport systems were designed and developed in the new industrial era, a time when people with disabilities had been socially segregated for centuries. Evidently, architects and planners would not have considered how these spaces were going to accommodate a broad spectrum of abilities, from sensory impairments to mobility issues. Instead, the 'model' passenger was figured as someone with a normative, conventionally productive body, like a non-disabled worker or leisure seeker. 'Bodies beyond those were, in many regards, illegible to the system,' explains Raquel Velho, a sociologist of science and technology. 'Therefore, their needs were not embedded within the infrastructure.' In short, disabled people were assumed to be housebound, unemployed, or institutionalised even, not your prototypical traveller. As a result, their access was never factored into the design process. Once again, our culture's unwillingness to see value beyond those perceived as 'normal', or standard fit, has created a legacy of oppression.

However, through the fearless activism of campaigners, by the 1990s many started to see the devastation that occurs when disabled people slip through the gaps. For the first time, society was forced to ask, as Sara Hendren puts it, 'Who is the world built for?' 'I realised then that buses should be for everyone, including us,' said Barbara Lisicki, the disability rights activist and stand-up comedian who founded DAN, along with her ex-husband Alan Holdsworth. 'Up to that point, I just thought it was my fault I couldn't walk and couldn't get on. It's actually possible to invent a ramp or a lift for the bus, whereas for me to be medically cured was not within the realms of possibility at that time.' Her words riff on that central tenet of disability liberation: look at the limitations of the disabled body as a product of the built surroundings, a thing that is socially constructed, not a medical concern or a personal failing. Ask how you can change society first, before you force the individual to navigate and butt up against an inaccessible world.

And society did change. After months of increasingly intense and ferocious protests, the Disability Discrimination Act (DDA) was finally passed in the House of Commons on 8 November 1995. This legislation made it illegal to discriminate against disabled people in relation to employment, the provision of goods and services, education and transport. The red-blooded fight for greater justice and equity that led to that moment has mostly been erased from our political history. But groups such as DAN played a crucial part in exposing, and then purging, the invisible power structures that are inherent in the spaces around us – the holy grail of the disability civil rights movement.

The rights of disabled people in the UK have changed significantly since that day. However, huge inequalities persist – especially when it comes to transport. Campaigners agree that the DDA didn't stretch far enough. Unlike the race and sex discrimination acts, the DDA did not establish a governing body with legal powers to regulate and police the new rules. Policies could only be enforced in a civil court, which left disabled people to fund legal action themselves with no guarantee of securing damages. What's more, some measures outlined in the DDA didn't have to be introduced for nearly a decade. In other words, it was a 'soft launch' on disability rights. 'Some people thought, well, we've won with the Disability Discrimination Act. We didn't win, it was never a victory,' laments Barbara Lisicki, on an episode of the BBC podcast, *Ouch*. 'The positive thing that most people agree on, is that it acknowledged in law, for the first time, that disabled people were discriminated against . . . That was pretty much it with the DDA.'

The legislative framework (which has now been rolled into the Equality Act 2010) did mandate a range of assistive measures around public transport. By the letter of the law, these include that taxi drivers must aid passengers getting into a taxi and help to load a wheelchair into the taxi when necessary. In the case of disabled rail users and people travelling aboard buses or coaches, users must be able to get on and off 'without unreasonable difficulty' and to be transported 'safely' and in 'reasonable comfort'. Almost three decades later, however, these laws are still not reliably implemented, with two in three disabled people experiencing problems using public transport. Most able-bodied commuters can expect some degree of friction when navigating transportation networks. But the hazards and the pitfalls simply aren't as exhausting or humiliating. Despite 'retrofitting' (attempts to make current transport systems more accessible through provisions like lifts and boarding ramps), disabled travellers are still thwarted by broken equipment, overcrowding and irascible drivers.

To paint you a picture: when the journalist Alex Taylor travels into Waterloo station at 6:30am for work every morning, he requires platform staff to manually lay down a wheelchair ramp at both sides of his journey. This is standard procedure. And yet, he is often left trapped inside the train when platform staff fail to arrive. On a recent occasion, he waited patiently as other train passengers departed, but no one came. 'I was left desperately shouting for help after finding myself completely alone and unable to get to work,' he said. He was struck not just by fear, but a familiar sense of frustration. Clearly, this is more than the soul-destroying discovery of 'severe delays' on the Piccadilly line or being smacked in the face by a wet umbrella.

When disabled travellers are put at the mercy of transport workers to secure a safe passage, empathy and understanding become imperative – something the actor Ruth Madeley knows only too well. In the summer of 2021, she hit the headlines after a taxi driver snatched her wheelchair without warning and refused to give it back. The driver had become increasingly agitated, telling her it was 'too difficult' to drop her close to an accessible entrance of Euston train station. Transport for London condemned the incident as 'utterly appalling', but when Madeley (who, quite prophetically, played the role of Barbara Lisicki in a BBC biopic) reported this harassment to police she was told no criminal act had taken place. It did not constitute a violation of the discrimination act. 'I was shut down [and] made to feel as though I was making a fuss over nothing,' she wrote on Instagram after the event. 'It is clear proof that the fight for disability rights is far from over.'

Madeley's sentiments were echoed just months later by the 26-year-old Paralympic medallist Jack Hunter-Spivey, when two Uber taxis drove off upon seeing that he was a wheelchair user. It was an appalling act of discrimination, but one that he endures 'regularly' from multiple taxi firms. 'My chair folds really easily, it takes thirty seconds to collapse down and it fits in any boot . . . It would be the same if it was somebody with a suitcase,' Hunter-Spivey told the BBC. 'Please think twice about it. We're not a burden, we're just trying to get around in our day-to-day life.'

Being unable to travel with confidence is having a harmful impact on disabled passengers: four out of five experience some level of anxiety or stress when travelling by public transport. I can't help but think, is it any wonder? The reality for disabled people 'just trying to get around' in the twenty-first century sounds more like the plotline of a second-rate slasher film.

For all its horrors, though, the dangers of this exclusion from transport services can escalate when people with disabilities are confronted with the alternative: navigating the city streets, unexpectedly, without protection or after dark. For me, it is an unthinkable position to be in. Every woman, in a similar predicament, is painfully aware of the risks that await – to be alone in a city at night is to put your body under threat. The tragedy of Sarah Everard's brutal murder in March 2021 as she walked home at night, and Sabina Nessa just six months later, was a stark reminder of the fact. The cultural discourse following these incidents pointed towards one unifying agenda: 'reclaim the streets'. But people with disabilities were, in my opinion, severely under-represented in this era-defining conversation. As a minority group that has, historically, endured restricted access to public spaces and is expressly vulnerable to these risks, disabled people should become central to the campaign for equal rights to move around the city.

Consider the experience of writer Lucy Armstrong, who is moderately deaf and cannot hear footsteps along the street. 'You see I am terrified when someone walks past me as I haven't heard them behind me,' she writes in a piece for the online disability publication *The Unwritten*. 'I have to alert myself to become hyper-aware of the spaces around me, using the streetlights to spot the shadows of anyone coming up behind me. My heart often stops until the human figure that has crept up on me moves well into the distance ahead.' Armstrong makes the valuable point that she doesn't have the luxury of calling a friend, as it is not always possible for her to speak over the phone. Much of the advice and proposed safety measures that emerged in the aftermath of Everard's death were targeted towards able-bodied individuals. Often, it is not feasible for disabled people to take a different, perhaps longer and more arduous, route home. It is not always possible to practice self-defence, to run away, hide or scream for help. It is not easy to stick to well-lit and busy areas – what if they have stairs, uneven pathways or are entirely inaccessible? The last resort of switching to a different form of public transport, or calling a taxi, is not a practical alternative either, due to the host of issues I have already unpacked. The only recourse to remaining vigilant and protected is steering clear of the city streets. In a society that refuses to give disabled people their right to travel seamlessly and safely, freedom has been usurped by fear and restraint.

This climate of fear reinforces the exclusionary power dynamics of our cities and dictates what type of body deserves access to public life. It is only by bestowing new freedoms and improving disabled people's access to spaces, that we can begin to disrupt the disabling politics of the past.

One day, my sense of scale and distance was blown apart. There were times after severe illness where even small distances felt entirely out of reach. Heart racing, I primed myself for that trip down to the hospital foyer like I was on an impending ascent to the moon. But the implications were far greater than feeling cut off from the fabled Stock-Shop. I guess, like a cartographic explosion, all corners of the globe were sent blasting into the cosmos. A moment of recalibration must have followed, where the ground was stretched out, resized and stuck back together in a way that left it slackened. My world had undeniably changed.

When I delve into memories of foreign travels, this extreme magnification of scale is most discernible; shocking even. It is a terrifying reminder of how unreachable these adventures are to me now, in my current state of orientation. To be stood, once again, on the rooftop of the Duomo in Milan, the city's filigree crown rising up from a pigeon-strewn piazza. Or looking out at that craggy cliff face, 12,000 miles away, in Kaikoura, where a rookery of sunbathing seals are laid out in ecstasy, having snubbed the surging Pacific waves. Or even tandem biking across the grassy banks of some ancient gardens in Rome, weaving between secret tombs and stone fountains – the last clinging vestiges of a civilisation past. It is startling. And yet these memories remain my most precious possessions. They give me anchor and alignment, illuminating the bounteousness of what exists beyond my present.

It is easy to amuse myself reminiscing about my travels, replaying the beautiful and bizarre incidents that have occurred when I've met the world. It all started with a small pink suitcase. Its proportions, however, were deceptive. It may have appeared babyish and futile but, filled to the gunnels, the case could comfortably house an entire global population of Sylvanian Families. The pièce de resistance? It rolled! In the age before the pervasive wheelie carry-on, these charming little wheels delighted me. I used to racket it around the house, ricocheting off doors and kitchen cabinets, leaving battered skirting boards in my wake. Each time I opened the case from the central black clasp, I was guaranteed an undiluted moment of theatre. First came the anticipation, the thrill, then a good five minutes of drama ensued, before giving way to utter relief and catharsis. See, I had not yet worked out the suitcase's volatile padlock function.

At the airport check-in desk, I would tuck in the retractable handle and hand over my case to a chirpy flight attendant in orange, habitually stepping past a family of five who, through groans and expletives, were disembowelling the entire contents of their five-piece suitcase set (everything from snorkels and flip-flops, to nappies and jars of Branston Original Pickle regurgitated across the terminal floor). I looked down anxiously at my suitcase's unblemished exterior, and into the eyes of the flight attendant: I could trust her, right? Her huge toothy smile might have put me at ease, had I not just seen my luggage crash down, thwack onto the conveyor belt, zooming off into oblivion. There was a violence in the way it hit the metal sides, briefly getting jammed before the flight attendant spotted, and revved up the belt speed to give it some extra welly. It was then gobbled up by that black-flapped orifice – the stuff of nightmares.

After several years of globetrotting – and many encounters with airport conveyor belts, taxi doors and the vengeful baggage handling of earmuffed Hulks on tarmac – the suitcase was a travelogue of its own. Each scuff told a story. The 6-inch thunderbolt, smack in the centre, told a story that was so surreal, I might not have believed it were it not for the battle scar. My family and I had just reached Paris. With suitcases in tow, we were heading to our hotel by the Métro. As crowds of people elbowed their way down white-tiled tunnels to the tracks, I threaded into a vicious throng, feeling that rush towards the steel synapses of the city. The speed picked up. The clamour was now booming off the graffitied walls, drowning out the reedy hums of a lone busker, hopelessly tugging at his accordion. As we made a bid for an already packed-out carriage, I tripped up, tumbling down onto the floor. A hand reached out to scoop me up and pull me out of the way of harried commuters. Next, we were fighting our way over to some green plastic seats at the edge of the platform. I had just perched down to examine my grazed hands and knee when a French madame rushed up to us, having just seen our struggle. She started cradling my mum's head and whispering something incredibly tender. 'Is she a friend from work?' I thought to myself. The madame then reached inside her crocodile-skin lady bag and pulled out a vial of liquid. '*Et voilà!*' she trilled, with a flamboyant hand gesture. My suspicions were immediately raised, spiking at the sight of this amber medicine bottle. Its homespun quality, the hand-scrawled label and cork bung, really did nothing to allay my fears. It looked as if it should have been locked away in the vanity cupboard of some nineteenth-century debutante – safely ensconced between the smelling salts and face creams laced with arsenic, where it belonged. And still, the silver-haired madame squeezed a pipette between her manicured fingertips and began drawing up some of the concoction.

'What the hell is it?' I thought, as the pipette came inching towards my lips (its crystal-clear colour spilling no secrets).

I tried to assess what was unfolding, PSHE lessons flashing before my eyes. Admittedly, it wasn't textbook – but I was sure that an elderly French madame plying me with an unidentified tincture belonged to the same school of thought as 'stranger danger' and 'never take drugs'. My French conversation classes, meanwhile, had lapsed in this area. Something told me that a *'non, merci'* would only excite her more. All I could do was grit my teeth and pray that the solution was merely decanted – not a lethal batch of bootleg hooch.

I remember its taste had a boozy quality, but was unmistakably herbal, while the syrupy texture made it nearly impossible to spit out. The madame, now shaking furiously at the medicine bottle, was focusing her 'healing' energies elsewhere. She thrust another unsolicited pipette into my mum – who, to my disbelief, was positively lapping it up. My sister had fair warning: she managed to dodge the loaded gun and I was envious to see it splashed all down her red duffle coat, not in her mouth. The madame then snapped her bag clasp shut, with a satisfying clunk, and disappeared off into the milieu. What had we just consumed? A question shared by my dad, who had been watching the full scene unfold in perplexed horror, from the other side of the platform.

Years later, on another trip to the French capital, I nearly left my suitcase behind in a restaurant. We were so distracted by a dessert menu that was more philosophically puzzling than any of the *cabinets de curiosités* we had seen in the Louvre earlier that day. It was, by definition, a menu, but not as we knew it. A tray of plastic replica desserts (mini *tarte aux citron*, *religieuse*, millefeuille and the like) was trundled out on a trolley across the restaurant floor. The excessive pomp and ceremony had something of the *Fawlty Towers* about it – particularly when, on the gruelling commute from the kitchen to our table, the wheels got tangled up in another diner's trench coat belt. When the maître d' reached us, I was struck by his composure, his dignity, and his continued respect for our decision to go à la carte. As he patiently talked through and gesticulated at the chef's selection of mock puddings, my mum returned from the toilettes. And so began her minute-long crusade to pick up a plastic, albeit disarmingly real, crème caramel that was glued to the tray. The maître d' looked on, mortified at the confusion caused by his sugary simulacrum – an experience almost as odd as being force-fed Rescue Remedy on the Parisian Métro by a French madame.

Though arguably, it was less dramatic than a dining experience that unfolded on another family holiday – where a covered patio, festooned with lights, descended into the crime scene of a so-called 'dine and dash'. The couple fled the scene, leaving no trace but a crumpled orange paper napkin, a cigarette butt, and the distraught wails of the restaurant owner. The police arrived, seeking witness statements. All eyes turned to my new handycam which had been rolling, amassing 360-degree footage, throughout the evening. Please, no, I thought to myself. I was terrified that it would be bagged up as evidence – or worse, that I would be subpoenaed to play back my recordings, in which I went full A. A. Gill, ranting about the manslaughterous amount of salt in the *confit de canard*. Had it been brined and preserved for consumption on the *Mary Rose*? Or dragged across 3,000 miles of Bolivian salt flat? The restaurant owner's ego, I feared, was bruised enough.

That suitcase rolled beside me on all these trips. To the hallucinatory dream spaces of Dalí's Theatre-Museum in Catalonia – the artist's subliminal world unravelling in red lip sofas, severed hearts and liquid clock faces – where, in the museum's ivy-covered courtyard, I saw levitating ships and vintage black Cadillacs filled with dead-eyed mannequins. I was, however, under strict orders *not* to touch any of the exhibits. My tiny, sticky fingers had been caught caressing a Picasso canvas during the last gallery tour. Its thick, impastoed oil paint tempting me in like a rough scab beneath my soft palm – that is, before it was torn away by a panicked museum guard, spitting something French and unpromising into his walkie-talkie. The suitcase was also a constant companion during my week-long campaign for a hair braid in the South of France. I needed those silver, lilac and baby blue threads woven into my long, sun-bleached hair. It was a ritual of any girlhood summer, as I pitched it to my parents. I successfully cajoled them into going on a two-hour round trip, from my uncles' farmhouse in the mountains to the braid stall, beside the bright lights and casinos of a clubby seaside resort. An odyssey via Avis rental car. I was soon begging for paracetamol from the backseat. The threads were pulled and bound so eye-wateringly tight as to bring on a hair braid-induced migraine. I looked over at my sister, our eyes locked through the half-darkness, in recognition of our hubris: we felt each other's pain.

My suitcase was miraculously there during our month-long ramble across New Zealand, sequestered in the boot of a light aircraft, which rattled like a tin can with strap-on wings as we flew between islands. '*Safe, reliable, rugged*' read the slogan painted in green across the fuselage. The emphasis being on rugged: it was a hell ride. Minutes before take-off, the pilot hollered out from the cockpit that passengers should switch seats. He'd sensed that the weight load was unevenly distributed across our twelve-seater craft. His laidback Kiwi charm, the casualness of his eleventh-hour disclosure, did nothing to supress the sheer disquiet of playing do-or-die musical chairs alongside a group of Filipino tourists.

Seafaring, in the form of dolphin watching, was equally emetic. As the rolling and surging motions of the ocean took our catamaran, hysteria swept the boat. Mothers and children, pale and retching, were bundled up into the darkened cabins below deck. Even at the tender age of nine, I could see that the skipper's call to relocate the sick onto the top bunks of two windowless quarters was much like steering the fated *Titanic* towards its iceberg – reckless. The waves heaved, just as the dry heaving sounded out across the boat. A Japanese man, meanwhile, had barricaded himself in the WC against the captain's orders. He staggered out an hour later looking ashen-faced, two stone lighter and in search of a refund. When the sun broke through the clouds and the storm calmed, we all gathered on top of the slippery, sea-splashed deck. In the clearing mist, I watched dolphins rise out of the blue waters, leaping up in their schools to lead our path. And as I braced myself against the wind, looking out into the gathering light, I thought to myself: remember this, *this* is what it means to feel free.

I love everything about these memories. But in the process of recollection, there is also a nostalgia for the freedoms that are entombed in my past. Where once lay colour and exploration, there is a blank. Wanderlust is now Netflix travel documentaries and dreamy, exotic panoramas splashed across Instagram posts.

This notion of past and present, then and now, openness and closure, is also probed by the American essayist and poet Molly McCully Brown. In her essay, 'Muscle Memory', she explores the psychogeographies of her disability: the ways that her cerebral palsy has remodelled the landscape and gradually colonised her body as 'a country of error and pain'. If she scans over old photographs from family holidays, McCully Brown sees a person who is almost an apparition. Familiar, yet unnervingly foreign to her. 'I can't bring up a map of the girl who did those things or remember what it was like to have her skin. I don't recall inhabiting her body until the point at which it started breaking,' she writes. 'But as I lose the girl I once was to forgetting, she takes with her a whole collection of places, her particular windows on the world. She saw things I never will.' It is in the third person that she writes of this younger self, the one trapped in the photos, the intrepid explorer who stands atop castles and spreads herself across uninterrupted beaches. After the years of surgeries, attacks of searing pain which began during adolescence, and now, with her reliance on a wheelchair, that state of litheness is an enigma. She can hardly remember the ease and pleasure that once existed in the fluidities of motion. It has all vanished. Her body is no longer able to compute the physical experience of climbing through ancient European cities, skidding across cobblestone streets, getting lost in the maze of night-time markets under canopies of glittering fairy-lights, or threading herself through tiny monastery doors and up flights of weathered stone steps. Now, she writes, 'I can imagine myself walking through the monastery only in the same sense I can imagine that I flew.'

When McCully Brown is faced with returning to Europe – a dreamy six weeks in Bologna for a writer's residency – it will be the first time since her childhood trips. As she contemplates revisiting the very sights that are etched into her past (like those inhibitive, taunting monastery stairs), it becomes a painful reminder of her body's decline. There is anxiety in the act of confrontation, in finding that she can no longer step inside these places – in being shut out. 'It's enough to be trapped at the thresholds of my memories. I don't think I could bear stalling at a real threshold: *Once you could be here*,' she explains. Even before she has landed in Italy, the travel experience is strikingly different. Hours are spent on the phone confirming doorway widths to ensure her wheelchair will fit and enquiring about lifts and the height of bathtub lips. An architectural apartheid ultimately takes hold when she discovers that, in Bologna, she can get 'almost nowhere' through the front door. Public libraries, botanical gardens, monuments and churches are a constant reality check – the psychological dimensions of her restricted body are played out in their steep stairs, blocked pathways and faulty signage. Despite her hunger to witness everything in the flesh, she laments: 'There are places I will never go. There are places I will never go again.'

For many people with disabilities, that burning impulse to see the world is met with a feeling of confinement and claustrophobia, not boundless possibility. Many are denied this window into a world outside the parameters of their own existence. Even before the coronavirus pandemic, over half of disabled adults in the UK had not taken a holiday in the previous year. An average millennial, by comparison, takes five trips annually. The tourism industry is breeding systematic discrimination by failing to address the barriers that preclude disabled people from going on holiday. It is shocking that, in our era of commercial travel, there remains a shortage of tailored information, accessible facilities and inclusive attitudes. The concept of accessible tourism is an encouraging one. But even within this emergent, niche industry, there is a tendency to treat disability as a monolith – an assumption that travellers who are visually impaired, deaf or have mobility difficulties would require the same blanket accommodations. When tourism companies are built on catering to a mass of able-bodied consumers, shuttling human cargo across continents as rapidly and inexpensively as possible, the depersonalised approach has become endemic. Comfort and flexibility are too often made a luxury.

To offer a glimpse into the hostile climate facing travellers with disabilities, I stumbled across a news article the other day describing how a man's passport application had been rejected because his photo showed an 'object in the background'. That 'object' was his wheelchair handles. But still, it 'didn't meet the standards set by the International Civil Aviation Organisation'. To resolve the issue, he was told to obtain a doctor's letter detailing, firstly, all about his disability, and, secondly, why he needed to remain in the wheelchair for the photo. This letter could only be sent by post, *not* submitted digitally (just to add to the inconvenience). He promptly rang his GP surgery to obtain the evidence, but was told it wasn't possible to make such a request over the phone – he had to fill in an online form! There would likely be a fee attached to his request. Okay, I digress, but this is just a small insight into the administrative hellfire that is being disabled in twenty-first century Britain. This constant pillar to posting is excessive and intrusive. And that's before you've even booked your flights.

Airports, though, are the epicentre of inaccessibility for disabled travellers. If you do not possess a standardised body, they expose the terrifying vulnerabilities and human errors that can arise while travelling across cities, countries and continents. In Emilie Pine's vigorous, probing essay collection *Notes to Self,* she touches on this crucial point while assisting her father on a flight. Their tumultuous journey – from Greece to a hospital in Ireland where he awaits urgent, life-saving treatment – gifts her an 'eye-opening' primer on the world of disability. 'At Gatwick we wait a long time for the wheelchair,' she writes, 'and when it comes, and when I start pushing it, I realise just how big an airport is.' This all ties into the idea of how disablement can disrupt and disorientate your perception of space. Suddenly, the space around Pine seems bigger, gross, insurmountable. When Pine comes to board the plane, Ryanair insists that her father must walk up the outdoor steps to board the plane – their policy being 'he can only board if he is able to do so by himself'. He looks 'defeated' as it is 'totally impossible for him'. But a stalemate ensues, only ending when they are put on a cherry-picker lift, normally used for loading food deliveries. 'It's a short flight but Dad is now exhausted,' she concludes in exasperation. After years of teaching Beckett plays as an academic, Pine admits wryly, 'I am finally living in one.'

While disability encourages us to think about spaces in a more open, adaptable way, air travel imposes a very rigid conception of how bodies should navigate their surroundings. According to a 2021 study by AbleMove, 62 per cent of disabled passengers restrict their food or fluids before a flight because aeroplane toilets aren't accessible. Meanwhile, it was reported that 60 per cent of people have their wheelchairs damaged during travel. A wheelchair, or mobility aid, is more than just a personal belonging. For many disabled people, it is an extension of the human body, part of someone's personal space, and it should be treated as such. Being stripped of this lifeline is not only a violation, but it can have devastating consequences.

It must be said that the aviation industry has overseen some improvements in accessibility in recent years, with enhanced regulatory frameworks for travellers with reduced mobility. However, in the experience of BBC security correspondent Frank Gardner the trial of disembarking the plane remains a 'tedious' and 'generic problem'. Since he was shot by al-Qaeda gunmen in 2004, Gardner has used a wheelchair due to paralysis. This means that, if the airline uses portable steps rather than a bridge connecting directly to the terminal, he requires special assistance to get off the plane. On a recent flight from the French Alps, he found himself stranded on the aircraft long after the other passengers had disembarked. In fact, the cabin was about to be cleaned. 'None of this is the exception,' he told the BBC. 'This is what happens frequently when there is no air bridge. I am pretty cynical about this because I have been travelling with a wheelchair for twelve years and I've not seen any improvement.'

Gardner's experience is indicative of the endlessly frustrating, often humiliating, hurdles facing disabled people who are simply trying to move through the world. It is a constant affirmation of one's outsider status. For work and repatriation matters, the battle is unavoidable. But for leisure purposes, it is different. There comes a point where, I believe, the anxiety of being left stranded in a vulnerable and potentially life-threatening position, dramatically outweighs the benefits of holidaying. Put simply, the pursuit of freedom is just not relaxing, nor restorative.

Urgent changes must now be overseen by the travel and tourism industries – whether that's reducing mountainous paperwork, creating accessible toilets, or providing disability awareness training to staff. These inclusive measures will allow more travellers with disabilities to experience new cultures and uncover the beauty of the world. It could mean the difference between staying at home and watching dolphins pirouette across the horizon once more.

So what does freedom mean now? Can I access that primal, energising sense of being-in-the-world by another means? I refuse to validate the destructive myth that disability and illness are forms of imprisonment. I still want to resist stasis. And, while my ability to run free is restricted, I need to fulfil my desire for motion. To be dispersed and obliterated by the world like a drop of water into a pond. To feel far away and make my way back home.

It is a reluctant truth that, in the face of travel constraints, the world feels colossal and unnavigable to many people with disabilities. I recently caught up with a friend who was telling me about her own transient experience of disablement – how life became a succession of exhausting hurdles when she suffered a deep cut on the sole of her foot. For the four months that it took to heal, she hopped around, no longer able to drive or walk long distances, let alone travel abroad. As a normally fit, healthy individual, she found herself winded and demoralised by her lack of movement. Fortunately, her ailment was only temporary. But my friend got me thinking: how does this lack of freedom affect the psyche in the longer term? And what does it mean to exist under the weight of an invisible restraint, or cloistered inside a fixed perimeter? What happens when you take away the right to move, safely and seamlessly, through the world?

There was a time when I feared that I could no longer claim to possess a free spirit. I had conceded to cultural scripts that dictate how freedom lies in white sandy beaches, string bikinis and exotic, spontaneous voyages to far-flung destinations. How I should be thriving along a perpetual quest for enlightenment and reinvention through jet-setting travel. There is romance in the idea of always arriving in new places, in spontaneity, flight and motion – and I do not deny that. But the escapist fantasy is a mark of able-bodied privilege. And racial, gendered, socio-economic privilege for that matter. In the past decade, our feverish desire for self-exploration through travel – call it, the *Eat, Pray, Love* complex – has been propped up by the capitalist, neoliberal agenda. Famously, Airbnb has tried to monetise wanderlust, selling us the dream that we too can jump out of our humdrum existence, up sticks and 'make anywhere a home' for seven nights at £199 per person (terms and conditions apply). Accelerated by Silicon Valley, it is a philosophy that has turned freedom and belonging into a commodity. The status of 'enlightened traveller' is now transactional – a personality trait that can be bought and sold.

To be untravelled, then, becomes a personal deficit or a lack. Your mind has not been broadened. You have not experienced that delicate 'balance between worldly enjoyment and divine transcendence' that the protagonist of Elizabeth Gilbert's *Eat, Pray, Love* waxes lyrical about. This warped delusion has fuelled anxiety around stillness and stasis for commercial gain. For many disabled people, who may not have the ability or resources to get across town independently, let alone cross continents, this manufactured vision of 'freedom' feels especially suffocating and out of reach.

Recently, however, I have found another meaning of freedom, of true freedom, and it is something more powerful, more abstract than touching down in a far-flung destination. Adventure does not have fixed coordinates, a latitude and longitude. It does not reject you on the basis of your limiting physical situation or corporeal position. This genuine freedom may be imperfect and messy, and it doesn't always feel particularly freeing at times, but I've learned there is another route to finding wanderlust and self-liberation.

Friedrich Nietzsche began to outline this alternative version of freedom when, in 1879, he carved a gainful prototype of the 'free spirit' after a period of ill health forced him to leave academic life. A free spirit, Nietzsche argues, is one who sees differently. One who can separate their thinking from the dominant views of their age. To be fettered and 'chained' has little to do with one's physical condition. Having dealt with physical and mental illness throughout his life (sensory and mobility impairments, plus symptoms of bipolar disorder), this is something Nietzsche would have known in the extreme. Indeed, it is sickness and pain – exhausting experiences involving solitude and suffering – that catalyse the breakthrough of the free spirit. 'The great liberation comes suddenly to such prisoners, like an earthquake,' Nietzsche writes. 'The young soul is all at once shaken, torn apart, cast forth.' This rupture sets the soul aglow, allowing the subject to bask in a 'sun of his own, with a feeling of birdlike freedom'. Armed with a new appreciation of life, even one's immediate surroundings seem changed and stimulating – 'to sit still, to exercise patience, to lie in the sun' can all incite joy because 'now for the first time he really sees himself'.

Nietzsche's image has been no more relevant to the public consciousness than during the recent pandemic years where, in the tremors and aftershocks of this global cataclysm, people were given opportunities to see and think in new ways. Overnight, the freedom to travel became prohibited by law. Stay-at-home orders were discharged from inside the red wine-sprayed walls of 10 Downing Street, and a national depression set in. There was a collective mourning for the loss of the right to move abundantly and at will. But, as the initial restlessness began to subside, many people discovered a reality that most individuals with disabilities and chronic illness had learned long before: the essence of freedom is present all around us.

If you engage the mind, it is possible to feel enlightened by what is local, nearby and immediate. To take pleasure in all the things that had previously gone unnoticed. While it remained a frustration to be tethered in the physical sense, there were other ways to experience escapism and expand our horizons. People were now getting their fix of 'divine transcendence' from the plucky chilli plant that miraculously survived a frostbitten winter. And they were getting 'worldly enjoyment' from watching the sunset under the cover of ten woollen blankets on a balmy April evening, an al fresco candlelit dinner laid out across plastic furniture. It could be anything. Daydreaming beside a newly bloomed wisteria, dancing in the kitchen, or the discovery of a fortuitously placed peephole to chat to your neighbours through the garden fence – anything to tap into the beauty of life. There was a new appreciation of how exceptional experiences – like this devastating, unprecedented period of confinement – can instil radical ideas about what it means to explore, exist and be free.

As restrictions eased, citizens regained their right to travel and wander. But many disabled people still cannot enjoy these recovered liberties. That feeling of existing with a restricted footprint is not a choice, it's a fact of life – whether that is due to inaccessible transport, or a pathology that imposes its own limits on the body. It's punishing. It's unfair. And it's hard to reconcile, especially if the key to someone's independence lies in the hands of policymakers who could, yet refuse, to expand the world for people with disabilities.

But, whatever your physical circumstances, I can offer you a freedom that is constant and unyielding. Something of a secret, something no one has authority over. Like Nietzsche's concept of the free mind, it has emerged, keen and inviting, in some of the most confining periods in my life – whether I've been rigged up to a dozen wires in hospital or, right now, as I write about the adventures that feel beyond my reach. Even in these paralysing moments, I take comfort in my power to delve into imagined worlds. To leave this earthly realm and enter the liberating dimension of my own mind. In transcending the material world, I cast off any physical constraints of my existence, relinquishing rigid categories for a world without boundaries. People may see this as an avoidance strategy, pure quixotism, or an act of renunciation; and I do not dismiss the possibility that there is some relief to be found in denial.

For me, however, this imaginative playground is not about silencing or shutting out the world – but clarifying it. The freedom to traverse the contours of my imagination has enlivened my present. It has taught me to continually see the world in new ways. How I can be the architect of my own existence. It is this very capacity for openness, fluidity and boundlessness that has shaped my creative outlook and my work – I know a place where everything feels more possible, and that's what constantly inspires my reality.

From within, I can reject the punitive idea that movement is synonymous with physical independence and autonomy. I recently came across a line in the book *White Girls* by Hilton Als, where he considers what it would be like for vital, spirited women to be suddenly confined or struck down by their bodies. 'Imagine', he writes, 'Holly Golightly or Sally Bowles or Maxine Faulk or Vera Cicero in the 1984 film *The Cotton Club*, infirm, not walking down the street or swimming with their boys in the sea, sick and feeling useless to themselves after all those years of creating such lasting, vibrant images in someone else's mind, artists and writers for the most part.' Here, illness and the inability to move freely are made incompatible with the role of heroine and effervescent muse. Lost freedom begets a loss of agency, action and therefore hope. While I cannot claim to be immune from this thinking, I know that it is possible to cut through the devastation. When you abandon inherited ideas about what it means to feel free and vigorous, you can start to seek beauty, movement and exploration from within. It is only by validating alternative modes of existence that we can redefine freedom. A freedom that is no longer dependent on the intactness of the body. A freedom that does not lie in 'someone else's mind', but a freedom where you are your own director and muse.

The most profound – and extreme – example of what I am pointing to, is perhaps located in Jean-Dominique Bauby's memoir, *The Diving Bell and the Butterfly*. When the glamorous editor-in-chief of *Elle* magazine suffered an abrupt stroke in 1995, he awoke from a coma twenty days later with locked-in syndrome, mentally aware of his surroundings, but physically paralysed with only some movement in one eyelid. Pushing against the waves of despair and isolation, Bauby came to one pivotal realisation: the world still offered itself to his mind. His memory and imagination take flight, the eponymous butterfly escaping the diving bell of his tethered, afflicted body. 'There is so much to do,' Bauby explains. 'You can wander off in space or in time, set out for Tierra del Fuego or for King Midas's court. You can visit the woman you love, slide down beside her and stroke her still-sleeping face. You can build castles in Spain, steal the Golden Fleece, discover Atlantis, realize your childhood dreams and adult ambitions.' Casting himself as explorer, lover and time-traveller, Bauby is now infinite – a free spirit wandering into uncharted territories and new perspectives. It is a voyage through which, he says, his condition 'becomes less oppressive'.

Bauby's memoir stands as an obelisk, its physical presence on bookshelves is a testament to the freedom that can be found in the most constrictive circumstances. In 200,000 blinks of the eye, Bauby propels himself into the world, occupying space and asserting his presence on us in a way that few people have. *The Diving Bell and the Butterfly* is not an in-person encounter, and it cannot erase his pain, but through the power of his subjectivity, Bauby proves, there are no limits on where we may travel. Even when you feel like there is nowhere else to go in life, there is always another claim to freedom. One that is indelible, transcendent and, most importantly, valid.

So, perhaps there is an irony here. It has taken me two years of shielding, rarely venturing outside the threshold of my home, to access this truth. As I lay down these final words, I can't help but smile at the absurdities of my life. It's now September, and a timid slant of sun strokes the balcony deck, where I am sitting above a Cornish seascape. It is the furthest I've travelled since the pandemic began and every detail in the scene is intensified after the months indoors – woodsmoke cutting across salty air, rattling wind and the soaring crescents of kitesurfers that rollick across the sandy lip of coastline.

Slowly, a walking group descends the steep, timber steps to the beach. One by one, the walkers stop to gaze up at an aerial display of swallows. Every face is hypnotised by the swoops and spirals of the murmuration – a vortex of wings in motion. Crinkled eyes strain against the light, and two women shriek as their woolly scarves attempt to join the flight. But something else has struck me.

It's the blue horizon – that solitary intimation of our planet, its subtle curves and cosmic scale. A dividing line, where the fullness of the Atlantic rises up to touch the skies. Today, the horizon is sharp. I stare out at the sunlight glistening across the indigo waters and I am filled with an irrepressible sense of the vastness of this earth – the promise of what's out there. Its pull is magnetic. All those unexplored sights that are concealed beyond that drop-off. Sights that we need to open up for people with disabilities, to ensure that anywhere – from the city street to the space beyond – is within reach.

But, for now, I have a new completeness inside me. In the process of writing this book, I've gone further and explored deeper than I ever have, or will, in a geographical sense. I already feel like an itinerant traveller, traipsing through the unmapped hinterland. Filled with hope and fear, I've got lost in the crevasses of my memory and fought my way back. Every word, a step. As I arrive on the next leg – straddling a nomadic mix of worldliness, exhaustion and the vitalising promise of the things I am yet to encounter – I have discovered the truth that lay inside me all along: freedom, its conditions and stipulations, is there to be rewritten.

# Role Call

'We have a surprise for you,' said Mrs Bell to the assembled class, her frosted lips coordinated, quite cunningly, to the exact shade of plum in her beaded earrings, which swung jauntily as she made her tease. I'll admit any hint of surprise is ominous in the scholastic context. A place where the unexpected rarely precedes anything pleasant – more likely an impromptu quiz on motte-and-bailey castles, than the rolling reappearance of that majestic TV on wheels. From the back of the classroom, I overheard speculative whisperings of a blustery hike up the quarries of Bodmin Moor. I instantly feared that it was something I couldn't partake in. On this occasion, however, I was wrong. Something was afoot that would sum up the majority of my school years – a sense of completeness, the persistent grip of possibility and belonging. A freedom to be whoever I was.

Right away, a gaggle of Year 9 girls took turns to monitor the surrounding roads from the top-floor computer room with green plastic binoculars ingeniously sequestered from the science labs. When confirmation came from above that a 'blacked-out' MTV van had indeed been circling the vicinity (and quite possibly, a bodyguard sighted in the local Somerfield clutching a Yorkie bar), the mood toggled from one of cautious scepticism to full-blown, raging hysteria. By lunchtime, we had gathered enough intel to deduce that there would be, firstly, a concert of some iteration, and secondly, a man named Shawn Emanuel was at the centre of it all. In haste, banners were made, 'I heart Shawn' scribbled onto torn Filofax paper in fizzy cola-scented gel pens. The precise spelling of Shawn inevitably drew ten minutes of intense consternation, appearing in eleven different guises until somebody located his Myspace page and the Tipp-Ex was disseminated. Like the self-respecting groupies we were, the banners were sealed with sloppy, watermelon Juicy Tube kisses. Clandestine trading of temporary tattoos ensued, as a kind of locker-room black market. Until, finally, squealing hordes descended into the assembly hall. Think Beatlemania, but considerably less chic. Instead of Mary Quant miniskirts, it was itchy polyester school skirts rolled up to new heights and chalky-white shirts knotted at the waist. In a puff cloud of Impulse body spray and thick, impasto slatherings of Maybelline Dream Matte Mousse – markings that constituted the taxonomic classification of noughties girlhood – we took our seats. The atmosphere was more feverish than the time a packet of Monster Munch serendipitously fell into the hands of a Spanish exchange student from the common room vending machine. It was hard to imagine that two hours ago, we had not heard of this rising R&B star, nor the smooth, honeyed vocals of 'U Better Believe It'.

That day, Shawn Emanuel must have left our school feeling like some kind of Casanova – his inflated ego straining against the locked doors of his getaway car. But it wasn't about him. As enemies and frenemies stood arm-in-arm, a cross-pollination of friendship groups swaying to the music, we were given a glimpse of a world that was outside our experience. An instant filled with all the possible versions of who we could become. The wild promise of metamorphosis pulling against the agitations of youth – a future that was almost, but not quite, ready to step into. In that surge of optimism and togetherness, I was not an exception. At school, I was like anyone else.

The knowledge I was gaining at school extended far beyond the index of hand-me-down textbooks, with their yellowed binding, suspicious staining and deliciously bitchy gossip from the class of '92 (Sally did *what* behind the bike shed?!). Those early school days were the prevailing influence on creating, reinforcing and developing my identity – one that was divorced from others' false or socially prescribed notions about what it meant to be disabled. An inclusive school experience meant that I was never held back or adversely defined by my disability. I was free to learn and grow in an environment where I was treated no differently to my classmates. I didn't need to be. Everyone, an equal.

At school I cultivated a fierce network of friends based on a mutual affinity for sticker books, belly laughs and all things fluffy. These bonds of love, I believe, held a seismic influence on my self-construction. They were a constant, giving me a sense of inclusion, of likeness and belonging, that ran parallel to my own refusal to be othered or limited by my body. To this day, these friendships continue to anchor me. To make me feel part of the world, even in the moments when ordinary life has felt more distant and untouchable than ever. Growing up alongside each other, swapping the skittish delight of those primary school days for the disorientations of millennial teendom, meant my friends lived through my difficulties. In their eyes, it was simply an intrinsic part of me. It was expected. It was normal. They understood. During my early school years, directly engaging with peers and sharing daily social interactions – like bemoaning the whims and fancies of our ill-tempered Tamagotchis, or expressing a mutual, green-gilled revulsion towards Copydex glue – enabled them to see through to my character and connect along the same emotional plane. The realisation that I couldn't easily walk upstairs or compete against them in the sack race at sports days wasn't anything alarming or tragic. It became immaterial to them.

This camaraderie strengthened by the year, cementing itself through our shared 'educational' experiences, such as a one-time performance from the modern languages department masquerading as a belly-dancing troupe. Like the HD footage of my friend's dad's hernia repair screened in our biology class, it was a sight that couldn't be unseen. Five midriffs jiggling and gyrating at a mortifying speed. The psychic damage was immeasurable, the entire lunchtime offering of pink jelly trifle untouched. But my friends and I were united in the wake of it. We sniggered from inside a packed-out toilet cubicle, attempting a comedic re-enactment – I, remaining inseparable from them.

This illustrates, to me, the power of an inclusive education. In capitalising on the malleability of children's minds, we have every power to teach future generations about the diverse spectrum of abilities, the value of tolerance and respecting difference. Why would I want or need to be marked out as disabled? It didn't feel relevant. It implied contrast where I felt communion. To be categorised as disabled seemed like an act of negation. A denial of the identity I was building for myself within the warm, fluffy cult of girl power – a cultural touchstone for the empowered self, the vestiges of third-wave feminism.

This was, in part, the privilege of not being as noticeably affected by my disability. At that time, I could, with the supportive arm of friends, negotiate the tall buildings that were slit through with dizzying networks of stairs. I coped with the physical demands of an eight-hour school day. It wasn't even too detrimental that the much-promised handrail on the stone steps of the main building was only installed by my school several months before I left. (Reader: I had been there for twelve years.)

But still, I cannot deny that I was shielded from stigma, far removed from any prejudice that lay beyond the classroom door. Within my school sphere I held influence and autonomy. I was expected to make my own decisions. To be outspoken, and in turn, be heard. When it came to my body, I wanted and, naïvely, always planned to exist just as things were – in a space where my physical differences were implicit and unspoken. Known, but not dwelled upon.

I am certain that my capacity to exist outside of labels, to feel there were no limits placed on what I might achieve, was critical for my self-construction. Later on, when illness threatened to erase me and snuff out my kindling ambitions, this stubborn sense of self was fine-tuned and encoded within me. In the ragged face of adversity, there alone stood the permanence of my identity – patiently lingering and, always, ready to fall back into. It was the one thing that could never elude me.

Education, by definition, is about discovering one's unique strengths and abilities while sheltered from the stigmatising gaze of the adult world. School should provide an antidote to the social perception of disability as synonymous with restriction and inefficiency – our education emphasising what we can achieve, over what we cannot. I've experienced first-hand how schools can positively shape attitudes by bringing together people of all abilities. How our education system wields the power to cut out and pre-emptively thwart the divisions of society. And yet, it has often done the opposite: encourage, rather than eradicate, segregation. The negative biases formed at school leading to a lifetime of public shame and fear towards disabilities. If we want to shift our view of disability away from abnormality to something integral, empowering and, most importantly, realistic, the assignment must begin inside the classroom.

Every child is a tabula rasa – a blank slate. At birth, the human mind is an empty vessel without inherited rules, thoughts or preconceived opinions. This theoretical framework, often attributed to the seventeenth-century philosopher John Locke, suggests that before receiving outside impressions, the mind exists in its original pristine state. In other words, we are not born with any concrete notions about what's normal and abnormal. We are liberated, and free from the tyrannical sways of stigma. It's only when experiences are gained through sensory engagement with our environment, education and social interactions, that it shapes a child's cognitive development and leaves a lasting imprint on who they become, what they believe. If knowledge is constructed through the personal experiences we've had since birth, the untarnished mind offers hope for enacting broad social changes. It is a reminder that we can rewrite the status quo for each new generation.

When the mind is in its metaphorical 'blank' state, it strikes me that this is a pivotal opportunity to reset attitudes towards disability. It's a kind of entry point whereby one split encounter, and its reverberations, can instil a whole new value system for humanity. It's a moment endowed with radical epistemological potential – if only we can see and nurture it. In a viral Twitter thread that received over 788,000 likes, one user recently described their positive interaction with a child and his mother in public: 'Yesterday I overheard a little kid asking their mum why I was using a wheelchair, and the mum simply replied, "Well, maybe his legs need a bit of extra help. You can ask him if he's happy to tell you more." No shaming the kid for asking, no treating disability as a hush hush topic.' Here inquisitiveness should not only be encouraged, but rewarded with a calm, empathetic response. 'If you give a simple, relaxed answer and give them the space to ask questions, disability is just another new thing they're learning about . . . then maybe their relaxed attitude about disability will be passed onto their friends.'

What's shameful is how this experience was felt to be a rare occurrence, an anomaly. In reply, a woman chimed in about how her son often experiences staring in public due to his cochlear implant or, alternatively, how people will theatrically avert their gaze. But, she added, 'I love little kids, because they will come right up and ask him what the things are on his head. He answers and the kids are like "oh, cool". Totally unfazed.' When we tiptoe around disability, impose silence and show discomfort, the more children internalise this and it gets transmitted on – propagating the ostracism currently experienced by disabled people of all generations. At a time when one-fifth of 18 to 34-year-olds are avoiding talking to a disabled person, the depth of this exclusion is palpable. Any desire to turn away from disability is devastating, but it is especially devastating that our 'flight response' arises from a basic lack of knowledge – the survey participants explaining they would rather avoid conversations because they 'weren't sure how to communicate'.

During our education, the value of experience-based learning – namely, gaining understanding about disability through direct, positive exchanges – cannot be underestimated when it comes to tackling ableism. Jean Piaget, the first psychologist to map out the cognitive development of children, claimed that the purpose of education should be to make 'creators', 'inventors' and 'innovators'. It was not about leading the child to resemble the typical adult in his society or manufacturing conformists. With this in mind he promoted the importance of experiential teaching, over a more didactic, textbook approach (like how tying a shoelace can only truly be learned when you physically immerse yourself in the experience, rather than reading or being told instructions). If experience is the key to imparting knowledge, Piaget's findings suggest to me that anti-ableist work to develop a more inclusive society will be dependent on early first-hand experiences, such as face-to-face encounters at school and beyond. Due to the psychological workings of children's brains, this will always effect more pervasive change than a ten-minute PSE slideshow or photocopied handout on 'diversity and equality'.

Including children with disabilities in a community of learners provides all students with opportunities to learn. In a process known as social constructivism, every spontaneous encounter or conversation is a chance to acquire knowledge about social norms, practices and values. Through reciprocal activities like playtime, for example, cognitive demands are placed on children to explain their actions to peers, negotiate shared understanding of the goals of play, and solve problems that give rise to new learning for all participants. While the influence of family and home life is significant, morality is mostly developed through these peer-to-peer interactions – concepts like equality, justice and altruism cannot be instilled by authority mandates alone.

As cognitive processes mature, the way children make sense of the world swiftly morphs and evolves. The mind becomes less elastic, tapering to a point where valuable opportunities to redefine disability are missed. By age seven, children have entered the 'concrete development period'. Now, their understanding of the world hinges on judgements and attitudes from people around them, not simply their own first-hand experiences. This is when prejudice and social bias will infiltrate and reach a peak. Children do not invent ableism; they are simply mimicking the patterns and stereotypes they see played out in society. As children progress into their teenage years and adulthood, their thinking becomes increasingly inflexible and prescribed. Changing mindset and rejecting systemic beliefs becomes a more deliberate, time-consuming process – one that requires conscious effort. Our intuitions may tell us that disability is strange, foreign, and thus does not belong. But we all possess the ability to step in, re-evaluate and override our intuitions with conscious reason. This very act is what makes us human. And yet, as much as adults can try to be inclusive, it will never be as engrained in the psyche.

It's only when disability is entrenched in our mental conception of life from infancy that we will find true liberation. Our failure to achieve this has bred intolerance and pushed people with disabilities to the margins of society. 'The main reason people do not want to be labelled as disabled, is because disability remains a stigmatised identity,' as Tom Shakespeare, a social scientist and bioethicist, explains.

'Nobody wants to be categorised in a way that seems limiting or negative. They want to stress their similarity to others, not their differences; what they can do, not what they cannot do.' A government research project corroborated this widespread hesitancy, revealing that more than half of people who could be defined as having a disability, did *not* self-identify as disabled – perhaps because we learn from an early age that disability is a limiting, ostracising word. Just last year, it was revealed that 45 per cent of the British public do not even feel comfortable saying the term 'disabled'.

This makes clear the urgent case for inclusive education. We possess the ability to shape lifelong beliefs: to mould the way a child sees disability, or any other stigmatised identity, that sets a precedent for the rest of their life. If we want to see disability as an integral part of society, classrooms must cultivate a safe, levelling environment where children can learn about the things that unite them – before they are bitten by the one-dimensional, destructive stereotypes that ravage our society. Learning should therefore be adapted so that all children have the chance to play and study together.

The petition to teach sign language in schools is a prime example here. If visual communication was taught on the curriculum, deafness would be framed as a welcome, integrated part of everyday life. In 2018, *The Silent Child*, a crowdfunded British film exposing the plight faced by deaf children in mainstream education, was awarded the Oscar for best live-action short film. Packing what the *New York Times* called 'an emotional wallop' straight to the audience's chest, the film shows how school can descend into a dystopian wilderness when the body exists outside of norms and doesn't slip into its rigid, striated systems; vertical and horizontal dividing lines between desks spiralling into a chasmic void.

We are instantly magnetised by the heartbreaking tale of four-year-old Libby who is deaf in a punishingly aural world – she is floundering, unable to communicate with her hearing family, sinking into a withdrawn state. However, when Libby is given the gift of sign language by a plucky social worker, the communication barrier is broken down. For the first time, she is able to meaningfully connect. At school, however, no one can sign. Libby is once again left isolated and cut off from her surroundings. In the interactive, dialogic space of both classroom and playground, her potential is waiting to effloresce. But time is running out, fast. We are left with a final haunting image of Libby backed against a brick wall, unable to join in as her classmates hopscotch and hula-hoop in front.

This is a narrative that overlaps with that of the lead actor, Maisie Sly. While Maisie's family relocated 160 miles just so she could attend a mainstream school that supported deaf children (a common predicament for families of special educational needs children in the UK), Libby represents one of the 78 per cent of deaf children trapped in mainstream education with no specialist support in place. The academic attainment gap is measurable, and damningly so. In 2019, the National Deaf Children's Society found that, for the past five years, deaf children achieved a whole grade less than hearing children at GCSE – the tremendous psychological damage remains unmeasured.

The dual afflictions of isolation and bullying also threaten to strike the mental well-being of children with developmental delays or learning disabilities attending mainstream school. The Anti-Bullying Alliance has revealed they are more than three times as likely to be victims of bullying than their non-disabled peers. In 2020, a documentary called *Amber and Me* traced the early school experiences of twin girls, born two minutes apart: Olivia and her sister, Amber, who has Down's syndrome. In what is a remarkably emotive portrait of sisterly love, the film enables a full-focus insight into their contrasting educational journeys as they tentatively step into and clamber up the school system. Getting dressed on the first day, their experiences are almost mirrored, giddily running alongside each other as they prance around the bedroom, tussling with blue, Peter Pan-collared polo tops. As the school term progresses, however, the narratives splinter and Amber is left behind: 'I feel a bit like why isn't she enjoying it, why doesn't she like it as much as she used to? I hope she stays at school with me,' says a young Olivia, observing how her sister is visibly overwhelmed. At home, Amber can flourish as a dynamic individual with wit and emotional sensitivity. But, for her, school is lacking the same baseline investment of love, compassion and security. 'Some people are being mean to her and teasing her, telling her to say things she doesn't understand,' notices Olivia. 'It makes me really angry. It's really unfair. I'm starting to think that's why she wants to play by herself.'

If we can design an education system with inclusivity and individuality at its core, I believe there is potential to teach children about the value of empathy and compassion – what really matters. One of the first times I recall experiencing the full intensity of kindness, with all its redemptive energies, was when my name was called out in the final minutes of a school assembly – familiar words rendered alien, as they reverberated around the stipple-painted stone walls. It began the way we spent most mornings, scratching coded messages onto our hymn books and trying to stay visibly conscious while our religious studies teacher read aloud, in bespectacled earnest, some morality tale. Aesop's finest captured in unflinching monotone. At least, I thought, it wasn't a repeat appearance from that local Morris dancer. A tall, waistcoated man with a salt-n-pepper beard who romped and gambolled around the assembly hall, performing his saucy, and positively unorthodox, take on the traditional folk dance. An untimely moment to be sitting on the front row, I was forced to avert my gaze as the curious man, love child of Patrick Swayze and Stevie Nicks, jangled his tambourine with all the airs and graces of a cat on heat. However, the events that unfolded on this particular day were of hair-raising proportions, something that even those jiggling hips and jangling tambourine couldn't touch. The instant my name was called to walk onto the stage and collect a prize, I gulped, peering up through a mass of 400 bodies and towards the creaky wooden steps with no handrail.

'I'd rather not,' I thought. Dread was now rising into panic, panic spiking into action. My route was uncertain, but I tried to play along and appear unruffled as I advanced towards the lit stage. A wing and a prayer, I guess. With the eyes of every assembled student boring into the back of my skull, I stopped, immobilised, at the bottom of those five menacing steps. They gurned at me, telling me it was never going to work. Still, I carried out a mental calculation of their height, depth and whether the surface appeared slippery, in the way that a Nepalese explorer plots a laddered ascent across an icy crevasse on Everest. Should I attempt the stairs by myself and risk plummeting back down? I'd witnessed the red-faced indignity of this at the biannual school fashion show, and it was not a look I was keen to replicate.

Or shall I just make a sheepish gesture and turn back now? Quick! Which was the lesser evil? My decision was interceded. In one of those favourable endings that seems as though you've written it yourself, a girl reached out from behind to offer a supportive arm. To make you moist of the cheek, it was a gesture requiring astonishing generosity – the courage to assuage her own fear of sticking out. It's this genuine awareness and empathy that we must nurture at all costs.

Altruism is embedded in our biological make-up, according to Professor Nancy Eisenberg who is a world authority on the moral development of children. From a young age the majority of us are 'able to pinpoint the source of another's distress and to help in ways that are appropriate', with children being exceptionally capable of 'other-orientated, prosocial behaviour'. This is clearly a huge developmental milestone, a child becoming aware that other people's emotions exist independently of their own. Consequently, they can take on another perspective, expressing empathy, concern or alertness towards what others may be feeling – like during that assembly. However, Eisenberg cautions that adolescents may not share this same willingness. Just as they might be inhibited by the fear of social disapproval, they also wrestle with the possibility that rushing to someone's aid will embarrass the recipient, cause offence, or fail to offer the correct support.

When education systems make moves to segregate children with disabilities, these altruistic encounters slip away from us. In promoting seclusion over integration, children can no longer hold out an unwavering hand, or assume their revisionist role. They are deprived of their potential to interrupt the cycle of historic marginalisation felt by disabled people – by default, feelings of alienation and estrangement are reinstated. If school represents a microcosm for wider society, to me, this covert form of exclusion sets a worrying precedent. In fact, disability activists, charities and human rights organisations are vociferous on this matter, united in the stance that the foundations for an inclusive, equal world are laid at school. The thinking goes: integration in classrooms should not only be fostered, but deployed as an effective agent in the fight for a more tolerant society.

However, diversity and integration among school children is not the only form of positive action available to us. The example set by teaching staff could, in fact, be equally valuable. The faces we see in front of the chalkboard, our teachers and educators, speak of power structures. As much as these authority figures wield influence to derail the lives of students, they also hold a potential to positively reframe our perception of disability. If children are the key to creating a more tolerant society, teachers are ostensibly the gatekeepers, offering passage into our new realm of inclusivity. In this respect, the impact of young people seeing teachers with disabilities could be revolutionary.

'As educators, we are the mirrors in which kids look,' explains 39-year-old Dayniah Manderson, an eighth-grade teacher with type 2 spinal muscular atrophy. 'They're going to look at me and find proof in the power of determination. They're going to see me get up every day and see persistence . . . and realise there is a strong tenacity that we need in order to reach our goals.' Speaking to the activist Alice

Wong during an episode of the *Disability Visibility Podcast*, Manderson, who teaches at Mott Hall Community School in the Bronx, New York, describes the obstacles she must negotiate to fulfil her role. From figuring out the best desk arrangement so she can navigate the classroom by wheelchair and grappling with keypads on locked doors, to securing a high-tech chalkboard that will digitise teaching materials and reduce the number of books she must carry.

There is a widespread assumption that any difficulty to perform physical tasks is a symbol of weakness, both of body and mind. However, I believe great power lies in these human vulnerabilities. To me, weakness suggests not failure, but the opportunity to expand our creativity and willpower. In fact, Manderson always wants to be transparent with her students, unafraid to show the physical toil or rely on their help for small practical tasks like distributing classroom materials. 'It doesn't matter if it's something embarrassing, it doesn't matter if it's something that other people find easy to do. The mere fact that they see me doing it, I think it's inspiring for them,' stresses Manderson. 'I want them to always remember that Miss Manderson went through a whole lotta stuff to get here, but she still got here, you know. She still showed up. And it's not a teacher who's walking who's there for them. It's the teacher that has a hard time coming out in the snow. It's the teacher that might not have gotten picked up by her paratransit that morning and had to take a bus instead . . . And when you have that level of commitment, it's something that . . . gets buried into them. They respect it.'

Manderson's philosophy applies not only to teachers with physical disabilities, but also sensory impairments. In 2020, the BBC reported on Brimsdown Primary School in North

London, where Alysha Allen, a deaf teacher, uses a combination of British Sign Language and lip reading to teach
her classes. Although it is a mainstream school, every pupil
at Brimsdown learns sign language. 'After a while they don't
even think about what they're doing any more,' explains
Allen. 'It just becomes natural to them.' Not only does this
foster an inclusive environment at the school, research has
shown that it can even benefit the children's language and
speech development. 'Alysha has inspired us all with her
positivity and resilience,' said deputy head teacher Eleanor
Painter. 'She has had much more to deal with in her life than
many of us but every day she comes to school with a positive
attitude and that's reflected in the enthusiasm of her class,
who love to learn.'

Teachers like Dayniah Manderson and Alysha Allen are
testament to the unassailable benefits of seeing authority figures with disabilities from an early age. Yet, children
rarely witness disabled people in positions of leadership and
power. Without these role models our perception of disability is subject to a kind of flattening, a two-dimensionality
which squashes social progress and leads to disabled people
being spoken for. We remain besieged by a crisis of under-
representation in schools, with a minuscule 0.5 per cent of
the teaching workforce self-reporting as having disabilities
compared to a population where 20 per cent of working-age
adults are disabled. This lack of visibility means our fear of
disability often goes unquestioned.

Most recently, a viral TikTok challenge played a disturbing prank centred around our hysterical abhorrence of perceived difference. Parents were challenged to show their
children photos of people, pretending it was of the new
class teacher. The sick twist? The pictures were of disabled

people, pilfered from the internet. Children recoiled at the images, with reactions ranging from fright to embarrassment, captured on video for comic intent. Upon discovering her photo was being co-opted by parents, the disability activist Melissa Blake, who was born with a genetic bone and muscular disorder, penned a defiant open letter. 'We need to teach the next generation that our differences should be celebrated, not feared or mocked,' she wrote. 'Disabled people aren't here for your ridicule. We're not punchlines. We're people.' If, from infancy, we are being socialised to believe the mere act of looking at disabled people is wrong and carries shame, this is a devastating scenario. The presence of disabled people among teaching staff could therefore be a valuable opportunity to stop the inheritance of these stigmas.

School is instrumental in reducing disability inequality but, as things stand, it is a breeding ground for ableism. From inaccessible buildings and bullying, to limited resources and an appalling lack of disability awareness among staff, schools can be exclusionary spaces for children with disabilities. These hostile conditions will limit opportunities for positive interactions between disabled and non-disabled children, denying us the chance to cultivate inclusive values inside a generation of growing minds. But, symbolically, they carry an even more malignant power. When learning environments pose difficulties for students with disabilities, it reads like a Blu Tacked sign declaring, 'You don't belong here.' Exclusionary classrooms, for example, are a glaring reminder of bodily difference, the very fact that being disabled can block your chance to succeed in the world. This implants the seeds of discrimination and disconnection among the student body, reminding everyone of that one precious currency in life that cannot be learned: able-bodiedness.

The United Nations has already expressed concern that progress towards inclusive education has stalled in the UK and disabled children are increasingly ostracised. Currently, there are two main educational models for parents and guardians to choose from: an inclusive education, where a child is placed into a mainstream school with non-disabled children, or a segregated education, where children with disabilities are educated at special schools or at home. Just as the United Nations object to the UK's growing reliance on special schools which segregate students with disabilities, in the same exasperated breath, they warn that our mainstream education system is unequipped to deliver high-quality, inclusive education. Criticisms include how teacher training is failing to meet requirements, with disturbing reports of school authorities refusing to enrol disabled students who are branded 'disruptive' to other classmates because teachers simply don't know how to communicate effectively with them. In response, the UN Committee called for urgent, bespoke measures to promote the inclusion of disabled children in mainstream schooling and end what they saw as the systematic violation of disabled people's human rights.

While the utopian ideal is to teach children together and eliminate internal biases, the reality of delivering these 'bespoke measures' is more complicated. Right now, we've reached crisis point. Over 1 million children with special educational needs (SEN) are at risk of being swallowed up and spat out by a system that wasn't designed for them. As an umbrella term, SEN encompasses everything from physical and learning disabilities to hearing and visual impairments. The question is to what extent it is possible to teach these children in mainstream settings so they can thrive, reach their full potential and are not left disadvantaged. Inclusion and participation are indeed essential to human dignity, and to the enjoyment and exercise of human rights. But at what cost? How far are we willing to push for the pursuit of these rights? When you consider the sheer range of disabilities that SEN applies to and the current shortage of specialised support in mainstream education, special schools will often be deemed preferable.

'Whether or not disabled children should be educated in segregated schools remains a contentious issue,' writes Professor Colin Barnes, an expert in disability studies who began his education at a 'special needs' school in Leeds. In Barnes' view, special schools are, for the most part, 'a form of positive action' and 'better placed' to give disabled children the targeted support they may require. This includes more individualised tuition, accessible teaching environments and greater access to therapies, like physio or speech and language specialists. For many, special schools are a life raft, promising buoyancy and sanctuary from the imminent threat of submersion in an education system that fails to recognise individual requirements, and by its making, holds everyone to the same inflexible attainment standards. Achievement must be quantifiable by grades, ratified by red ticks. Often parents, in sheer desperation and panic, are forced to prove that their child's specific needs will never be met in a mainstream classroom, believing they require intensive support within smaller classes to maximise their potential. In this catch-22 scenario, the constant fear of drowning may just overshadow any social benefit of a 'normal' educational experience.

But, at the same time, special schools are 'a fundamental part of the discriminatory process', according to Barnes. By categorising and syphoning children based exclusively on their ability, these educational environments are anathema to their inclusionary project. Special schools construct, and then immortalise, artificial barriers between disabled children and their able-bodied peers – barriers that will likely be sustained far beyond the school walls, potentially lasting a lifetime.

Most of all, they solidify the idea that disability is abnormal, rare, exceptional and indeed 'special', instilling a public mindset that is false, yet almost unredeemable. For this very reason, the term 'special educational needs' has come under fire; the labels 'special' and 'needs' denote rarity and create an image of dependency that may unduly impact on policymaking in education. According to Katherine Runswick-Cole and Nick Hodge writing in the *British Journal of Special Education*, the phrase educational *rights* must be adopted in its place. Rights-based discourse, traditionally used by activists to challenge exclusionary practices, 'shifts the "problem" of disability away from the individual and into the collective responsibility of society as a whole'. In positioning accessible education as entitlement, not an act of clemency, it would value all children as equals and better reflect how school is a basic human right.

'My younger self resented being sent to a segregated "special" school. I recognised that I was being treated unfairly and felt that I had been rejected,' says Michelle Daley, who attended the Elizabeth Fry School for children with physical impairments in Newham, London, during the 1980s.

'I, like many others, am a living testament, a survivor of this deeply disturbing structural system.' The reputation of special schools as safe, liberating and equalising environments is, in her opinion, a myth. Daley observed a hierarchy in her school, one where disabled students were not only ostracised from abled-bodied pupils but also divided among themselves. Students who could walk and do certain activities received priority treatment, and they would often bully others who were perceived as 'more disabled'. She also felt isolated because there wasn't any emphasis on social development or sustaining meaningful friendships; 'the building didn't allow for that'. Students always had adults known as 'welfares' hovering over them, which Daley saw as excessive. 'Young people need to be free, even if you do need support, they need to know when to step back.'

Daley, who left her special school without any formal qualifications and has since gone on to become Director at the Alliance for Inclusive Education, believes that neither her social nor educational needs were met – despite that being the main justification for segregated learning. 'They didn't think about our future,' concludes Daley. 'There wasn't a focus on learning. It was very basic. It didn't prepare us for anything.' After school, she would spend four hours reading and writing just to have a chance at gaining entry to college – something that she realised would be crucial to securing a job in future.

Daley's observations are matched by Zara Todd, who attended a special school in the 1990s before transferring to mainstream education. As a wheelchair user, Todd's family were encouraged to go down the route of special schooling: 'It was basically said to them that I wouldn't achieve anything, so that was the best place for me to be.' But, by age four, Todd was thrown into a class of six and seven-year-olds because they couldn't cater for her within her peer group. 'I was so far ahead of my classmates, I used to be sat in the corner with a workbook and just left to get on with it.' If the raison d'etre of segregated education is its ability to offer individualised, flexible teaching to every pupil, Todd's experience refutes that fact. 'I didn't fit the model that they were used to operating on,' she says. In reality, she later excelled in a mainstream school, before enrolling at university and going on to secure a postgraduate degree. 'We were incredibly protected' and wrapped up 'in cotton wool' at her special school, Todd remarks: 'We weren't really challenged.'

The view that special schooling curtails academic excellence and is not geared up to equip students for the real world is prevalent – but not universal. For Damian, a fifteen-year-old young man with autism, his ambition to become a pastry chef has been encouraged by his residential special school, where he regularly bakes for his housemates and members of staff. Having previously attended three mainstream secondary schools, he 'hated' their lack of structure, the limits on his personal liberty. 'One minute you'd go in there, the next minute you'd be going somewhere else and you didn't even know,' says Damian, who used to lash out at other students and teachers when he felt overwhelmed. 'They didn't understand what I was trying to get across.' But the structured, supportive environment of his new school has been both calming and transformative. 'It's easier to get along with people. I have somebody to support me all the time. They just know the way that I like to do things and know that I have to find things out for myself.'

These split experiences show that a personalised approach is paramount – and how educational pathways must be adaptable, changing as children grow and progress. 'When I was four, I started at special school where I was taught by a lovely teacher and made good friends,' says Jonathan Bryan, a fourteen-year-old with cerebral palsy in an interview with the magazine *Inclusion Now*. 'In reception this was fun, but as the years went on it was obvious that there was no expectation of progression and no teaching of literacy . . . This was frustrating and demeaning.' As a result, Jonathan's mother took him out of school to teach him at home for a couple of hours a day. As someone who is non-verbal, he communicates by looking at letters of the alphabet stuck to a Perspex board and spelling out everything he wants to say.

Ultimately, these basic literacy lessons enabled Jonathan to attend his local village primary school in Wiltshire. 'Being included as part of the class and school is great,' he says, describing how the staff went out of their way to include him. '[It] makes you feel valued in the community.' His desk had table raisers, for instance, so his wheelchair fitted under the table, the layout of the classroom was adapted so he could access different areas of the room and, where possible, teachers sent lesson plans in advance so they could be adapted to make it easier for him to join in. 'In games my peers took it in turns pushing me. As far as I was concerned the faster the better,' he says cheekily. 'Sometimes I would take my walker in and my friends would whoop and clap when I managed to move it.' When Jonathan transferred to secondary school, he designed a little pamphlet explaining who he was, why he needed a wheelchair and, crucially, how he communicated. This pamphlet, which included some handy FAQs, was given to everyone in the school the summer before he joined. As a result, everyone at his secondary school talks in a normal voice, knowing that he understands. 'If everyone valued inclusion, it would be more of a reality,' Jonathan believes. 'It takes belief in the importance of inclusion and a can-do mindset to enable it to happen.'

Here lies the crux of a complex debate, to which I can offer neither a definitive, nor actionable, answer. Michelle, Zara, Damian and Jonathan are a prime illustration of how nuanced the issue of disability really is, and a necessary refutation of generalising labels. You can never impose monolithic, all-encompassing rules. You must listen, empathise, collaborate and accommodate to develop a hyper-individualised plan. A versatile, person-first approach that respects aptitude in all its forms could positively redefine how we perceive academic potential, failure and ambition. Fundamentally, it would establish the underpinnings of a world that accommodates, and wholeheartedly believes in, the real power of diverse abilities.

Our reliance on segregated education is preventing this utopian vision from becoming a reality. If mainstream schools can divert anyone who doesn't fit into their set model towards a special school, there is little incentive to offer any form of individualised teaching. Ultimately, the presence of segregated schools 'weakens' the responsibility of the mainstream sector and 'stifles' our imagination about how to accommodate diversity, according to the Centre for Studies on Inclusive Education. Perhaps this is most clearly visible in the sheer lack of provision for disabled students. By law, all school governing bodies must prepare an 'accessibility plan' – self-written guidelines on how to improve the physical environment and boost participation of disabled pupils. But a study found that, awkwardly, 65 per cent of education professionals had never even heard of such plans.

When it comes to decisions about schooling, rather than pushing for a unanimous consensus that can be rehashed across the entire disability spectrum, strategies must be driven by parents or guardians, in the best interest of each child and never on the basis of government resources. Scant budgets, underfunding and vanishing social provision should not be held up as a legitimate excuse to define the course of a child's future. Just as we cannot rest any schooling decisions on the scourges of expired patience and low expectations. This is a screaming injustice. Yet it's one that is creating irrevocable fractures in our society today.

It feels natural, imperative even, to argue against any ideology of segregation. However, on the subject of educating children with disabilities, it unleashes a tsunami of gainsaying and murky waters. Always, it must be a case of what's the most suitable, comfortable fit for the individual child – and we should be uncompromising in this respect. Even in exceptional cases where children are placed in special schools, their education should never be 'entirely segregated', according to a UNESCO report on special education, which is regarded as the definitive framework for action. Part-time attendance at regular schools must be 'encouraged', for instance during social periods like playtime.

With creative thinking and adequate investment, all children will be given the inclusive, successful education they deserve. An education that lives up to the best of human values, allowing children with disabilities to build an identity that is joyously free of stigma and deflated prospects. I refuse to accept that it's an impossible or futile endeavour.

To sit back, vacillate and fail yet another generation of disabled youth is inherently amoral.

For all the obstacles that currently fester in our two-tiered education system, there's no denying that we have come a long way. Historically, children with disabilities were denied access to regular schools, severed from the family nucleus, and forced into residential special schools under a practice known as institutionalisation. At twelve years old, Mary Baker became part of this lost generation of disabled children. In the 1930s she was separated from her father and brothers and sent away to Halliwick Hall for Crippled Girls, an institution for the physically and mentally disabled in Edmonton, London. 'I had entered a different life. My father was far back home and I thought that everyone had forsaken me. I think I cried most of the night,' she recalls of her initiation at the school where she was stripped off, scrubbed with carbolic soap and her hair was cut short, right above the ears. 'The next morning you were given a number and you had to remember it . . . We never had names, we were just numbers there. It was all very disciplined.' Her account lays bare the dehumanising effect of living inside an institution, how she was denied the right to learn and grow up alongside her siblings – all because she walked with a limp.

While there remain exceptions – the Enlightenment bringing about the first British school for deaf people in Edinburgh (1760) and Louis Braille's invention of a tactile alphabet (1829) – until the latter part of the twentieth century disabled children were thought to be largely ineducable.

It took the philosopher Mary Warnock's report on special education in 1978 to propose urgent, radical change. Addressing government, Warnock advocated for the inclusion of special needs children in mainstream classes, introducing formal procedures and pathways that would allocate vital support to those deemed eligible. Three years later the Education Act was inscribed into law, and to this day, it remains a landmark for inclusive education in the UK. But these ideals are not always put into practice.

Despite its evolution, the education system is still a place where existing inequalities are played out and aggravated – particularly when it comes to the successful integration of disabled students. In the developing world, for instance, education divulges, and exacerbates, the contours of global inequality. A third of out-of-school children are disabled, with UNICEF suggesting that nine out of ten children with special needs in developing countries still do not attend school at all. In Bangalore, India, a mother of a girl with cerebral palsy told a news publication how her child was denied entry into the two mainstream schools near their house in KG Halli. 'The school authorities said that she was not normal, so they can't give admission to her,' she laments. Despite scoring well on the entrance tests for acquiring a place, the management said they would not 'enrol her in the school for even one day'. Fizarullah, a local boy who has epilepsy, was enrolled in mainstream school at first, but was forced to drop out when the school principal told his parents that they did not want to be responsible if something happened to him. When the teachers couldn't understand his condition or his seizure episodes, they would say to his mother, 'There is something wrong with your child,' dismiss his behaviour as disobedience and fail him in classes.

Inclusive education cannot be treated as a Western issue, when the available data shows it is plainly a matter of universal concern. From the financial burden of schooling and lack of accessible infrastructure to the reduced access to education in general, the lives of disabled children, a future of independence and economic security, hang in the balance. Families will often be forced to choose which of their children can go to school on account of financial circumstances. In this scenario, children with disabilities, disproportionately girls, will lose out.

The developed world is not immune to this phenomenon either. Often, structural biases will emerge and infiltrate the education system which can, therefore, become an incubator for lifelong inequality. In the worst cases a nexus forms between disability, racial and class discrimination creating an overarching bias which has led to children – both past and present – being ensnared in a scandalous cycle of neglect.

In a *New Yorker* exposé, 'The Forgotten Ones', the journalist Rachel Aviv investigates the toxic repercussions of a 'insidious, shadow education system' that has rocked the US state of Georgia. Known as the Georgia Network for Educational and Therapeutic Support (GNETS), these schools are currently attended by around 4,000 children with a range of disabilities under the umbrella of emotional and behavioural disorders. Far from a progressive space of learning, classrooms are segregated, punitive spaces surrounded by fences. Teachers often have no specialist training and predictably there is only a 10 per cent graduation rate, compared to 78 per cent for other public schools in Georgia. At one particular site, a grandmother discovered her son sitting on the floor handcuffed to a classroom chair 'like a chained animal'.

He routinely came home with a swollen face after episodes of being restrained. At another school, a teaching assistant was reportedly arrested after knocking a fourteen-year-old boy to the floor, choking him, and shouting, 'I will kill that little motherfucker!' With a vastly disproportionate number of African-American boys trapped inside these underregulated schools, questions and accusations are mounting. Is the label of disability being used as a smokescreen to further an unofficial, yet sinister, project of racial segregation?

According to Beth Ferri, a disability scholar at Syracuse University, the Individuals with Disabilities Education Act (IDEA) offers a sort of loophole to the 1954 Supreme Court ruling which outlawed racial segregation in American schools. 'You don't need to talk about any race anymore. You can just say that the kid is a slow learner, or defiant, or disrespectful.' She believes racial segregation has now continued 'under the guise of "disability"'. Set against a culture of low expectations and racial bias, Black students exhibiting any sign of learning difficulties or nonconformity are at risk of being written off by teachers. Behaviours cast as aberrant are reprimanded, shuttled through a covert pipeline into these segregated schools, all under the pretence of positive action. But, in addition to exposing institutional racism, this abuse of power betrays a great deal about our perception of disability – the notion that disablement is tantamount to a write-off.

There is obvious danger in falsely engineering our definition of disability for this abhorrent practice of racial discrimination. In twisting our classification of special needs and packaging it up as an excuse for social exclusion, it doesn't only trigger systematic cruelty against racial minorities. It painfully disfigures our whole understanding of disability, suggesting it is a negative force that can be abused or remodelled like wet clay to promote discriminatory agendas. Ultimately, students are prevented from accessing a suitable level of support, imprisoned in a system of fear and injustice, awaiting its urgent reform.

The repackaging of special schools as an aggressive form of discipline finds parallels in the historic UK school scandal where, throughout the 1960s and 70s, Black British children were unjustly removed from mainstream education. Instead, they found themselves thrust into so-called 'dustbin schools' for those deemed 'subnormal'. With Black children four times as likely to be enrolled as white children, this practice was 'underpinned by eugenics and the belief that Black children were somehow lesser than white children', according to the journalist Micha Frazer-Carroll. Over half a century on, a BBC documentary unearthed the lasting trauma of this disturbing period in British history with former pupils speaking out about their experiences for the first time. At the age of six, Noel Gordon was labelled as having learning disabilities. Despite no evidence or explanation of his disability being given to his parents, he was sent 15 miles from his home to a state-run ESN boarding school for children with learning and physical disabilities. All so a matron could supposedly take care of his 'medical needs'. 'That school was hell,' says Gordon, who still struggles with the psychological impact. He was sold the lie that he was inferior, and it stuck: 'I spent ten years there, and when I left at sixteen, I couldn't even get a job because I couldn't spell or fill out a job application.'

Stories like Noel Gordon's are dramatised in *Small Axe*, a masterful anthology film series from the Oscar-winning director Steve McQueen. In the final part, titled 'Education',

McQueen's most personal film yet, the narrative follows a bright twelve-year-old boy called Kingsley who is also foisted into an ESN school by his headmaster. Here teachers routinely fail to show up to class. Children are left untaught, scribbling on chalkboards, slamming desks and running amok. Kingsley dreams of one day being an astronaut (at the very least, a Tottenham Hotspur player). But, as his friend puts it, 'Once you're in those schools, you're finished.' Judged on the basis of his skin colour, Kingsley is rigorously policed and assigned this most punishing existence – an existence that could only be enforced by his illusory learning disability. In this scenario, the label of 'special needs' was a Trojan horse, concealing a rotting core of racism beneath its façade of benevolence. 'When you're in an environment of possibilities, then you feel like you can achieve anything and there are no limits. But when you're put aside, you're already being told you're not the same as the rest,' explains Steve McQueen. 'This started to happen to me when I was thirteen and already my path was sketched out for me. It is very important that [segregation] doesn't happen. It is disgusting. It makes that person feel like they're nothing.'

The intersections of ableism, racism and classism scream through these personal histories. Authority figures exploited their power, manipulating the classification of 'special' needs to curtail the lives of minority children. Kingsley is eventually rescued and enrolled in a Saturday school by a group of West Indian mothers who were exposing these schools for what they were: an unofficial segregation policy. His real-world counterpart Noel Gordon, and many other disabled children, aren't so fortunate. Today, Black boys are still being disproportionately excluded from school on the basis of disability. The Timpson Review of School Exclusion 2019 reported that Black disabled pupils in education have a 58 per cent chance of receiving a fixed period exclusion in the UK. This shameful reality illustrates how humanity's gross failure to be inclusive can spawn the most lethal prejudices. A poisonous spillage of lies seeps into the education system, wiping out children's lives before they've really begun.

I am quickly realising that an important issue at stake in the matter of segregated schools is the question of normality. The core principle of inclusive education is that human diversity is *normal*. Learning should therefore be adapted and expanded to meet the needs of *all* children, rather than forcing each child to fit into inflexible educational environments. But our two-tiered education system proves just how tightly we cling on to our conception of 'normal' versus 'other'. Every time schools fail to provide individualised learning, these punitive categories are defined and instilled in younger generations. This is a definitive issue when it comes to the exclusion of disabled children in education – and one that shows why we need to obliterate our reliance on stigmatising labels.

Integration can only be achieved when we choose to expand the parameters of normality. In many ways, school doesn't just hold a mirror up to our cultural obsession with standardisation, it positively engenders, encourages and enforces it. From obeying accepted rules of comportment to digesting the curriculum, schools can be conveyor belts of compliance. It's where we are first tutored to become prodigies in toeing the line – the necessary preparation for a conventional life of productivity and conformism. To be positioned aslant or off-grid in this one-way juggernaut of a system means you risk admonishment and destruction. Individuals with disabilities, through no fault of their own, can easily become unsuspecting casualties of an environment where every student is presumed to possess a healthy, pliant, standard-fit body.

A fierce level of protection swarms over our yearning for normalcy, to the extent that school has structures in place to reward obedience and reprimand early warning signs of irregularity. Prizes for perfect attendance, the triumph of not missing any school days, are surface-level evidence of a system where ableism is in-built. Flawless health is expected, and a degree of presenteeism assumed. This accolade is not just a public certification of a compliant body, of not needing to attend hospital appointments or being impeded by any illness that necessitates time out. It implies that absenteeism is elective, an act of malingering or, at worst, a moral failure. This is clearly the mark of a capitalist society where from an early age, we are coached to become obedient workers with an innate understanding that productivity determines human value. Spontaneous dysfunction, and the uncontrollable machinations of the body, are the enemy of a bureaucratic state. For the advancement and progression of our society, whip-smart intellect and conformity are highly sought-after (not to mention profitable) attributes. We are made to believe they guarantee success and wholeness. But this means we overlook, and criminally underestimate, the power of our innate differences, imaginations and unique minds.

In the creation of a better, more tolerant world, academic accomplishments are no substitute for content, free-thinking and empowered individuals. These are the vital characteristics we must instil and inspire in the next generation. School is the unifying experience of our life. It's where we do the earliest work on our self, from learning who we are and what we stand for, to mind-mapping our desired role in the world. It represents our best shot to fix the underpinnings of a stable identity and confront our fears and self-conscious feelings in a sheltered environment. Later, this indestructible sense of self will prove invaluable in a society where we are continually labelled. In my view, it holds more currency than an intimate knowledge of potato batteries, river drainage patterns and Queen Anne's preferred tipple (apparently brandy – but that's what Wikipedia is for). To leave school with a sharp awareness that you are worthy of being seen and heard is perhaps the greatest intellectual achievement.

During our early school years, children are becoming increasingly self-aware, preoccupied by their perception under the intractable public gaze. Knowledge of the self is no longer a single, reliable entity. It's a rapidly multiplying, increasingly layered behemoth that is warped and wrangled by the arrival of self-conscious thought. In the classroom, children start to realise there is an alarming gap between who they are, and how they are perceived in the minds of others. Multiple, distinct versions of the self are suspended in the ether – dancing between the chalkboard easels, squirting glitter glue and ever-pummelled beanbags. The certainty that once surrounded a child's identity is now lost, as they concede to the anxious possibility that classmates have assumed the role of judges and evaluators. This new awareness of their public appearance generates what Philippe Rochat, Professor of Psychology at Emory University, calls 'a devaluation or a delusion' as children flick between opposing emotions of shame and pride. 'A self-conscious self is expressed: an entity that is simulated and projected in the mind of others.' How each child learns to navigate this fragmentation – ideally how to push back against the barrage of false projections on their identity – is the germination of assertiveness and self-esteem.

To a certain extent, everyone, regardless of their ability, is required to maintain this external awareness of their identity. It's a precondition of a society that is addicted to normalcy and gets high on magnifying minor aesthetic or behavioural flaws. But when you have a disability, Judgement Day holds grave and potentially life-changing consequence. The first, excruciating instance of being confronted with your difference is an experience that unites all people with disabilities, across generations. Whether it's through classmates, the contorted prisms of mass media or the hostile gaze of unthinking strangers, the intimate relationship to our bodies has always been subject to interference and intrusion. Once you've been shown your difference, it feels as if there's no going back. The ability to reject these harmful interpretations of who you are, based on the sight of your body, becomes an important lesson. It is the key to success while society remains fixated upon inspecting 'flawed' bodies, gazing at them with the curiosity of 'a child watching a new fantastic animal at the zoo', as the writer Flannery O'Connor puts it. Self-assurance is the only form of counter-attack when we fall prey to autocratic decrees of who we are, and who we can be.

This desire to diagnose or categorise bodies illustrates society's obsession with conformity – and how it can cruelly infringe on our identity. When you look at me, you might draft a hypothesis to explain my disability as a way of controlling and demystifying the unknown. In philosophical terms, this is what the French thinker Michel Foucault termed the 'clinical gaze' or *le regard medical*. What he means by this is that we have all become amateur physicians – believing that our own eyes hold the key to detecting and diagnosing 'problem' bodies. It's a distinctly modern phenomenon that has arisen from the emergence of science, medicine and the microscopic world, where the observations of one individual have become a means to extract absolute truth. But the 'clinical gaze' is inherently ableist; it creates a field of power where the observer must seek out problems and concoct imaginary cures.

My identity at school, among peers, was, for the most part, divorced from any medicalised version of the self, unbridled by prejudice or bigotry. I had space and privilege to conjure up a narrative of my body where I was no different. I'll admit I had some logistical snags to find ways around – like negotiating a rickety flight of stairs one step at a time or filling up those heavy hours when everyone else decamped to the sports field – but disability was acrobatics with schedules and logistics, not any negative reflection of my personhood. If the school day collided with the medical sphere, usually, it was dipping out of school for an outpatient appointment. A biannual event that somehow always involved waiting in a puddle-strewn street for a furious taxi driver, butterflies in my stomach and a victory Crunchie bar for the dusk ride home. Otherwise, it was accompanying friends on a riotous jaunt to the sick bay. Without fail, our school nurse was propelling herself out the door, a hiking bag full of medical supplies strapped to her back after receiving an emergency SOS call – anything from someone scratching their oesophagus on a partially defrosted Findus Crispy Pancake (never to be seen on the menu again), a student peer-pressured into snorting a flake of Tipp-Ex (certain death), or a *Fargo*-style massacre down in the wood tech department (blood splattered across the Hegner saw). God knows what horrors the woman was attending to, but you could rest assured that the cure to all these terrible ailments was to be found in the liquid embrace of Milk of Magnesia. Was she on commission? In a packed-out waiting room, not much bigger than a broom cupboard, fake groans went up upon the realisation that her mercy mission would add a substantial wait time. The maths test could wait, I guess.

On one particular trip, I was stopping by to visit a friend in the darkened backroom. These were close quarters with camp beds reserved for only the sickest patients, or those who didn't fancy the scheduled cross-country run. Greedily, we pawed through the stack of well-thumbed magazines, reading out the neon pink coverlines brandished across *Mizz*, *Sugar* and *Shout*. Their 'true story' headlines were the primitive form of clickbait – you'd see everything from the hilarious, *Jealous Mum: She Had Surgery to Look Like Me*, and the obscene, *I'm 13 and Still Breastfeed*, to the frankly Kafkaesque, *My Mate's Got Mad Cow*. I was engrossed by every twist and turn in the epistolary narrative of *Why Did My Boyfriend Fake His Own Death?* (the unflattering conclusion being, with no attempt at sugar coating: he hates you), and had just flicked over to the rather more concerning, *My Mate Crashed My Sleepover and Shot Me in the Head*, when the returning nurse bursts into the room. Magazines were thrown under the pillow, patient scrambling back into the bed, resuming her repose of looking like a meek kitten, half-comatose, under the scratchy crocheted blanket.

So when the medicalised self did rear its ugly head, projected through the clinical gaze, it was humiliating and baffling and made me feel itchy. Like a creeping sense of formication, it's something I desperately wanted to shake off. I'll admit one particular incident is repressed in my memory. It begins, as most childhood dramas do, with a school trip and ends in a tacky souvenir shop.

Up with the larks, our coach was packed up and sent wheezing down the M4 on a cold February morning. I remember the insides were decorated with all the garish insanity of a 24/7 Las Vegas casino and strip club (surely mood-boarded by Llewelyn-Bowen on acid). Every right turn down a bramble-lined Somerset lane was so incredibly laboured, rumours that we'd be making a pit stop at some services for a mechanical check spread like wildfire. Naturally, as much time spent away from the sulphur-stenching Roman baths and in the service station arcade was a prospect to be lauded, encouraged even, by a coachful of twelve-year-olds. After an ominous snapping sound arose from seat B24 and one little poppet puked in the aisle, the coach driver (whose eyes read 'sign me up to a union, now') made the call. We were elated. I think cheers went up. But after an hour of frenzied investigations and no identifiable cause, our time to sniff the 'healing' waters of Aquae Sulis could be deferred no longer.

We plodded through the lofty museum doors in silence. The sight of the crumbling pillars, bilious-green bath waters, and their accompanying pong, was a far cry from the spa-like oasis we'd learned about at Key Stage 3. By noon, we had made our presence known. To the extent that I overheard a posse of WI ladies lamenting why 'on God's green earth' they didn't just schedule their biannual day trip for last Thursday when Margery was having her colours done. As the day progressed, their displeasure was palpable. My friend swore blind she was nearly tripped up – with *mens rea* – by the walking stick of one cantankerous woman with a wicked grin. During our tour of the baths, one student went MIA, her jam sandwiches and Peperami mysteriously uneaten and no confirmed sightings since the tepid plunge pools. A full-on manhunt was instigated – tannoys and all. Our once unflappable teacher was caught wailing into the hiss of an overhead speaker. When it transpired the bolter was in the group all along (the jam sandwich, a red herring), the mood shifted from one of sheer panic to giddy relief. We seized the opportunity to swoop in on the souvenir shop. A place where a bucket of £1 plastic key rings and a 10-inch stick of rock could rouse infinitely more enthusiasm than the chalky relics of Caecilius, Metella and the canis from 1100 AD – much to the chagrin of our teachers.

That day, unbeknown to me, I was being observed. A fact that became clear when I was accosted by a boy with his attempts to 'diagnose' my condition, spluttering something about MRI scanners. Trying to ignore it, I stood motionless and silent, scared that a huddle of tourists might overhear. I refused to attract more attention, given that I was now cast as a museum artifact. But the clinical gaze already felt like an out-of-body experience. An uncanny, surreal instant that scoops you out and transplants you straight into the clutches of an anatomy theatre. While I encourage openness about my disability, this was not sensitive, empathetic enquiry. It was a one-sided exchange that instantly disabled me, more than any of my physical difficulties on that day. After some withering looks from my friends, it was deduced that this boy was clearly off his rocker and he skulked off. We never spoke of it again. But it was a reminder that how I look is regulated, perhaps more so than other girls and women for whom society already places a premium on their attractiveness, health and vitality.

Each jarring and spiky word reinstated to me that disability was something to be ashamed of. In that moment, my disabled self existed outside of me, exposed and terrifyingly public. It appeared like its own entity – an uncontrollable, spawning nucleus of false meaning which could be extracted to create awkward encounters, at the whim of others. I didn't want to be caught off guard again or play the role of victim in another unsuspecting attack. Instead, I subconsciously, and without ever articulating it, pushed away from disability. Ghosting it, believing it to be antithetical to the best parts of who I was.

It would be a lie to say I still don't buy into this delusion. When we're conditioned to believe that normality defines our worth – especially in these formative years – our standing as human beings is defined by how far we can emulate normalcy. To what extent we can live a 'normal' life. And how convincingly we can claim that universal icon of a line-drawn wheelchair user, suspended in a void of Pantone Blue 294, doesn't apply to us. As twisted as it may seem, any declaration of our value becomes tied up with a painful rejection of our bodies – a task that requires hard labour. Not only are we trying to minimise the physical difficulties of being disabled, but we portray ourselves as an exception, rationalising the ways in which we are unlike other people with disabilities. It's a relentless fight to prove that our lives are full and fundamentally worth living – a campaign that is made necessary from an early age when schools equate conforming bodies with social and academic success.

This internalised need to downplay our disability to gain acceptance is even more disruptive than external prejudice. As the writer Jenny Morris explains, this defensive practice – known as 'passing' – is one of the most serious threats to selfhood. 'We attempt, of course, to avoid the oppressor's hateful distortion of our identity,' she says, but it carries the risk that 'our true identity, never acted out, can lose its substance, its meaning, even for ourselves. Denial to the outside world and relief at its success blurs into denial of self.' Knowing that our life prospects depend on how we are perceived, people with disabilities learn to appraise themselves first. The habit of concealing disability therefore becomes not just a standard imposed on us by society, but a standard of our own. Complicit in a system that tells us disability is shameful, our internal soundtrack begins to ventriloquise discriminatory voices. This can lead to a tragic erosion of the self – a gradual chipping away, until a landslide threatens collapse. As a result, Morris rallies against this obstructive need to 'pass' as normal, in both appearance and function: 'I do not want to have to try to emulate what a non-disabled woman looks like in order to assert positive things about myself. I want to be able to celebrate my difference, not hide from it.' It's clear to me that nobody can be expected to live their whole existence straining, squeezing and sculpting themselves into a shape they just won't fit. This is exhausting and serves no one.

If there is any realistic hope of alleviating this burden, the solution must surely lie at its inception: our school years. When we grow up in an educational environment that demands conformism – with comparisons being drawn between peers – there is increased pressure for children to 'perform' whatever is an acceptable, mainstream identity simply to avoid sticking out. Alternatively, when schools encourage individuality and self-expression, this desire for sameness is reversed. Like flexing a muscle, it becomes instinct to stand tall against the pressure to cover up or be anyone other than yourself.

This was a skill I began to acquire at school. One incident springs to mind: it was October, and I was lined up in the lunch queue, awaiting my plate of grey and gloopy chicken fricassee, splattered across white rice with grains like 17-caliber bullets. Quite enough to crack a molar. But not enough to elicit any concern from the health and safety inspectors, who once pitched up unannounced at the behest of a friend's mother. Despite the alarming optics of their undercover raid – clipboards, hard hats, visors! – both food and service were deemed 'exemplary', much to our annoyance. On this day, however, half-term was on the horizon so there was an air of jollity that felt uncharacteristic of a Tuesday lunchtime. Until everything unravelled. The queue was running at a sluggish pace, so to save me standing for twenty minutes, my friends and I were invited to slip ahead. As we crossed in front of a logjam of hungry ten-year-olds, a voice cut through the din of jangling cutlery. 'How come that cripple gets allowed through?'

'What?' I thought, performing a mental double take. It was as if I had caught sight of myself in the side mirror of a fitting room – that disorientating, somewhat mortifying instant when your blind spot is laid excruciatingly bare. You see yourself locked in an entirely new dimension screaming to get out. The refracted self, a haunting unknown. For the first time I was shown a vision of myself I had never seen before, with all its weird, disarming geometries. I instantly feared this could be how everyone saw me. The humiliating possibility that others were too polite to say anything, too censored. My self-constructed identity began shrinking and shrivelling to a chimera in my head. Was I deluded in thinking of myself as a strong and capable being? Was it all a fallacy? Was I *abnormal*? It was comical, even, for how it lay at extreme odds with my version of events.

Once the sting wore off, in some peculiar way I transgressed a boundary. Those ugly, caustic words were a galvanising force – pressuring me to see my life and everything I'd constructed with hyper-clarity. I had a decision to make: would I relinquish myself to someone else's view? Or would I refuse to bend to this distorted vision? I quickly vowed that nobody would define my body, my abilities or who I am. No one could impose these things upon me, not least someone I didn't know, or hadn't spoken to.

In these formative moments, growing up with a disability becomes a balancing act. When reality doesn't align with the self-made version of who you are, it smacks you off your axis. It forces you to confront the external assessment of your identity. This realisation that my security and happiness are indebted to the perceptions of the people beside me, threatened to undo me. To rewrite everything I'd come to know about myself. My schooling shielded me from narrow-minded thinking and gave me a solid sense of self. But these sobering instances show that the hostilities of the real world are ready to gust into your life – everything could snap in seconds.

In Judith Heumann's memoir she recounts a similarly traumatic, 'blinding flash' incident as she crossed along the street to a sweet shop with her friend. Out of nowhere, a young boy stared aggressively at her wheelchair and repeatedly shouted 'Are you sick?' in a booming voice. Left speechless, Heumann instantly desires to cover herself. She is thrown off-kilter and forced to reconcile her own understanding of who she is with how she is perceived by the world. Like me, Heumann believes this moment was filled with phenomenological significance. She was ripped from a mental space where she 'never felt different' from other children and suddenly held hostage in the realm of other. The boy's barrage of probing questions sparked an internal reckoning, a new self-consciousness: 'I became uncertain of myself. *Was* I sick? I saw myself through his eyes . . . everything in my life made a perverse kind of sense. I couldn't go to this school, I couldn't go to that school. I couldn't do this, I couldn't do that, I couldn't walk up the stairs . . . I *was* different. But I'd always known that. It wasn't that. It was the world and how it saw me. The world thought I was sick . . . I wasn't expected to be a part of the world.' This encounter – the anger, the pain, the injustice – changed the course of Heumann's life, planting the seeds of her activism which ultimately brought about revolutionary human rights legislation for the disabled, including a landmark act that reduced barriers to education. As Heumann says, 'Some people say that what I did changed the world. But really, I simply refused to accept what I was told about who I could be. And I was willing to make a fuss about it.'

Heumann's experience reminds us that real liberation originates from inside our own consciousness. As Jenny Morris writes, 'Just as no feminist would think of trying to change discriminatory laws and conventions of society without first changing her own attitudes to her personal inheritance of conditioning, so no disabled person should see liberation from prejudice as solely a matter of changing others.' We must no longer be pulled towards a desire for normalcy, herded by the grip of our self-consciousness. To believe we are seen for who we are is the biggest step towards eliminating shame – regardless of whether false stereotypes and distorted views tint the vision of others.

This, to me, is where school offers a tipping point. We must create environments where children with disabilities can find the courage and freedom to resist these fears, to be themselves. The tools we need to be liberated exist within us. It is only when education arms us with the courage to assert our true self that this personal liberation can become a reality.

If education lays the foundation for a prosperous life filled with opportunity, children with disabilities face an uncertain future. Already, if you have a disability, you're three times less likely to hold any qualifications than your non-disabled peers. But I do not believe academic attainment is the only thing at stake here – in fact, there is something more valuable, more metaphysical, to be lost when students are capsized by barriers in the education system.

Our culture has a fixed and unflattering perception of disability, like it's a passive 'sick' role to play. It is only by abandoning this restrictive mindset that children will have the confidence to occupy the truest, multi-dimensional versions of themselves – I am testament to that fact. My education allowed me to escape prescribed roles. I was given the power to unwind and unfurl my character away from the negative cultural fabrications of disability. It placed me, starry-eyed and arms aloft, beside my classmates as we gawped up at Shawn Emanuel and imagined our futures.

This, I now realise, was a luxury – and, quite possibly, one I could no longer possess. It is painful to admit that my own experience in education would now be out of reach, due to the physical demands of an eight-hour school day, and some frankly Everestian architecture. However, the early knowledge that I could choose who I wanted to be is the reason why I can now embrace my disability in a way I have not done before, knowing that I have the strength and courage to resist assaults on my identity. Without those formative years, making secure friendships and developing my selfhood without fear of intolerance, I would be a distorted pixelation of who I am today. A sliding doors scenario that would set me adrift on an entirely different path towards a less enriched reality.

This, of course, is all hypothetical. But for many children with disabilities right now, it is a present reality. Through unwarranted segregation, exclusion and a lack of investment, school forces them into that role. This should not be permissible in our liberal twenty-first-century society, or elsewhere across the globe. The material body, with all its terrifying, random instabilities should never hold such dominion over our lives, our opportunities, our chances.

Education is where we will flesh out an evolutionary blueprint for a more inclusive society. Schools must become spaces that nurture empathy and self-expression among every new generation. We must empower all children to see that whoever they are, there is no role they cannot play.

# Varsity Dream

What does it *really* mean to be disabled? A blank UCAS form and a sweaty school computer room hold the key to this eternal, probing question. For this was the exact moment I was counted, present and correct, as having a disability. Growing up, I refused to give the term any airtime. I staunchly declined to be labelled as 'disabled', believing it to have only negative connotations that were far removed from the identity I had forged for myself. Disability was a cold, privative, reversing force poised to threaten my agency. Even a sibilant whisper of the word was enough to mortify me. But now, rendered in black size 12 Arial font, it was painfully inescapable. My fate foretold by a drop-down box.

Perched on a swivel chair in front of a glaring PC screen, I suddenly belonged to 'Category H – Disability, impairment or medical condition not listed above'. What a time to be alive. I was a physical anomaly; I didn't even have a place within the listed categories. In that moment, I felt exposed and stripped of agency. The philosopher Judith Butler once explained how recognition of oneself can only take place through a set of social norms. And here, by dint of a blank UCAS form, I was faced with a tick box scenario of the highest degree. I was no longer simply the sum of myself, but under the gaze of society I was now categorised by my physical abilities. I had just come to terms with the reality that it would be 'advisable' to change my email contact from lottsarellaxoxo66@msn.com to something less spunky, more vanilla. And now there was yet another hoop to jump through.

Sitting motionless, I watched my classmates zipping three pages ahead to the declarations of 'criminal convictions and felonies'. Meanwhile, across the room, our teacher was cautioning a mop-haired boy who wanted to pepper his 4,000-character personal statement with a wince-inducing pun or witticism. 'They rarely land,' I overheard Sir squawk from where he was leaning against a squat filing cabinet. 'Total waste of space' (the comedy, I assumed, not the boy). Hands already trembling from my narrow mishap of selecting a course in Animal Husbandry (campus: Outer Hebrides), I decided to log out and return later.

It felt awkward, yet strangely cathartic, translating into words the physical limitations I had lived with since birth. Years later, the wearisome process of explaining, over and over, my disability would become a rote script – from last week's restaurant booking to future job opportunities, the occasions are numerous. But right then, aged eighteen, I was forced to accept that according to the official record I was different, part of the category 'other'. Perhaps the realisation that the world isn't designed to accommodate me was an existential reckoning that was long overdue. As children we are ideally praised for uniqueness and shielded from prejudice, but the transition to adulthood is like being thrown into a dystopian hinterland where your physical strength callously determines your chances. For the first time in my life, the milestone of applying to university, I could no longer ignore the inconvenient truth: my disability was a part of me.

After missing out on the majority of my sixth form years due to long spells in intensive care, the prospect of university and 'my future' were deadbolt-locked in a parallel universe. The world was sadly not my lobster, it was a skimpy crayfish from a petrol-station sandwich and it was on the turn. Life was eclipsed by a constant feeling of slipping behind, social isolation and gruelling hours of self-study just to catch up. But, irrespective of the card I was dealt, I refused to allow this period of illness to define or limit the direction I wanted to take in life. If anything, the allure of education made me desperate to distance myself from the plastic hospital ID bands that had recently handcuffed me. When the world outside felt further away than ever, I needed to carve a future for myself and a reason to get better.

But there is nothing quite like a seemingly innocuous tête-à-tête with a careers counsellor to smack you off your perch. After contacting their PA for my twenty-minute slot, I arrived to an empty classroom for my allocated time of 4:52pm. I peered around nervously at the archaic flip-top desks (a dying breed) and the walls plastered with historic timelines charting the rise of Industrial Britain ('Ten ways to work a loom', chronicled in wavy Microsoft WordArt and felt-tip pens). Naturally, Freud would attribute my creeping unease to a much earlier encounter with the school careers service, which was, to put it lightly, a complete riot. After five tedious hours spent box-ticking on a never-ending questionnaire, the test papers were collected up and sent away for analysis. Six weeks later and the verdict was in . . . I was a natural-born podiatrist. I couldn't conceal my horror. One friend with a pathological fear of birds was also on the verge of tears after being told her dream career lied in butchery. Another, who had ill-advisedly ticked the box 'I like working independently', was announced to have all the innate talents of a mortician. Anyway, I digress.

When the sixth form careers counsellor bolted through the door, he began speaking with a tone of stark pessimism about my ambitions to study English at Oxford. He flicked through a pile of course brochures with an arresting speed, reiterating the words 'competitive' and 'highly selective' through some dismissive hand gestures. Suddenly, a life devoted to cankerous ingrown toenails and bunions was looking slightly more appealing. Then, as a dénouement, he whipped out an impressive array of facts and figures about the improbability of me ever stepping foot onto an Oxford quad. The word 'counsellor' should not be used anywhere in the job description, because the resounding experience was far from therapeutic.

Low expectations blight people with disabilities. A study published by the *British Journal of Sociology* found that disabled adolescents are 15 per cent more likely to have low expectations about going to university compared to able-bodied pupils of similar socio-economic backgrounds. The root of this pessimism is hard to tease out. It's often far more covert – and pierces much deeper – than the glib predictions of a careers advisor. Perhaps the most disturbing cause is that intellectual aptitude is often falsely equated with physical stamina. When we fail to separate the bodily condition from the mind, it's unconscionably easy to underestimate those with disabilities. Disabled school students may therefore give up on pursuing an academic pathway – even though many impairments are not linked to cognitive limitations.

However, when researchers surveyed further into what was driving these low expectations, they came to a surprising conclusion: the prospects of young disabled people are over-whelmingly curtailed by the fears of parents and guardians. Concerned about the potential for discrimination at university, parents perceive higher education as an unsafe environment for any young adult with a disability. This widespread fear of prejudice and inequality is contributing to a society in which disabled people are still only half as likely as non-disabled people to have a degree. I am fortunate that I could find my greatest advocates at home, always ready to dispel any fears with a chorus of 'you have nothing to lose'. Or engage in some sassy backchat about the loose professional morals of the careers counsellor. But without that baseline encouragement (or any reassurances about the support available for undergraduates), success is reliant on disabled applicants being able to single-handedly circumnavigate the logistical and emotional hurdles that arise when transitioning to university. Unlocking one's potential therefore becomes a test of mind *and* body.

So, my early aspirations to study at Oxford were seen as doubtful, off-the-wall even. Was my ambition down to self-belief or wanton denial about the challenges that lay before me? It was hard to tell. But I left the careers counsellor's office with a hefty stack of university prospectuses, a feigned smile and even greater resolve.

When you have any kind of disability, choosing a university can be a minefield. Glossy prospectuses with their intoxicating inky smell are like an elaborate sales pitch: they may espouse their 'inclusive ethos' on page 26, but will they really tell you if the only accessible accommodation is in the arse-end of nowhere with a fifty-minute bus ride to the main campus? I don't think so. I desperately wanted to imagine myself beside the dreamy-eyed freshers in those photos, dashing to check books out of the library or hobnobbing in the SU bar. But instead of seeing the silhouettes of my future, I felt rising apprehension. For disabled applicants, accessibility must always be top of the agenda when deciding on a university – something that many able-bodied people are privileged to take for granted. You might be hellbent on taking that niche module on midwifery in medieval Gaelic literature but if the seminar room has no lift access and a vertiginous flight of stairs, it's a non-starter.

A campus tour and high-grade sleuthing is the only real way to determine how each university will cater to specific accessibility needs. But in the case of 21-year-old veterinary student Sarah-Marie Da Silva, even this wasn't foolproof. In February 2020, still only a fresher, she tweeted a photograph of herself in a wheelchair attending a typical Friday morning lecture. The image, taken by her lecturer at Hull University, showed Da Silva isolated in a stairwell at the back of a lecture theatre, unable to get down the stairs to join her peers. 'I turned and saw the stairs and panicked,' Da Silva recalls, 'then I realised people were wondering why I'd suddenly stopped and I was in people's way. I just told them I can't get down and to just go past me.' Physical disability left Da Silva degraded and unjustly segregated from the crowd, at a time when mingling and making connections with her classmates was paramount. Her plight went viral. 'Jesus Christ it's 2020,' read one of the many exasperated comments. While it's encouraging to see an outpouring of support on social media, 280 characters of consolation cannot enact change.

Prior to the incident, Da Silva had raised the issue of poor accessibility numerous times. She was told, however, that the only viable alternative was changing to another room where the 'accessible' seat obstructed fellow students, requiring her to constantly wheel in and out of the lecture theatre. Waiting, crammed in a claustrophobic stairwell, seemed like the least-worst option. Da Silva described the experience as 'humiliating' and 'othering'. Hull University promised a 'full investigation' (yes, one of those) but when BBC News followed up on the case, Da Silva reported that there had been 'no improvement' in disabled access. Still she was unable to sit with other students during lectures: 'I'm either isolated at the front or I'm stuck at the back by myself,' she laments. 'I just feel so disheartened that they think it's OK to treat us like this.' Despite Da Silva's repeated appeals, plus the fact she is paying full tuition fees for a sub-par educational experience, nothing has changed.

Similarly, for nineteen-year-old Meelina Isayas, who has cerebral palsy, it was exasperating that admissions offices could sell the dream of an inclusive student life, but then have little regard for the practical help you would need after visiting the site in person. When Isayas selected her university choices, diversity was top of her criteria: she had always been frustrated by her position as the only black disabled person in educational spaces. However, when visiting their campuses, some explicitly admitted they were 'not the best' for physically disabled students and she should apply elsewhere. These were institutions that proudly advertised themselves on their diverse ethos, yet brazenly admitted that they couldn't make adequate accommodations for disabled students. On another university tour, however, Isayas was blown away by the support on offer: 'I was reassured by the staff that if there were any problems with the infrastructure of the building (such as unwieldy door handles) that I would just have to let them know once I arrive and it would be changed.' These gestures of flexibility and foresight have real potential to encourage students with disabilities into higher education – but, frustratingly, they remain all too rare.

Isayas's case shines a light on why it is so important for educational institutions to take accessibility seriously. 'Something that has never left my mind is the employment discrimination disabled people face,' she admits. 'If you combine this with being a Black, working-class woman, getting a degree was somewhat non-negotiable.' Her words pull us towards the bigger picture. In a society that is liable to write off disabled people in the jobs market, there is an urgent need to prove your productivity and aptitude, to shield yourself from that appalling, yet prevalent, assumption that disability is synonymous with inability. For individuals with intersectional identities, like Black women or members of the LGBTQ+ community, this pressure can indeed multiply. A university degree, a rubber stamp of excellence, is one of the few options to certify your intellect. If disabled people wish to be competitive in the careers market, a successful university experience can be make or break.

My earliest reconnaissance mission to the dreaming spires of Oxford fell on a sweltering June open day as coaches packed full of bushy-tailed sixth formers descended on the winding, cobblestoned streets. After a quick scroll across Google Maps, I convinced my mother into going on a road trip. 'It's really not a difficult route – so easy to find!' I said with youthful optimism, and she was game. But with a mystifying one-way traffic system, it proved impossible for my mother (designated driver) to negotiate the streets by car. As the Bonnie to my Clyde, we rode around for several hours flouting multiple red lights, tooting horns and cautionary signs reading 'BUSES ONLY'. I took out my iPod headphones as a gesture of support, but morale was at rock bottom and it did little to achieve its aim. Reluctant to give up, we eventually befriended a genial road worker called Steve with a dazzling high-vis vest and majestic long grey beard: 'You wanna take a left here, ma darlin', circle back to Pitt Rivers, then it's on yer left.' In that moment, Steve appeared like Gandalf's enigma showing us the hallowed path – or perhaps it was a dehydration-induced mirage.

After being hurled around in the passenger seat for hours, under Steve's expert tutelage it was a mere five minutes until we had embarked on the final student tour of Wadham College. I crossed through the ornately carved Jacobean archway to get my first glance of the towering battlements and square lawn which lay in perfect symmetry. Instantly, I was fearful that the imposing buildings would be a literal fortress to me – entirely inaccessible. I'd be forced to confront the devastating reality that my body was going to blight my ambition. That powerless feeling of injustice. The agonising frustration. The flash of anger. It's something I'll never be desensitised to.

Yet, I was encouraged by the number of rooms with level access or a lift. I was mindful that some areas would not be accessible, but the college's flexible, inclusive attitude was reassuring enough. I just had to tackle the small feat of getting an offer, right? I returned home fired up with determination and feeling content about the opportunities that might await me. Well, until the Oxford City Council traffic fines started to arrive in the post.

Oxford interviews are traditionally held in those heady first few weeks of December. But, by the time the tinsel was dusted off and advent calendars were ensconced on mantelpieces across the country, I still hadn't learned my fate. Again, the bunions were calling. Just when I had resigned myself to the fact that I wouldn't be debating the beatniks' use of parataxis, an invitation dropped into my inbox. It read, 'Come for an interview next week, prepare to stay for five days . . . and bring your woollens.'

Aside from a raging fear of the unknown, the experience was at once enjoyable and surreal. The college allocated me an easily accessible ground floor room, where I heard the muffled crunch of a snow-scattered quad and the fanfare of rolling suitcases that trailed along the ancient stone pathways. At night, I peered out from the window seat onto the silvered, moonlit gardens. Whatever was to follow the next day, this was the victory.

Contrary to folklore – and those little shit-stirrers of thestudentroom.co.uk – the interviewers did not deploy Secret Service recruitment tactics. I was relieved to find it was an intellectually stimulating conversation with a convivial mood, and not a discussion about whether I'd rather be a novel or a poem, how to poison an enemy without the police finding out, or my preference to be a seedless over a non-seedless grapefruit. During those thirty minutes, I felt listened to: at times, the interviewers' mandatory poker faces slipped to betray a look of excitement or enthusiasm at something I had said. However, just minutes before one of the two sets of interviewers arrived, it transpired that the chairs were too high for me to sit comfortably. The student ambassadors ran in and out with a couple of seating options for me. I felt like the protagonist in a bedroom farce, trying to quell my escalating panic as I was plonking down on the conveyor belt of seats. But their kindness and ability to find humour in the situation blew off my nerves. 'These are my people,' I thought.

The eventual news that I had received a place was, therefore, exhilarating and a relief. The next step involved a mandatory Disabled Student's Allowance (DSA) assessment. From computing equipment to library assistants or travel expenses, the allowance aims to cover extra costs associated with long-term illness or disability during university. Exclusive to Oxford, I was also required to have a 'fitness to study' meeting. Now, this was scarier. I had visions of walking into a HIIT bootcamp scenario with an aggressively stout man with a buzz cut, cargo pants and tank top swinging some kettlebells up to his ears and screaming into a megaphone. In reality, this meeting was just an opportunity to enquire about the support on offer and discuss outstanding concerns.

It is often the small adaptations, along with people's willingness to embrace them, that make the biggest impact on university experiences. In many cases, it is these tailored, seemingly insignificant adjustments that are the difference between success and failure for disabled students. During her psychology degree at Glasgow Caledonian University, Rachel Townson, who has autism, struggled with the overwhelming sensory experience of examination halls. 'I just couldn't walk into the exam room,' she recalls. 'The floor felt like waves of movement, physically rolling up and roaring towards me, and the desk looked so far away I couldn't walk to it without nausea kicking in.' Although she was found to be on the autistic spectrum after leaving university, her grades were severely impacted by this undiagnosed condition. 'There were noises in the room I couldn't switch off from, the invigilators walking up the room had me on edge. One exam my eyes were streaming from a girl's perfume. And on my worst exam I was in the toilet being sick, with an invigilator making sure I wasn't trying to cheat.' In her final year, a lecturer expressed concern about why there was such a disparity between her written coursework and exam grades. After explaining her difficulties, student services were able to allocate Townson a smaller exam room with only five other people. 'From then on, I scored top grades in all my assessments. A small reasonable adjustment took away the social anxiety and sensory discomforts that I couldn't face.'

For the zoology graduate Lizzie Huxley-Jones, it was only during the second year of her degree at the University of Liverpool that she became severely disabled. The acute onset of recurrent, unexplained seizures caused major disruption for both her work and social life. 'It was really tough,' she concedes. 'My seizures were out of control and I was waiting for a number of scans and tests to be done to give more of an idea of what was happening. I had extremely low attendance and missed a bunch of exams.' Suddenly, she was extremely vulnerable and forced to be dependent on others. 'The staff were amazing though. They moved my deadlines, sent me extra material to study if I missed lectures, and even helped make sure I had a morning to sit the exams last minute so I didn't have to miss the third year with my friends. Thanks to their support, I came out with a first.'

Calls for reasonable adjustments, however, are regularly disregarded or bound up in red tape, forcing disabled students to overexert their bodies while they to fight to prove their eligibility – or else pioneer innovative solutions for themselves. The truth is that learning to self-advocate and find unique ways around poor access are a large part of navigating the world with a disability, at university and beyond. Almost always the responsibility lies with the individual, rather than the institution. The triumph of Haben Girma, the first deaf-blind person to graduate from Harvard Law School, is a testament to the power of creativity and perseverance against all odds. Without a means to communicate with her teachers and classmates, her early experiences of education were exceedingly isolating. Upon arriving at Harvard in 2010, Girma was determined to give more colour to her surroundings and so invented a cunning device that connected a Braille computer to a keyboard. An interpreter could then translate her lecturer's speech into its tactile form. She was even able to take the device to campus bars where fellow students could type conversations and describe the surroundings for her – though, she admits, the typed chatter became much less coherent as the night rolled on and the tequila was flowing.

Girma raises a critical point about the privilege and security able-bodied people possess in a world that is built for them. 'It felt overwhelming because the burden would fall on me to come up with solutions to pioneer my way through the unknown,' she revealed during a BBC radio interview.

'That gets incredibly exhausting, but it was also thrilling. It's an adventure. I am creating more opportunities for the students who come after me.' When disabled people are falsely perceived as helpless and passive, our culture denies this power – the ingenuity and courage that is constantly drawn upon in everyday life. Like Haben Girma, I am often left empowered when finding creative solutions or breaking down any physical obstacles that are thrown my way. This has given me not only an assertiveness, but an ability to think critically and without limits which I have always been able to utilise in my work.

The reality of having to strive for every solution, though, is not always so generative. The lack of extra support available has resulted in the regulatory body, the Office for Students (OfS), warning that disabled students are dropping out at a 'concerning' rate in the UK. 'It is time for universities to ensure genuinely equal opportunities for disabled students,' said Chris Millward, Director for Fair Access and Participation at OfS. 'This means not only meeting their legal duties to individual students but learning from each other to create learning environments in which all students can thrive.' As world-leading universities are being called out for institutional ableism, his comments are unsurprising. A new report by UCL found that 67 per cent of disabled students experienced ableism, while a shocking 58 per cent felt unwelcome during their degree. 'You are made to fuss for little concessions which is dehumanising,' one student revealed. 'You then magnify your vulnerabilities of being disabled as a result of being forced to fight for each and every measure of support.'

Adjustments – whether that's alternative seating, extended deadlines on assignments, or exam papers in Braille format – can transform educational experiences. But these concessions remain the exception, rather than the norm, meaning that people with disabilities are silenced or ostracised for reasons that are entirely rectifiable.

With a month to go until fresher's week, I made the heavy decision to purchase a mobility scooter. My original intention of taking taxis around the city was looking unrealistic and, admittedly, I was still triggered by my past ordeal of negotiating Oxford's labyrinthine streets by car. Could I really rely on another chance encounter with Steve and his marshmallowy beard? Likewise, I had heard horror stories about the challenges of getting around at other universities. One particular story about a designated 'bells and whistles' minibus service for disabled students incited a feeling of dread. After multiple breakdowns, late arrivals and a steadfast refusal to drop passengers off anywhere that didn't require a hike to rival Scafell Pike, it fell short of its grandiose promises. The dismount from the minibus via ramp also came with a cacophony of emergency sirens, as if to herald the Queen of flipping Sheba. The relative ease, and quiet, of zooming down the cobbled pavements on a scooter became too tantalising to ignore.

While it shouldn't be perceived any differently to hopping on a bicycle, in reality mobility scooters are stigmatised and held up as symbols of vulnerability. There is a persistent cultural narrative that portrays mobility aid users as 'bound' or 'confined' by their disability. It's inescapable. 'Be anyone you want to be at university!' is a freedom that consequently was never going to apply to me. I could not be a blank canvas – whether I liked it or not, first impressions would be formed on the presence of four wheels and a chassis. It felt scary to be perceived as someone who was visibly disabled when the stigma attached to this felt so far from my true identity. I feared initial awkwardness and longed to be accepted on my own terms. But ultimately, I was fortunate to be surrounded by thoughtful, inclusive-minded people. The truth is almost every student will have internalised fears and unseen vulnerabilities to grapple with. My weaknesses were simply surface-level, immediately visible to external gaze.

In my case, the customary fresher's nerves were split – 80 per cent is access going to be problematic; 10 per cent will people be accepting; and 10 per cent am I going to handle Oxford's notoriously ferocious workload? I was so apprehensive that illness or poor access was going to derail me, every coming day felt like an achievement. Certainly, there were moments when I didn't know whether I'd juggle everything that university demanded. Caffeine-fuelled all-nighters in the library researching Derrida's post-structuralist theory followed by 5am jaunts to the Purple Turtle bar were rites of passage that weren't possible for me. While this sparked sentiments of FOMO, I knew that there is not one archetypal or 'valid' university experience. Whether a college tutor was ensuring I had a comfortable seat for our tutorial on Victorian realism in *Middlemarch*, or I was meeting my friends for cups of tea and routine evening debriefs over a G&T in my room, or a formal dinner was specifically held in an accessible location, rather than the usual top-floor venue, with the generosity of others, I soon learned to navigate university in my own way. I relished my new independence, clinging onto the magic combination of being proactive and trusting the force of my ambitions.

From surviving exam pressures and living away from home for the first time, to forming new friendships and keeping up with a hedonistic nightlife, navigating university life with a disability requires true mettle and enterprise. But, beyond the everyday demands, university means a fight to be seen, heard and understood. Personally, I felt empowered by my autonomy, the ability to leap along the stepping stones to the real world and prove to myself what I am capable of. However, with so much to gain, there is enormous potential for complications to arise. What is an opportunity to strike out and discover a new order of experience can quickly become fraught and isolating.

Overnight, the Covid-19 lockdown radically opened up the academic landscape for students with disabilities. Lecturers who were once adamantly against recording lectures or virtual teaching became reliant on such methods – and, as a result, disabled students benefitted. However, many questioned why it took a global pandemic to improve these aspects of disability access. Why was progress only possible when able-bodied people demanded it and universities were facing financial pressure? Social media blew up with people expressing their disbelief about the hypocrisy and double standards at play. Take, for instance, Cambridge University, who announced they were moving their lectures online for a whole academic year. One graduate felt rightly aggrieved: 'I and many disabled students fought tooth and nail to try to get Cambridge to put its lectures on [the online teaching platform] Moodle,' she tweeted. 'Almost always we were told it wasn't possible.' If anything, the pandemic provided a once-in-a-lifetime insight into ableist structures still present in society. The rights disabled students had fought so hard for suddenly became a reality, illustrating how the power to change the system lies in a collective force.

But, in a rapidly evolving public health crisis, the implications of Covid-19 policies did not remain static for long. As restrictions eased, progress was reversed. When universities returned to in-person teaching, for instance, the introduction of infection control measures posed major issues for disabled students. Intricate one-way systems on campus proved disorientating for those with autism, unnavigable for the visually impaired. The presence of lengthy queues, lift closures, and removal of seating spaces to promote social distancing were exclusionary for some physically disabled students. According to a survey carried out by Disabled Students UK across sixty-nine universities in 2021, over half of disabled students were considering leaving their degree, interrupting their studies, or switching to part-time studies due to the pandemic.

It may be cynical to admit, but the early benefits plainly arose out of universities making urgent adaptations for *all* students. It was purely coincidental that learners with disabilities were disproportionately advantaged by it. When it came to hands-on support and targeted disability inclusion policies, most institutions were left severely wanting, with many students saying they felt 'left behind', 'alienated', and 'forgotten' by university staff. Is this acceptable for institutions that are designed to inspire progress, innovation and freedom of thought?

To date, there remains a persistent gap in accessibility and success for disabled students in higher education. It is shameful how the transformative powers of academia are frequently ringfenced and blighted by discriminatory policies. A diverse student body will only be achieved by fostering an environment where everyone, regardless of their ability, is given support to unlock their potential, empower their self-belief – and finally live out their varsity dream.

# Fashion-able

What I remember most vividly from the summer everything changed is not the fear, shock nor wrenching despair, but a blue dress. A slinky silk floral number with a nipped-in waist, artfully laced back and a near weightless skirt that graced the knee. At a time when I was forced to re-examine everything I'd known about my body, this dress was the one silky-damn thing I had to separate me from the identity of a patient. Wearing this dress and feeling the lustrous slip of the fabric cleave to my skin was restorative. It allowed me to regain control of the narrative, tearing me away from the lingering trauma of the coarse, boil-proof hospital gown knotted at the back with twill tape – a dreaded reminder of my own vulnerability.

When I agreed to meet my friends for an end-of-year celebration, arriving to face a gaggle of partygoers, shrieks and shrill laughter, this dress became my armour. I stood nervously tugging at the hem, in many ways feeling like a different person, before my friends spotted me, swooped in, and took me back into the fold. It was the outfit of someone who was living the life that I was not. And, for a moment, I could step into that carefree, buoyant existence – the one that I was starting to believe was not destined for me. While we ultimately grew apart, the dress still dangles regally in my wardrobe, secure in the knowledge that she's performed a lifetime of dutiful service.

At every chapter of my life, I've used fashion as a protective shield that allows me to shape how I'm perceived by society. It's always fascinated me that the way I dress can prohibit people from imposing false constraints on my body and appearance – defying other people's labels and unsolicited assumptions. It's a common misconception that people with disabilities do not care what they look like. But this simply isn't true. From styling myself in a mohair Fair Isle knit and gold hoops for the tentative first day of university, to wearing a cornflower blue shirt teamed with hot pink high-waisted trousers when setting out for an internship, dreading that I wouldn't be able to access the workplace, I wholeheartedly subscribe to the Zadie Smith philosophy: 'Women often believe clothes will solve a problem, one way or another.' In most cases, they do. Clothes have always been the silhouettes of my reinvention.

For as long as I can recall, I've expressed this fierce sense of style – but that's not to say it has always worked out. Age seven, I decided to impulsively cut myself a side fringe. Insert alarm bells. Where I was thinking just a couple of stylish tendrils to discreetly frame the face, this tuft had its own agenda. It bobbed – making wild, erratic movements from its blunt cut edges. It refused to lie and repelled the rest of my brunette locks. To say it was a *Fleabag*-grade haircut emergency would be no exaggeration – it was neither modern nor chic, and it certainly wasn't 'French'.

My friend who was complicit in this tinpot experiment gazed on in horror, yet still proceeded to cut her own. As she drew fire with the kid's plastic craft scissors, she accidentally nipped it 2 inches above the agreed length. This wouldn't do. She impulsively grabbed the scissors again and macheted the whole section at its root, as if to make the problem go away. The following morning everything caught up with us, and we were dragged out of a family party after her mum spied the hairy remnants of our night of debauchery languishing in the waste-paper bin. While our parents were less than pleased, we paid the ultimate price – condemned to flick hair out of our eyes until it was time to throw a snap clip on the sproutlings. This hair disaster, an event that fortunately predates the advent of camera phones and photo sharing apps, became folklore . . . well, until my sister's horrific mullet struck.

My gravitation towards fashion couldn't even be derailed by some traumatic experiences in the school textiles classroom – a place where absolute anarchy was expected, and infliction of bodily harm was to be presumed. If there wasn't someone slicing their fingers open with the pinking shears, there would surely be second-degree burns from the steam iron, or a diplomatic incident centred around a Bernina Overlocker. Tasked with the ambitious project of crafting 'embellished jeans', our school nurse was primed on speed-dial, first-aid kit at the ready. After an hour-long queue, I headed over to the sewing machine to seal my fate. Just as I'd revved up the foot pedal, however, I caught sight of our teacher charging towards me. She was waving ferociously and screaming like a banshee. 'What the hell is going on?' thought I and the rest of my classmates, who were looking up from their sewing stations in hot anticipation of a showdown. Earlier in the day, this same teacher had tripped over an errant bobbin that was left in the gangway (her bête noire) and writhed around on the floor for minutes, as if to prove a point. She was not messing around. It transpired that I'd neglected to put on the obligatory hairnet and protective eye googles – a 'flagrant disregard of safety protocols' – and was unceremoniously thrown out of the classroom for my sins. The embellished jeans were a disaster, but the appeal of self-fashioning and creating identities through clothes has always stayed with me. I was back the next year to try my hand at a revolting faux leather peplum skirt (the optics of which may have constituted a human rights violation), mercifully with a new teacher, the previous one having taken early retirement to open an out-of-town bed and breakfast.

No matter the outcome, my personal style has always been about more than ephemeral denim fashions or the punishing quirks of an ill-executed haircut. It's an act of defiance, self-assertion and a declaration of who I am – which isn't going to be dictated by anyone but myself. Fashion and beauty are too often held in contempt as objects of vanity. In the context of global strife, my preoccupation with that age-old dilemma 'what to wear' could be seen as a moral failing. But this refuses to acknowledge the freedom and empowerment that style can bring people with disabilities.

It's illogical to me that 'style-conscious' and 'disabled' are still viewed as mutually exclusive entities. Many wrongly assume that if you have a disability, it radically defines your taste – a pair of thermal sweatpants or greige orthotic footwear is about as stylish and sexy as it gets for you. God forbid anyone with a disability would actually want to look good. In reality, our wardrobes can be a place of emancipation. The magic that lies behind its doors allows disabled people to write the narrative, unleashing their style and asserting their individuality in the face of a society that tries to flatten it.

Yet people with disabilities are routinely overlooked by the fashion industry. From billboards and glossy advertising campaigns, to the bulb-lit catwalks and retail departments, images of able-bodied models dominate the visual landscape. What's more, these images often contain a subtext of choice – with capitalism upholding the false promise that, if you can mimic the look, you are on the path to gaining higher social status. The ideal feminine body, almost always non-disabled, is presented as an object for consumption, a means to buy success, self-sufficiency and approval. It is an irrational notion that sets everyone up to fail. But people with disabilities will often become the first casualties in this oppressive culture.

Style is often maligned as vacuous and insignificant, our clothes being no more than 'vain trifles'. However, if we view fashion again for what I believe it to be – a site of independence and expression, a means to lay claim to our own narrative – then many disabled people are being torn away from an enriching part of life. For too long, consumers have been sold the idea that style belongs only to the prescriptively beautiful, the lithe and the able-bodied. This belief system has been pummelled into the recesses of our subconscious by fashion media, Instagram feeds and advertising agencies the world over. Here anyone who cannot remake themselves in fashion's image, or replicate its strict aesthetic ideals, is rendered almost invisible. If we desire to live in a diverse world where disabled people no longer feel segregated and hidden away, the definition of what constitutes an acceptable, normal body must expand and evolve – right now.

From razor-sharp cheekbones to bee-stung lips and Barbie doll waists, society has long been ruled by the myth that beauty lies in a monolithic ideal. For generations, individuality was cast away, or concealed under layers of exhausting artifice. Any aesthetic quirks were to be bundled out of sight like a pair of ripped granny pants on a communal washing line. In its place came this crazy thing called 'beauty', of which you can never have enough. Slick on that scarlet red pout (but only if it complements your eye colour), strap on those sultry stilettos (over forties beware!) and soak up those hour-long roastings on the sunbed to get that supermodel glow (just don't miscount your Mississippi's and come out resembling a sun-dried tomato). Beauty is a seductive delusion, a masquerade where individuals, whatever the cost, must manipulate their image to squish into a perfect mould.

Modern life compels us to desire sameness. Governed by our desire for normality, we scuttle along an axis, pushing who we are into who we must become – discarding little pieces of ourselves along the way. We're all compelled to act, look and be normal at every turn. Consider that one-size-fits-all minidress from Brandy Melville, the rigmarole of a seven-day Special K diet, or the cyborgian look of the 'Instagram Face' only achieved by the sharp scratch of Juvéderm filler. People must slot into pre-existing templates, categories and structures. Uniformity – as much an addiction as a legal requirement – has become a form of social capital that expunges the individualities of who we are. In our quest for this cookie-cutter lifestyle, however, we've developed a collective aversion, almost a sickness, towards abnormality. This makes disability a perilous state of being.

The sight of disability 'breaks the rules we live by', according to the disability theorist Rosemarie Garland-Thomson. It just doesn't fit. In a line-up of people, the presence of a wheelchair, an amputated limb or a facial disfigurement jars awkwardly. It refuses to slot into place, leaping outwards much like my once unruly side fringe. Disability is hyperbole where we seek understatement. It is this preference for quiet conformity and the jarring nature of disability that, Garland-Thomson says, can 'render novelty in human form repugnant to us'. Bodies that deviate instantly become 'spectacles of otherness'. While able-bodied people may exist away from this alienating gaze of society, if you have a disability your body is unwittingly, and without consent, branded as abnormal.

I've felt this dichotomy in action – whether I use a mobility scooter or not. If I'm able to slip into an accessible restaurant without a long walking distance, I can almost exist like someone 'normal'. I sense my body is unmarked, or under the radar. I am part of the collective throng. In this moment, I delight in the freedom and limitless possibilities of an existence away from the weight of public scrutiny. Whereas if I am riding the streets by mobility scooter, wind in my hair, this iconography of abnormality forces me to be segregated from others. I am painfully visible, exposing a part of myself that others are conditioned to fear. You, my reader, might clap eyes on my mobility scooter and hastily misinterpret it as a sign of suffering. In this scenario, feelings of angst, pity, even guilt, may bubble up. You might prefer to look away. Choosing to develop a blind spot, rather than the self-reflective task of contemplating what it all means. Or you might react in frustration. Tutting and exhaling loudly as I attempt another botched reverse out of a crowded lift without so much as a wing mirror, or a 'mind those doors!' while the hefty steel mechanics clamp shut. You may even scan my body furtively, trying to work out what the hell went wrong, eyes rolling up and down in an act of empirical deliberation. Here you momentarily refuse to see me as a person, but instead as a transgressive body that cannot be codified or interpreted. While society views any mobility aid as a mark of weakness and frailty, ironically, I am a lot more able with it than without it. These outdated misconceptions may be potent and persuasive enough to deceive you, tearing you away from the reality of who I am. But we cannot forget that they are illusions conjured from the flimsiest of foundations.

There is truth in how the visually impaired poet, Lynn Manning, describes disability stereotypes as a kind of sinister 'magic'. They can bewitch us, despite having no logical or rational basis. In his autobiographical poem 'The Magic Wand', Manning portrays himself as a 'quick-change' artist who is hexed by violent stigmas: 'I whip out my folded cane/ And change from black man to blind man/ With a flick of my wrist'. A spell strikes in the eye of those who surround him. They gaze on, sifting through hostile interpretations and selecting a category by which to identify him – race? Gender? Disability? He is stamped with whatever label feels most relevant to the time, place and viewer's preference. 'My final form is never of my choosing; / I only wield the wand; / You are the magician', writes Manning, reminding us that he holds no power in this scenario. Stereotypes are not only transfigurative, but they encourage us to single people out and make impulsive judgements based on incomplete, visual markers of identity. This must change.

Disabled bodies are disruptive simply because they defy our need for what's familiar and predictable. They don't conform to our expectations of how a body should look or behave – owing to the fact we have hidden disability away, redacting it from the annals of history. When we encounter the disabled body on the street or in the workplace, we still don't know how to interpret it. It is this social illegibility that causes anxiety and tension. 'It's not that disability itself creates unease,' confirms Garland-Thomson, 'but rather people's inability to read such cues disrupts the expected, routine nature of social relations.' There is no flat-pack manual here.

It strikes me that the stigma surrounding all disabled bodies can be further understood, and perhaps more easily eliminated, when you look at it in relation to the 'Beauty Myth'. This premise – outlined in Naomi Wolf's seminal text from the 1990s – describes how a woman's value is determined by her ability to act out society's definition of 'flawless beauty'. She is assigned a place in a vertical hierarchy based on how convincingly her body can pull off this performance. Is she a Hollywood starlet at the Oscars or Worst Supporting Actress at the Razzies? Hurry, her life depends on it! This tyrannical thinking now sits at odds with the emerging era of body positivity. We are finally exposing the absurdity of the 'Beauty Myth' and toppling this hierarchy. Yet, when it comes to disabled bodies, the same old diktats remain. Body fascism prevails.

Naomi Wolf's *Beauty Myth* is based on an able-bodied individual – untouched by impairment, injury or deformity. While she makes no mention of the disabled experience, parallels are drawn between 'ugliness' and 'disease'. To be ugly or diseased are 'insults' that women must seek to avoid. They will diminish your value. Wolf cites an article from the *New York Times* in 1988, where an expert in dermatologic and cosmetic surgery says: 'It would benefit physicians to look upon ugliness not as a cosmetic issue but a disease.' Today we respond to this comment with outrage. It's clearly absurd. But if we flip the statement around and are asked to look upon disease as ugliness, the statement doesn't incite the same degree of horror. Whether we admit it or not, we are still conditioned to see disease as a mark of ugliness.

The link between disability, deformity and beauty ideals is put under the microscope in Jennifer Egan's acclaimed novel, *Look at Me*, in which she writes ferociously about self-image and spectatorship. We meet her character Charlotte Swenson – a *Vogue*-approved model from New York – after she is pulled from the flaming wreckage of a car and has her skull screwed back together with eighty titanium bolts. Before the crash, she adored being admired by strangers. Their 'jabs of interest' strike her 'as an unharnessed energy source'. As a girl who once sat obediently within accepted beauty norms, being observed was life-giving. But things inevitably change. Charlotte's reconstructed face renders her a spectacle of otherness and she is now ashamed to be seen in her 'present grotesqueness'. She cannot slip back into that cookie-cutter lifestyle; she is made 'less visible', yet also 'darkly conspicuous; a dour visitor, a drug-ravaged starlet incognito'. Egan's novel is a reminder of where disability and deformity are on the slider scale of body oppressions we all face in a world where value is judged on our exterior. Despite surviving a devastating accident, we're so invested in beauty and outward appearances that the miracle of her survival is made irrelevant.

Physical perfection is culturally synonymous with living a charmed life. It becomes difficult for Charlotte to comprehend a viable existence outside of our normative borders of beauty. Is being stripped of one's 'pretty privilege' a fate worse than death? Well, almost, says Egan. What is clearly satire, exposes a truth that we all know – how women are often willing to put their bodies at risk just to erase their perceived defects. Plump, suck, snip and tuck is all it takes to buy an off-the-rack, glossy life. In our desperation to cover up signs of abnormality, we gloss over the disabling side effects and complications of cosmetic surgery. It is startling how the act of inflicting pain and violence on the body through invasive treatments, sometimes demanding weeks of recovery (euphemistically termed 'downtime') has been normalised. I remember tuning in to makeover programmes like *10 Years Younger* when I was growing up: a mainstream show that advocated several bruising rounds of plastic surgery, simply so that a few bewildered strangers on a high street might proclaim you the real-life Benjamin Button. It made the life-threatening risks of bodily manipulation seem entirely necessary – ordinary even. Flick over the channel and you could see 23-year-old reality TV star, Heidi Montag of *The Hills*, unveiling her 'new body'. She had undergone ten figure-altering procedures in one day. Procedures that, in her words, nearly killed her on the operating table, left her requiring twenty-four-hour nursing care and opioids to dull the extreme pain. Anything to attain, or hold on to, beauty.

In late 2021, the devastating toll of restrictive beauty standards was again brought into sharp focus, when the nineties supermodel Linda Evangelista revealed she had been left 'permanently deformed' and 'brutally disfigured' by a cosmetic procedure. Once the most photographed person on the planet – a feline-eyed woman who famously didn't get out of bed for less than $10,000 – Evangelista was now disclosing that she had been living in seclusion for almost five years, unable to look in the mirror. The treatment known as CoolSculpting, designed to reduce 'fat bulges' under the chin, jawline, arms and thighs, had left her with a condition called paradoxical adipose hyperplasia. This occurs when the fat-freezing process inadvertently causes the fatty tissue to thicken, expand and harden. 'I loved being up on the catwalk. Now I dread running into someone I know,' said a tearful Evangelista. 'I can't live like this anymore, in hiding and shame.' Her words buy into the beauty myth, implying that her 'deformed' condition diminished her value. It is yet another cautionary tale of what happens when you are forced to deviate from the norm, a body refusing to bend to the socially desirable vision of beauty.

The task of defining beauty standards – the very idea of what constitutes an aesthetically beautiful sight – has been an intrinsic part of the fashion industry since its modern inception. Rather than promoting individuality or teaching us to embrace our quirks, fashion has encouraged us to buy into one specific 'look'. Whether it's baguette bags and nineties blowouts, or gravity-defying low-slung jeans, trends are, by definition, about forecasting a dominant pattern and then shuttling consumers towards one direction until it becomes the norm. This has often buttressed our human desire for sameness. It has also taken the industry into a realm that's inflexible, oppressive and, sometimes, dangerously unattainable. Consider the Kim Kardashian-endorsed waist trainer which promises to squeeze in the waist, while giving the illusion of more curvaceous hips and bigger breasts. MRI scans of the wearer tell a less seductive story: the liver and kidneys being crushed, and the ribs pressing into digestive organs. When it comes to the many torturous ways of being 'worth it', the list goes on . . . lip fillers, microblading, skin bleaching, mail-order Botox, Brazilian waxes, vampire facials, cosmetic dentistry, blisteringly high platform heels, bandage dresses, flat tummy teas, vacuum packing your flesh into Spanx, and IV vitamin therapy to get that glowing complexion.

These dictatorial mandates on how we must look have historically excluded disabled people and other minorities, who cannot easily perform the masquerade. The inherent 'abnormality' of the disabled body clashes with the need for a normative, malleable figure. The fashion industry's idolisation of able-bodiedness lies at the heart of why individuals with disabilities have long been disregarded as both models and consumers. But is fashion finally ready to confront its historic erasure of disability? To use its autocratic power to end the painful stigma that still plagues disabled people?

In recent years, I've watched fashion gradually open itself up and embrace a wider spectrum of identities. Designers are showcasing models who don't conform to the tall, slim, white, cisgender archetype – finally eschewing rigid beauty ideals in favour of inclusivity. Fashion's new dawn arrived in 2017, a time when conversations around diversity in visual media were starting to effloresce and produce visible results. Progress was accelerated, in part by the appointment of Edward Enninful to editor-in-chief at British *Vogue*, but also because of a wider cultural awakening to the disgraceful power that unconscious bias has wielded over us. Suddenly, a diverse cast of models could spark more elation, and column inches, than the latest It bag – the values once espoused by the sartorial elite were undergoing a radical revision.

Arguably, Valentino's Spring/Summer 2019 couture collection has come to define this reckoning, with its cast of predominantly women of colour throwing down the gauntlet. The spectacle of frothy floor-length gowns gliding in and out of the chandelier-strung halls of the Hôtel Salomon de Rothschild, Paris, was at once electrifying and radical. If the most exclusionary bastion of fashion, haute couture, could be reshaped under the inclusive values of new generations, there was no time to wait. 'Since the Middle Age, there has always been a canon of beauty,' reflects creative director Pierpaolo Piccioli. 'Now, you cannot have canons. Humanity is the canon. Everything is valid.' Versace followed next, with 'plus-size' models making history as they stormed the catwalk at Milan Fashion Week in 2020. Behind the scenes, landmark appointments at the luxury fashion houses of Balmain and Louis Vuitton flung open the door to ateliers that were once impassable to people of colour, with Black designers Olivier Rousteing and the late Virgil Abloh consistently pushing for greater diversity in design. But it was the September issue of *Vogue* magazine in 2021 that provided the most striking affirmation of just how far the pendulum has swung. Under the strapline 'In Real Life', the image featured Ariel Nicholson, the first openly transgender cover star, among the likes of 'plus-size' Asian model Yumi Nu and supermodel Kaia Gerber. Their megawatt smiles and animated hands implored us to join the party, to embrace this new era where the concept of style being defined by strict categories of body is irrelevant – laughably passé.

We are at the beginning of a cultural shift towards what the Pulitzer Prize-winning fashion critic Robin Givhan calls a 'big-tent beauty'. Writing for *National Geographic* in 2020, Givhan outlines how we are venturing through a new, untrodden landscape of beauty where all are represented. Herein lies utopia and anyone can pitch a tent: 'Everyone is welcome. Everyone is beautiful. Everyone's idealized version can be seen in the pages of magazines or on the runways of Paris.' But where does disability fit into this diversity agenda?

It seems that beauty is slowly evolving to mean something more than a superficial set of aesthetic ideals. Beauty is being liberated; no longer codified, but multiple and expansive. However, when it comes to disability representation, exclusion remains stark. One fifth of the UK population is disabled, yet research has shown that, in the past, only 0.06 per cent of adverts featured disabled people. It's clear to me that disability is still execrably under-represented in fashion media. As Givhan confirms in her article, many of 'the clubbiest realms of beauty' still don't include disabled women. But why is this? How can we continue to reject some minority bodies while endorsing and affirming others? It just screams hypocrisy.

'Disabled difference, it appears, is not frequently seen to be the kind of difference that societies value,' says Professor Lennard Davis, a renowned voice in disability studies at the University of Illinois at Chicago. While disability is the type of diversity that should be cherished, it still falls outside the ever-expanding parameters of inclusion. I sense something complex going on, with centuries of entrenched stigmas prohibiting change. Trying to dissect these falsehoods is the first step towards their eradication.

The suffocating stigmas around the disabled body find their origins in the so-called 'Ugly Laws' (1867–1974) when people who were regarded as 'diseased, maimed, mutilated, or in any way deformed' were cruelly prohibited from appearing in public in several US cities. Put simply, it was illegal to exhibit one's disability in public spaces and being deemed an 'unsightly or disgusting object' could result in your forcible removal or arrest. Diametrically opposed to this was the freak show, where disabled individuals were exhibited as specimens of biological curiosity for middle-class spectators to ogle. But as one of the most abhorrent forms of disability discrimination and systemic ableism, the 'Ugly Laws' expose how the shame and public policing of visual difference was once enshrined in policy. For nearly a century, disabled people could be excluded from social power and status under these restrictions. They were unjustly segregated from the general public, demonstrating how one's physical appearance has long been a measure of our value, influence and the kind of life we can expect to live.

Although the last known enactment of these laws was in 1974, I've observed how the surveillance of disability remains shockingly rampant. A hostile gaze on the streets can escalate, spilling over into a full-blown hate crime. In 2009, a 22-year-old British student famously took the fashion brand Abercrombie & Fitch to court for 'lookism' and disability discrimination while she was working at their London flagship store in Mayfair. As someone who wears a prosthetic arm, Riam Dean did not conform to the company's archaic 'look policy' – athletic, tanned and long swishy hair. She was therefore condemned to work in the stockroom. Well, until the winter uniform arrived and she could wear a concealing cardigan. You couldn't write it. While her shirtless male colleagues romped around and paraded their slicked abs on the shop floor, Riam was screened from public view. Able-bodied workers held up as paragons of aesthetic perfection for aspirational teen shoppers, a disabled individual consigned to the shadowy backroom where the screeches of Cyrus's 'Party in the USA' were muffled, yet punishingly audible. Their actions appeared indefensible. But in the judgement of Philip Davidoff, a discrimination lawyer at the global firm FordHarrison, Abercrombie's attempt to safeguard its image was not illegal: 'There's nothing that prohibits discrimination against ugly people,' Davidoff preached to ABC news. '[Abercrombie] wants to have people out on the floor who project a certain image, and that kind of public perception is closely related to their business model.' Under a carefully constructed veil of exclusivity and the all-American ideal, capitalist structures uphold an ableist conflation of 'ugliness' and disabled bodies – to detrimental effect.

'It was the lowest point I had ever been in my life,' Riam told the tribunal, where she later received £9,000 in compensation. '[It] pierced right through the armour of twenty years of building up personal confidence. I am born with a character trait I am unable to change, thus to be singled out for a minor aesthetic "flaw" made me question my worth as a human being. Abercrombie taught me that beauty lies in perfection, but I would tell them that beauty lies in diversity, for I would rather live with my imperfection than to exude such ugliness in their blatant display of eugenics.'

Riam's experience is eerily reminiscent of the BBC presenter Cerrie Burnell, who faced a disturbing hate campaign after she appeared on children's television exposing her amputated right arm. Hysteria ensued. Multiple parents lodged official complaints with the broadcaster, expressing fears that it was – and I'm not making this up – mentally scarring their children at the expense of fulfilling diversity quotas. One parent had the gall to describe the inconvenience of having to switch channels because their daughter was 'so frightened of Cerrie' that it was 'giving her nightmares', while another bleated, 'I don't mind disability, but I don't want to deal with it at 9 o'clock in the morning.' Apologies, is post-watershed more convenient for you to 'deal' with it? What was potentially a quiet opportunity to educate their children on disability, to show the value of diversity and place a full stop on these inherited stigmas, was rejected. Instead, the prejudices of these parents were cloned and transplanted into the next generation, allowing the cycle to perpetuate. In a BBC documentary, *Silenced: The Hidden Story of Disabled Britain*, Burnell reflects on the furore: 'I'm a mother, writer and actor but to some people I will always be remembered as the woman on children's television with one hand.' For almost a decade, her public persona has been dominated by one facet of her body that, in an ideal world, should be viewed no differently to having a particular shade of hair. But this discrimination was by no means exclusive to the public realm. Age seven, Burnell recalls being encouraged by a doctor to wear a prosthetic arm (she was offered two options: 'a hook covered in plastic' or a non-functional prosthetic 'like a dolls hand'), which she resisted. 'Well,' her doctor said, 'the other children might not like it if you don't wear it, or you might not have any friends.'

The ugly face of ableism is still shooting daggers at society – just look at the recent experience of the model Jue Snell. A month before the pandemic hit our shores, Snell waited in line with hundreds of other models vying for a slot to appear at London Fashion Week. The casting was held by Fashion Scout, an agency that organises off-schedule shows for up-and-coming designers. They are, according to their website, 'renowned for empowering and showcasing the future of fashion'. But the events that unfolded could not be described as empowering, nor nurturing by any stretch of the imagination. Snell's excitement soon dissipated when she walked up to the auditioning table. 'What is that?' said a casting agent, gawping down at her amputated lower left arm. 'No, move on.' Another woman said bluntly, 'We don't do disabled, move on.' Here, the line between aesthetic preference and ableism had become dangerously blurred – leaving discrimination unquestioned and seeping through the cracks.

All three women illustrate how the pervasive stigmas surrounding visual difference are being met with attempts to erase disability, and how the fashion and the media industries are often lying at the hinge of this injustice. To me, it's unacceptable that any deviation from able-bodiedness is seen as strangely perturbing, and something to be feared or hidden away. This is causing untold harm to disabled people, to the point where the fractures of our collective anxiety are being internalised. A study by the disability charity Scope confirmed that 66 per cent of disabled people expressed the need to hide their disabilities as a consequence of the negativity and discrimination associated with them. This, of course, is the prerogative of each individual. Sharing one's disability should be on your own terms, not dictated by social committee. But, with our narrow understanding of what constitutes a beautiful, 'normal' body, the majority would prefer to expunge their true self – opting for a façade of normalcy over people's irrational hatred. And so these stigmas against disabled bodies continue, unchallenged.

Today, fashion remains one of the most persuasive and lucrative visual mediums with a market value of $2.4 trillion worldwide. It wields the global reach and commercial responsibility to rip up and reconfigure the visual politics of disability. To undo the rash impulses that tell us deformities are abnormal or ugly. One of the philosophical reasons we keep erasing disability and react to its sight with such unease is that disabled bodies are a mirror of our own existential angst. That, on a subliminal level, looking at disability forces us to confront our biological instability. This contradicts everything the fashion industry strives to sell us, where what's 'in vogue' is a byword for desirability, influence, poise and futurity. Disability is a mimicry of the very fleshiness of our being, the incalculable workings of our component parts that might easily malfunction the way a MacBook thrums and whirrs until the lit silhouette of the apple blackens. Why would this be considered desirable, aspirational or 'luxe'? As much as society tries to make us believe we have agency over our health and well-being, disability is a reminder that this is, ostensibly, a marketing ploy. Our health is regulated by the mercilessness of fate, not a three-day juice cleanse or collagen-boosting facial. Your genetic material cannot be realigned like an off-kilter chakra, and immunity from disease will not be bought or sold like a mini-break at a Shamanic healing retreat. There is discomfort in contemplating our corporeal vulnerability – in the same way that we are averse to the clinical starkness of a hospital or the hurried scrawling of a will. As a defence mechanism, strategies of avoidance are devised to repress these fears. Fashion is ripe for disrupting these deep-rooted prejudices. It can start by refusing to hide disability away. But too often the industry has reproduced these social stigmas, rather than remedying them.

Sometimes I find myself thinking, why can't we collectively agree to 'get over it'? To accept disability as a beautiful and natural part of the human condition. Not as an 'unruly sight'. A blot on society. An aesthetic flaw so shameful that it must be thrust into oblivion. Yet it's proving near impossible. Is there any effective route forward? And what can be achieved if, and when, we finally tackle this? To see beauty where we have long seen absence and lack. In this moment, a revolution is waiting, expectant.

There's no denying that we are required to look uniformly beautiful – or face up to some dire consequences. But how about if we just eradicated this addiction to normality and beauty, would this in turn solve the 'problem' of the disabled body? In Jia Tolentino's essay collection *Trick Mirror*, she writes of how 'the default assumption tends to be that it is politically important to designate everyone as beautiful, that it is a meaningful project to make sure that everyone can become, and feel, increasingly beautiful. We have hardly tried to imagine what it might look like if our culture could do the opposite – deescalate the situation, make beauty matter *less*.' This is a radical and tempting proposition, yet it fails to recognise that beauty is the promise of confidence, power and sexuality. As I argued in an opinion piece for an issue of *Vogue* Italia, 'a world without beauty is an infinitely poorer one . . . It's only by stretching out the boundaries that we can rebuild the very idea of beauty in its most powerful and rawest form.' Instead of abandoning the pursuit of beauty, we must tackle the stigma surrounding disabled bodies and plot a new way of seeing.

Throughout the history of fashion, we've witnessed pioneers who have attempted to deconstruct the social taboos afflicting disabled bodies – simply by making them visible and desirable. The late Alexander McQueen recognised fashion's potential to redefine negative perceptions of disability. His electrifying Spring/Summer 1999 fashion show thrust disabled models into the spotlight, with double amputee Aimee Mullins emerging onto the catwalk in a pair of ornate, hand-carved prosthetic legs. McQueen first caught sight of Mullins on the cover of a luxury design magazine in America, and instantly she became his muse. 'Before I knew it, I was flying to London and turning up on set,' Mullins recalls. 'I told a make-up artist that Alexander McQueen wanted to work with me, and she said, "Girl, be prepared to walk along the razor's edge, because that is it."' As the creative world's enfant terrible, McQueen used shock tactics and radical spectacle to incite reaction. This provocative spirit was reflected in his otherworldly designs, which included futuristic spray-painted dresses and haunting corsetry. Both legless and strikingly beautiful, Aimee Mullins represents a disruptive paradox – challenging the viewer to see a vision of beauty that had never been seen before.

In the run-up to the show, McQueen oversaw the publication of his guest-edited issue of *Dazed & Confused*. 'In a world where the mainstream concept of what is and isn't beautiful becomes increasingly narrow,' read his self-penned introduction, 'you have to be young, you have to be thin, you should preferably be blonde, and of course, pale skinned.' Inside the magazine lay a fourteen-page fashion editorial dedicated exclusively to disabled models. It was shocking and revelatory – it cut deep. Even before the advent of Facetune, which has given millennials the Swiss army knife of cosmetic tweakments, McQueen was prescient in exposing how fashion's emphasis on bodily perfection plays a devastating role in marginalising disabled people. Late twentieth-century fashion magazines, in particular, were 'a powerful symbolic system' and 'a major force in producing' the identity of its readership, according to academic Leslie Rabine. Given that a vast majority of their imagery subscribes to able-bodied beauty ideals, McQueen was right: the ostracisation of disability in fashion media is parroted in wider society. As the *Dazed* editorial hit the newsstands, journalists reported that McQueen had done it! He had broken down 'one of the last bastions of body fascism'. And while McQueen's legacy is defined by this uncanny ability to subvert prescriptive ideals of beauty, twenty years later, progress in the trenches of fashion remains painfully sluggish.

As a model, Mullins often experienced people coming up to her saying, 'You know, you're really beautiful . . . you don't feel disabled.' She became privy to an 'us versus them' dynamic – what they were really saying was, 'You don't feel like one of them, a disabled person, you feel like one of us.' This made her think about the hypocrisies of visual culture. 'What we put on our bodies is a prosthetic – it can change our mood and make us feel like we are revealing a different facet of ourselves. People feel confident in clothes that look great on them.'

Her words point to a curious contradiction, a conspiracy that lies at the heart of the fashion industry. When glossy images are digitally Photoshopped or stylish clothes, corsetry and plastic surgery are deployed to 'augment' and 'enhance' the body, it's deemed an act of beautification. But if you amputate part of someone's limb and attach a prosthetic, it's automatically stigmatised as disability. This exposes just how superficial and gossamer-thin the tightrope really is. Fashion and beauty have long endorsed editing, reconstruction and augmentation of the body – so long as it's the socially prescribed kind. Removing part of the nose for a rhinoplasty procedure? Implanting silicone into the chin to reshape the jawline? Even wearing stilettos to elongate the legs, and Wonderbras to fake a perky bust-line? Here, the artificial is positively encouraged. When it comes to disability-related prosthetics or adaptations, don't expect to receive the same approbation. Such double standards do not only incite shame and a suspicion of failure, but they sustain the polarising system – 'us versus them' – where disabled and beautiful cannot co-exist. 'This tribalism where people only want to cosset themselves with the familiar and the known is like wanting to return to the Dark Ages,' Mullins tells me. 'I thought fashion would be a perfect place, with its seeming triviality, to have a conversation about something substantive, because we all know how much power and influence the fashion industry wields over our society,' she reflects. 'The more we see the extraordinary spectrum of human experience all around us, the better.'

This is how change begins, with the act of seeing a disabled body in sharp focus, flickering into view from the blurry depths of social obscurity. To see a disabled person unfiltered holds enormous, mostly unawakened, potential. Instead of being distressed by someone who appears unlike us, we must challenge ourselves to look past our social conditioning around 'deformity' and seek out a path of identification. It is the responsibility of the fashion and advertising industries to stage-manage this revolution by presenting us with disability. But progress lies in the palms of the individual, too. Educating ourselves on visual difference is a personal journey. One that requires conscious effort and a fundamental willingness to change. With commitment from the media, the public can embark on this process – and I do not exempt myself from this charge. Only then will the diversity of our world be valued in its totality, and we can all become unmoored from the oppressive anchors of the past.

The value of 'exposure therapy' cannot be underestimated – as the writer and civil rights activist Audre Lorde argues in *The Cancer Journals*. Documenting her own breast cancer diagnosis and subsequent mastectomy, Lorde rebels against the societal pressure to hide the physical scars of her illness behind 'silicone gel' or 'a pathetic puff of lambswool'. In her view, the attempt to present a 'normal' body would make her complicit with society's misogynistic attitude towards women – diminishing her to the role of 'decoration' or 'externally defined sex object'. Instead, Lorde transforms her body into a site of progress, upholding that central tenet of feminism: the personal is political. Imagining herself as part of a vast army of one-breasted women descending upon Congress, she turns an individual struggle into a politically useful one. 'The first step is that women with mastectomies must become visible to each other,' Lorde writes. 'For silence and invisibility go hand in hand with powerlessness.' By using her experiences to educate others, Lorde proves how, in the simple process of making something visible, perhaps even beautiful, there lies a politically generative act.

One glance at Stella McCartney's #NoLessAWoman campaign embodies this radical potential. Shot by Pulitzer Prize-winning photojournalist Lynsey Addario and filmmaker and activist Alice Aedy, the campaign posted images of twelve undressed women who have lived through breast cancer diagnoses to the designer's Instagram account. From Mel Bastien, whose radiant smile steals your eye from the purplish slit that embellishes her chest, to Lizzi England, who clutches her baby daughter Violet at her breast where a pink crescent-shaped scar lays visible, exuding an almost talismanic aura. Each portrait captures the raw, unfiltered energy of seeing bodies that defy our preconceptions. As emblems of feminine beauty, breasts must sit symmetrical, plump and unblemished. It visually jolts us when a body disrupts these fixed ideas of how they should look, when we see a raised scar in place of a nipple or the insistence of a blunt scalpel line. We are stunned and speechless – not from the spectre of disease, but because we don't yet have any knowledge of how to interpret it. To encounter a wound or void where we anticipate the soft curve of a breast, calls for a revised definition of womanhood, sexuality and desirability. As much as social media can play into the autocracy of modern beauty ideals, it also offers up a space to process these images of bodily difference. The longer your eyes linger, or your finger retraces the image, you can expand these aesthetic margins, developing a counter-narrative where once unruly bodies are finally made coherent.

Sororal outpourings of pink and red heart emojis were posted beneath the photographs, alongside the adjectives 'positive', 'healing', 'beautiful', 'powerful' – illustrating how the beauty of resilience, power and courage can be incredibly enriching and, in some ways, magnify our own sense of self. Their bodies implored us to not look away and voyage inside our own minds. Compare this to the controversial 1993 cover of the *New York Times Magazine*, where the artist and activist Joanne Motichka appeared in a diaphanous head wrap, her one-sleeved dress slashed low to reveal a scarred hollow in her chest where the right breast had once lay. The self-portraits 'stopped you in your tracks', recalls Janet Froelich, the magazine's art director at the time. 'No one had seen this scar before, unless you had it, or a close family member had it. We were riveted by the images . . . Nothing had caused quite as much of a stir.' In the days following its publication, the editorial team received hundreds of letters – some expressed positive sentiments, but many were disgusted and appalled to see such an image splashed over their Sunday paper. Even breast cancer survivors believed it violated their privacy, exposing what they themselves looked like to the public. We were not yet ready to welcome this new vision of what beauty could be.

In the three decades since Motichka adorned the cover, the cultural mood has undeniably shifted. But why, now, can the public respond so empathetically to the sight of bodily difference? I suppose it began with the internet. As we developed a 24/7 online presence and voracious appetite for sharing everything from the momentous to the mundane, the boundaries between what is public and private rapidly dissolved. In 2010, this climate of openness and self-expression gave rise to fourth-wave feminism: a consciousness-raising exercise where women were emboldened to speak up about their experiences of oppression, mainly via social media platforms. Here personal issues like body shaming were no longer private, but collective and shared. For the first time, many were inspired to seek connection with other's experiences – even those that lay outside of, yet strangely paralleled, our own. It was just like Audre Lorde had once said: 'I am not free while any woman is unfree, even when her shackles are very different from my own.' McCartney's #NoLessAWoman campaign exemplified this bridge-building action. Separated by nothing but a smartphone screen, we stood united against society's unrealistic body ideals and validated everyone's claim to beauty.

A total gestalt shift, from aversion to admiration, may seem ambitious to you – far-fetched even. But this is something that, I believe, the fashion industry is already poised to oversee. More proof of this disruptive potential can be found in the tragic ordeal of Olivier Rousteing, the 37-year-old creative director of Balmain. In an unfiltered essay for British *Vogue* in 2022, Rousteing explains how his recovery from a freak fireplace explosion – which engulfed the front of his body, leaving him hospitalised with first- and second-degree burns – forced him to reckon with his philosophy of perfection. Struck by 'a new and powerful shame' about his appearance, Rousteing kept his disfigurements under wraps – literally. He styled himself in oversized hoodies, applied make-up to obscure his scars, turned off his Zoom camera, and posted strategically filtered images to his 8 million followers on Instagram. 'My deceptions worked,' he writes, explaining how, despite the physical agony, he desired to conceal his injuries from friends, family and the press. Until he was hit by a profound mental breakthrough while sketching in his sunny Parisian studio.

Uplifted by the 'unconditional love' of his colleagues, Rousteing's experiences began to filter into his designs – the trauma bestowing creative inspiration in the form of gauze, dressing and grunge-inspired details. He even incorporated 'worn, patched, asymmetrical and irregular twists' into Balmain's signature tailoring. 'Those additions, just like my own scars, may surprise at first – but, ultimately, they help to make clear that a thing of beauty, in its entirety, often relies on the embrace of distinct imperfections,' Rousteing reflects. 'In fashion and beauty, we tend to overuse the word "flawless", helping to set unreal standards that, ultimately, push many to cover up, cut away and filter out.' Perhaps what it takes is a life-changing event to blow apart our definition of flaws, to seek out the beauty in imperfections – whether that's a global pandemic which forced us to confront our own mortality, or a devastating injury like the one suffered by Rousteing.

At last, exclusive members of the fashion community were seeing through some of the most entrenched beauty mores – and it was more than lip service. On extremely rare, but poignant occasion, disability was represented in editorial campaigns. First, there was a trailblazing Gucci beauty campaign starring Ellie Goldstein, a British model with Down's syndrome. Next, Haleigh Rosa starred in an Off-White activewear ad, where she posed in her wheelchair wearing monochrome swimwear, and Savage X Fenty cast Lyric Mariah Heard, who has a visible limb difference, to model their line of lingerie. Then came Aaron Rose Philip, who was hailed as the first Black, transgender and disabled model to front a Moschino campaign. Critics will still question whether this amounts to performative activism; yet more tokenistic posturing to snaffle column inches and placate consumers who want to buy into brands that are vocal about social justice. While it remains to be seen if these historic castings have laid the foundations of lasting change, it did achieve something irrevocable. Each image proposed to us an alternate, enticing reality where beauty could exist beyond able-bodiedness and, more importantly, a new way of seeing.

Redefining how we see signs of deformity and disability through the lens of fashion is not a trivial matter – it's bound up in the fight for equality. In fact, according to the late disability theorist Tobin Siebers, the urgent political struggle of disabled people will only succeed when there's a realistic conception of their bodies. 'Disabled bodies are so unusual and bend the rules of representation to such extremes that they must mean something extraordinary,' Siebers wrote. 'They quickly become sources of fear and fascination for able-bodied people, who cannot bear to look at the unruly sight before them but also cannot bear not to look.' This is the paradox of the stigma around disability: our brain craves unfamiliarity and abnormality. In brain imaging studies, the neurotransmitter dopamine flows at an increased rate, rushing through our neurones, when we confront an unexpected sight. When faced with a photograph of the disabled body, for example, this jolt of pleasure hormone instantly gratifies us – but it quickly dissipates at the hands of our social conditioning. Pleasure replaced with overwhelming dread. As the visionary examples of McQueen, McCartney, Rousteing and others illustrate, the fashion industry has a unique opportunity to rewire our psychological response by presenting disabled bodies as both readable and beautiful. By showing that functional prosthetics and mobility aids should really be no more stigmatised than the clothes we wear or the makeup we apply. Our failure to capitalise on this opportunity and cauterise visual streams of physical 'perfection' has a high cost for disabled people in terms of how the public perceive disability and beauty.

Excluding disability from fashion catwalks and editorials has implications that stretch beyond our philosophical notions of beauty; its ripples can be felt in the everyday, not just in the media streams we absorb but also in the clothes we buy and the way we dress. Decades of endemic under-representation in visual culture has given rise to marked discrimination – from a lack of accessible clothing options to poor shop access on the high street.

Many retailers have neglected the UK's 13.9 million disabled consumers and, subsequently, fail to accommodate their specific accessibility needs. For me, a typical shopping trip is replete with physical barriers. One particular outing remains etched in my memory. I loitered outside shop windows in the Baltic air, desperately trying to catch a store assistant's gaze through a line-up of towering mannequins so I could ask for a portable access ramp. This basic piece of equipment is a gatekeeper: it's vital for allowing my mobility scooter to zoom over the stepped entrances. But in most cases, I was turned away feeling somewhat degraded. Attitudes of shop workers varied between severe embarrassment – with a perplexed expression that read, 'Why haven't we thought of this before?!' – to defensive and confused about why I'd be interested in browsing their store. I resisted whipping out my best *Pretty Woman* impression – 'Big Mistake! Big! Huge!' – and reluctantly gave up. As I faced the humiliating ride of shame, I was an underage teen being turned away from a club by a bouncer after spotting her fake ID belonged to a 41-year-old with the nominal millstone of Connie Lingus. I now prefer to shop online.

My negative shopping experience is outrageously commonplace, with research revealing how three in four disabled people are encountering problems with accessibility on the high street. This includes everything from inaccessible changing rooms or no step-free access, to a lack of Braille signage or hearing loops. For those with sensory impairments, the toxic combination of poor lighting and loud, thumping music makes the retail experience distressing – in some cases, prohibitive. Although the Equality Act was passed a decade ago to legislate against disability discrimination and ensure public buildings provide reasonable access for disabled people, many shops are still resistant or oblivious of such laws. But retailers who flout these obligations are overlooking the largest untapped consumer group. Colloquially known as the Purple Pound, the UK's disabled population has a collective spending power of £249 billion. Clearly nobody is winning in this scenario.

When it comes to the realm of trend-setting clothing design, I've observed a similar neglect of the needs of disabled consumers. Sinéad Burke, a disability activist with achondroplasia who stands at 3 foot 5 inches, has always desperately wanted to wear the style of shoes sported by her non-disabled friends. But with children's size 12 feet, she has been confined to shopping in the kids' department. 'I've spent my whole life trying to convince the world that I am intelligent, articulate professional and an adult,' explains Burke, 'and yet the fashion industry, unintentionally or not, [suggests] the absolute inverse by what it offers me. I'm not accommodated for.'

The recent rise in 'adaptive fashion', however, does indicate a burgeoning awareness of this need to design more inclusively. Adaptivewear is clothing purposely created for those with disabilities and chronic conditions. Think discreet elasticated waistbands that are pinch-free when seated, adjustable hems and nifty magnetic fastenings for independent dressing. Nike's hands-free footwear technology, for instance, was first inspired by an American student with cerebral palsy who wrote to the brand about his dream of tying shoelaces independently. 'At sixteen years old, I am able to completely dress myself, but my parents still have to tie my shoes,' Matthew Walzer's letter read. 'As a teenager who is striving to become totally self-sufficient, I find this extremely frustrating and, at times, embarrassing.'

We exist in a culture that glorifies self-sufficiency – take for instance, the *veterstrikdiploma*, a diploma that children receive in the Netherlands only after they manage to tie their shoelaces by themselves. While undeniably cute, this form of glorification brings a harmful side-effect: the repulsion and embarrassment that surrounds dependency, the very act of asking for help. Adaptivewear can mitigate some of that shame. Every aspect of the garment is fabricated with the wearer's everyday difficulties in mind, illustrating fashion's potential to empower, not denigrate.

In a feature for *The New Yorker*, 'Adaptive Fashion on the Red Carpet', a disability-focused fashion stylist speaks of the system she developed for designing inclusive clothing. According to Stephanie Thomas, there are three fundamental requirements: a garment must be accessible when dressing, medically safe, and look fashionable. Her trademarked Disability Fashion Styling System has become the definitive guide for adaptive fashion design.

We cannot underestimate the role of accessible fashion for advancing disability equality, as Jillian Mercado, an actress and model with spastic muscular dystrophy, hints to the *New York Times*: 'For the longest time I've had to make time, maybe an hour, to complete an outfit by myself. With accessible clothing it's maybe fifteen minutes.' The so-called 'grooming gap' is already a notorious form of gender discrimination. It refers to the disproportionate amount of time and money women feel compelled to spend on their beautification. But compare this to the additional hour that Mercado must devote to getting dressed when clothes are unsuitably made. Here accessible clothing becomes not just a labour-saving convenience, but a human right. Every day disabled individuals are forcibly stripped of time, money and precious energy without the option of easy-access adaptivewear.

Make-up application may also pose huge challenges for those with limited dexterity and visual impairments. Following her multiple sclerosis diagnosis, the actress Selma Blair posted a mock Instagram tutorial illustrating the near-impossibility of applying make-up without fine motor skills. Bare-faced, she swipes a super-sized kabuki brush over her complexion, and with a mischievous glint in her eyes, announces, 'There! Done.' Due to her difficulties with precision gripping, an indiscriminate dusting of glow-enhancing bronzer must suffice. Right now, there are a growing number of disability-focused beauty brands that embrace make-up's capacity to empower regardless of ability. Innovations include everything from easy-grip make-up brushes and rubberised accessories you can attach onto your mascara wand for better precision, to a stamp-on eyeliner tool that promises symmetrical feline flicks without fail. This breed of stylish yet inclusive design could herald a new era for disability equality where physical limitations are no longer a barrier to one's confidence, agency or self-esteem.

Here fashion and beauty will expand our conception of a 'normal' body and its abilities. Ingenious product design not only offers ergonomic solutions, but it gives social validation, the sense of finally being *seen*. I am certain this can improve disabled people's lives immensely – hell, it could improve everyone's life immensely. But only if we are prepared to go there.

I can hear the small, initial rumblings of a cataclysmic change in how we conceive disability – in fashion, beauty and beyond. Once we finally acknowledge the validity and beauty of all bodies, it will be a moment of true liberation.

I've never forgotten the energy of a school fashion show where for one night, and for one night only, everyone gathered around a makeshift catwalk. Budget lighting, usually reserved for the biannual themed disco, was casting its garish rainbow all over the school hall as I stood agitatedly backstage. Next to me, one 'model' was throwing a diva strop, protesting that her allocated feather boa was bald as a coot after some very emphatic booty shaking from its previous custodian. Our textiles teacher (this might well have been what finished her off) scuttled around with a haberdashery kit in the near-darkness, trying to pre-empt any indecent wardrobe malfunctions. Stage left, another model was hitting the catwalk on her metallic platform heels with all the uncontrollable vigour of a butcher pounding raw meat. The funk rhythm of Chaka Khan's 'I'm Every Woman' was electric, but to our collective horror the girl tripped and cracked her coccyx on the stepped dismount. Fortuitously, her scream was muffled by Chaka's belting top notes of 'whoa, whoa, whoa', and two teachers could haul her off the floor and bundle her out of view from the concerned faces of prospective students and parents in the front row.

Then, it was my turn. As I walked out through the curtained threshold in my mock-denim monstrosity, the spotlight was bright and expectant. Trying to suppress the urge to shield my face, I looked across to my friends who were already executing a choreographed twirl. Intuition took over – I was gliding. The vibrations that ran along the plywood walkway propelling me forwards. As I hovered above the crowd of spectators, it unleashed a new sense of courage. And, in that moment, I saw fashion for what it can be: it brings joy and empowerment beyond the ill-conceived boundaries of our differences.

# A Virtual Reality

It's Saturday night, and we are divining the future amid a constellation of stars in the ink-blue sky – in other words, the glow-in-the-dark stars Blu Tacked across my bedroom ceiling. Five sleepyheads, tucked up under the push and pull of a rumpled, paisley duvet, are waiting to meet the future. It's coming – tomorrow, under a haze of gold confetti, we'll say goodbye to this millennium and enter the open expanse of the twenty-first century. But, for now, we delight in our limbo, reclining back into our pillows and chattering about the mind-blowing gadgets that exist in our futurama.

'Will we be piloting flying cars on the school commute next year?' someone yells out, in between dispensing handfuls of Haribo Starmix. 'Strapping on jet packs, perhaps?' another voice cuts in. 'Or maybe the garden shed will be upcycled into a teleportation device?' Suddenly, there's a noise from the corner of the room, where a friend who, after receiving some morbid news on her palm reading, was cowering on a rolled-out futon (famously, an apparatus that is as conducive to a restful night's sleep as a medieval torture rack). 'Might we get to spend our holidays in resort hotels under the sea?' she entreats, clearly animated by the prospect of a future that did not feature thirteen hairless cats and a hostel in Skegness. 'I'd imagine so,' I say in encouragement. And one thought that inspires all-round exhilaration: would we get to step inside the big white tent, that colossal feat of engineering, our very own Great Pyramid of Giza raised on the Greenwich Peninsula? The future, with all its infinite, cosmic promise, was looking good.

But I was unaware that the revolution, in a 26-inch cardboard box, had already infiltrated my home. Downstairs, in a shadowy corner of the kitchen, sat a Bondi Blue Apple iMac computer – the future inserting itself into our lives. That night, its lights, like all other appliances in the vicinity, were switched off, owing to my mother's psychological manipulation at the hands of conspiracy theorists. (She was unsure what the millennium bug was, or where it was crawling in from, but she did *not* want it in our house.)

I will never forget the moment I first pressed the 'power on' button in early 1999. As the processer booted up, I gazed into the computer's plastic casing, a translucent sea-green shell that denuded some of its nuts and bolts – its secrets. I tried to be patient, rolling the mouse back and forth across its purple foam mat, but it seemed to be taking a while. A spinning pinwheel had stalled proceedings, invading the computer screen with Technicolour pirouettes. 'Was there some sort of commotion going on in there?' I thought to myself, returning to peep into the shell, half-expecting to see tiny magic hands at work. I was now on the verge of hypnosis by the curious pinwheel, while my dad was frantically leafing through a first edition of *Mac for Dummies*, trying to make a diagnosis. Was it just a benign beach ball? A signal of total system malfunction? Hurry!

After ten minutes of inconclusive investigations, I made safe passage to the desktop and opened Internet Explorer. Its screeching dial-up had me in raptures, as I admired each fuzzy pixel with glee. In fact, the entire house was abuzz with anticipation as the wider world greeted us through a small glass screen. What was brought in on the proviso of being a device for playing 'educational' games – a form of digital tutelage by the respected likes of Dorling Kindersley and Mavis Beacon – was soon co-opted as an amusement centre. Raucous nights fighting the apocalypse as fire-breathing dinosaurs, fending off crashing meteors and exploding volcanoes. Hours spent nurturing litters of puppies, seeking out giant omelettes on Neopets and creating psychedelic artworks on Paint. An education, but not as my parents envisaged.

As we embraced this other dimension – another texture of human existence – reality began to change, speeding up and splitting in two. Suddenly, relationships were being redefined by the net's promise of 24/7 interconnectivity. Gone were the days of twiddling your thumbs for the piecemeal dispatches of a Bordelaise pen pal (riveting as it was to decipher scrawl about the latest diplomatic bust-up at l'Hôtel de Ville). Now, in a clickety, clack, clack, you could log in to AOL and seek out friends anywhere – from down the street to across the globe. Households were strung together by phone cables and modems, decoding text into audio signals and back again, like a kind of mystical Morse code.

Let's not rose-tint here. In its embryonic form, the World Wide Web offered neither a sophisticated nor seamless user experience. After the credits had rolled on *Top of the Pops*, it took twenty minutes just to tell your friend, by email, that you were horrified by Fatman Scoop's continued monopoly of the number-one slot. And to express a mixture of disgust and glee that Robbie Williams – pre-watershed – was permitted to romp around on stage naked, but for a pair of tiger-print pants and a lollipop. A cultural reset that was overshadowed by a disappointing supper of burnt fish fingers and microchips. And not forgetting the many chilling experiences that haunted our new digital citizenship. An innocent search for children's winter coats that yielded 10,000 suppliers of crispy coated chicken, courtesy of the now defunct Ask Jeeves.

Inter-generational dynamics were also shifting. While millennials quickly grasped the intricate workings of the online terrain, the boomers – not so much. My friends and I were coding reams of HTML for custom-built Myspace layouts, while our elders were still spending five minutes contemplating a copy and paste. Reader, it was hard to watch – heart-rending in moments. It triggered a devolution of power as, for the first time, parents and guardians saw us as service providers. If you knew where the 'on' button was located, you were suddenly a little genius, with room to renegotiate pocket money rates.

The whip hand was finally ours. How we sniggered at the story of my grandparents frantically shutting down and unplugging their desktop computer at the mains, after they received a spam invite to join a 'lonely hearts club'. 'Cherry-Ann is waiting for you . . .' the 'racy' email read. And how we sniggered harder at my grandma's foray to the cyber café; her vivid tale of venturing down a cobbled back alley, up a rickety fire escape and into a brave new world of email domains, double clicks and jacket potatoes. With her youngest son jetting off to travel the world, she needed a swift, convenient way to contact him in an emergency. 'Get yourself a Yahoo!' her friend Joyce implored at their weekly bridge night, recommending the local 'cyber caff' as the place to go (but not to be seen). She was under explicit instructions to ask at the counter for a hedgehog-haired man who went by the name of 'Dez'. 'Dez will sort you out,' her friend said.

So, the following week, my seventy-something grandmother

dutifully fought her way across a caff floor, littered with torn-up flyers promoting 'Thursty Thursday' club nights and hungover students passing out on neon blow-up chairs. The 'workstation' consisted of a printer and three desktop PCs, screwed together from salvaged parts like Frankenstein's triplets. And, as with any respectable IT set-up of the early noughties, a Xerox fax machine, firing out copier paper like shrapnel, and making enough clangour to prompt groaning from a shirtless man sprawled across an inflatable sofa. Meanwhile, Dez, like a creature prematurely woken from hibernation, emerged from a red-lit backroom, his entrance heralded by the soft clatterings of a bamboo-beaded door curtain. Now Dez was clearly no stranger to the sight of errant pensioners, trembling beside his plastic potted plants and empty fish tank. He rubbed his eyes, readjusted his crumpled T-shirt, and scooped my grandma off to the workstation – only stopping to ask, rather chivalrously, if she would prefer a more comfortable chair to the hard metal bar stools? She took a discreet glance over at the menagerie of blow-up furniture, and said she'd be fine. Once Dez was fully caffeinated, it took five minutes to set up an email account. However, his speed, his swing, his groove were foiled by my grandmother's frequent interjections. Having personally attempted to teach her predictive text on a Nokia 6210, Dez had not only my respect but my full sympathies. She wrote down step-by-step instructions in her lined notebook, returning home long after the six o'clock news with an email address, the smell of burnt toast in her hair and a sense of triumph.

Unlike my grandma, I was coming of age with the internet. And, although I wasn't aware at the time, this nascent technology would one day be my lifeline. From building a career to staying in touch with friends, the digital era has placed the world under my fingertips and given me opportunities that would not have existed over a decade ago. In the immediate face of life-changing illness, a phone and laptop became like my own diorama – the illuminated screen was an aperture through which I could view the outside world, housed inside a square threshold and rendered in miniature scale.

Cyberspace has revolutionised my reality, giving me a 24/7 means to connect and exert my presence in society, without which I would likely be left powerless and cut off. It has become a necessity for times when physical connection isn't possible – especially so during the recent pandemic years. When I finish writing this paragraph, I will tap on that tiny, sunset-coloured Instagram icon and the world will unfold itself before me. I'll watch clips of the aurora borealis dancing over the skies in Reykjavik last night, cast judgement on this season's Miu Miu collection live from Paris Fashion Week, 'like' a new philosophy meme about Dostoevsky's alleged haemorrhoids, and even get a repartee going about a kitten wearing a crochet onesie shaped like a mushroom ('for medical purposes'). It's deliciously unpredictable. Then I can cross over to WhatsApp and see a video of my friend's newborn niece that she has sent from her office in London during her lunchbreak. While it may feel small, and it may not compare to seeing all these things up close (Dostoevsky's haemorrhoids notwithstanding), this instant connection is joyful and restorative, a blast of fresh air.

At a time when millennials and online culture are increasingly vilified, internet technology has given me a route to freedom and made life less insular. For all its imperfections, it's been one reliable, constant, ever-evolving thing in my life. This is a love letter to the World Wide Web.

Humanity radiates an aura of blue light. Along the street, swarms of people gaze into glowing palms, light pressed into their face, as they err into the path of angry traffic, seemingly cut off from the urban bustle. In kerbside cafes, purring laptops cast a luminous halo around bodies at work, hands furiously typing, while lovestruck teenagers, dazzled by the digital dispatches of secret crushes, slurp coffee in darkened corners. Beside the window, the heartbroken are entranced by the bright glare of dating app downloads, heads down, robotically swiping right. Human experience is now increasingly played out in scrolls, clicks and cursors. This climate has transformed our lives and, more importantly, delivered unprecedented access and opportunity.

But society's reliance on technology, in the form of the internet and social media, is widely perceived as unhealthy. An addiction, much like a smoking habit. This very analogy was invoked at the World Economic Forum, where the billionaire net entrepreneur Marc Benioff proposed that companies like Facebook must undergo fierce regulation, 'exactly the same way you regulated the cigarette industry'. We are told time and time again of villainous tech companies who engineer algorithms to encourage such addictive behaviours, to keep us a-scrolling. This human foible has, indeed, been exploited by tech and social media companies, with our addiction opening the door to many of the heinous scandals that the industry has presided over. Most notably, a hijack on our democracy that buttressed populist agendas, Trump and Brexit. And, more recently, the lethal misinformation campaigns that fuelled anti-vaxxers during the pandemic. And yet, we cannot seem to quit.

It was the writer Nicholas Carr who first described how the net 'turns us into lab rats'. How we sit there, as passive subjects undergoing our transmogrification, 'constantly pressing levers to get tiny pellets of social or intellectual nourishment'. In *The Shallows: What the Internet Is Doing to Our Brains,* a modern classic of internet criticism, Carr observes how our capacity for concentration and reflection is being diminished by digital life. We are powerless to its seductions: that promise of instant gratification accessed through our fingertips, the blast of dopamine that never fully satisfies. It seems we are trapped in a state of, what the cultural theorist Mark Fisher calls, 'depressive hedonia'. That is, an infinite loop of joyless stimulation. This is the dominant cultural narrative – one of backlash and betrayal, where the internet has fallen spectacularly short of its early promise.

It's true that the internet has made its claim on our reality. In the space of two decades, it has infiltrated almost every facet of day-to-day life, no longer confined to sluggish PCs in communal corners of kitchens and spare rooms. On an existential level, it has achieved the impossible: simultaneously assuming the dual role of creator and chronicler of our everyday actions. The internet can exert its power by influencing what we do and think, as much as it can offer an archival record of what we've done and thought. It is past, present and future. This inescapable cycle is as looping and unbreakable as the frenetic stream of activity that spews out of our phone screens – breaking news, deaths,

50-per-cent-off sales, thirst traps, engagement announcements and the repeat. It has reached a point where the net has been crowned, as millennial philosopher Jia Tolentino puts it, 'the central organ of contemporary life'. But, in her view, it is not a healthy one. It is metastasising inside us, rewiring our minds and overdosing us with more sensory input than is humanly possible to assimilate in a five-minute scroll. It's making us sick.

In Tolentino's now-seminal essay collection, *Trick Mirror*, she presents a forensic examination of how, in capitalism's greedy mitts, the internet went from whimsical dancing hamsters, geeky movie reviews and dads creating golfing websites (what she lovingly brands the *You've Got Mail* era), to something of a panopticon that is 'so bad, so confining, so inescapably personal'. There is punishing accuracy in Tolentino's description of logging on: 'I have become acutely conscious of the way my brain degrades when I strap it in to receive the full barrage of the internet – these unlimited channels, all constantly reloading . . . blitzing our frayed neurons in huge waves of information that pummel us and then are instantly replaced.' To her mind, without exerting immeasurable self-discipline, the virtual world is dizzying, corruptive, and an impediment to a better, healthier state of being. 'This is an awful way to live,' she decries, 'and it is wearing us down quickly.'

For Nicholas Carr and Jia Tolentino, online life has become dystopic, a source of entrapment and despair. There is part of me that agrees with their arguments. I cannot deny that digital life is, at times, distortive. Or that it has swept us up into a paradoxical state of distraction and hyper-awareness. But I am not entirely on the same bandwidth. Carr and Tolentino's analyses, I fear, are not as readily applied to the disabled experience. Their stance just does not stretch. It is especially interesting that both authors lionise our health and well-being as the prime justification for why we must step away now, why we must 'detox' to protect our 'frayed neurons' from the battering onslaught of the net. The diseased human body – the vocabulary of metastasis and organs – is pulled up as a metaphor to convey the web's poisonous role in our lives. The critics seem to be drawing a causal link between poor health and internet usage, yet their arguments fail to factor in the different life experiences of users. For those with already compromised health, there is a different story to be told.

In 2020, the *British Medical Journal* circulated new research looking at the impact of social media on adolescents with chronic disease. The cross-sectional study took 212 patients, aged thirteen to twenty-four years, with conditions like cystic fibrosis and inflammatory bowel disease, and observed the role of Facebook in their daily lives. Typically, excessive scrolling of social media is shown to incite feelings of anxiety, depression, isolation and low self-esteem in healthy adolescents. But here, the patient group bucked the trend. Time spent on Facebook became a protective factor. It gave the adolescents a way out from thinking about their disease. It made them feel like a 'normal' part of society. And it offered them a portal to reach out, sharing their experiences with others affected by the same conditions. In healthier periods, the patients were spending around five hours a day on the platform. During periods of flare-up or hospital stays, this screen time was hitting an average of eleven hours. The internet was a place to escape *to*, not *from*. Almost unanimously, participants agreed that 'they are never alone thanks to Facebook'. When you are faced with extreme health crises or feel desperately shut out from the world, the internet's promise of instant connection simply outweighs its perils. The corruptive actions of data-harvesting tech firms, who surveil our thoughts and position us as docile consumers, become easier to ignore. To many, this may appear short-sighted. But there are times when the internet, and its bustling social networks, have been proven to be fundamentally good.

Where Tolentino is critical of how the internet minimises the need for physical action, how it deceives us by feeling 'like an astonishingly direct line to reality', for many people with disabilities, who refuse to live like an Austen heroine, these factors are game-changing. The virtual world is not flattening experience, it's finally offering it – bringing with it a sense of involvement and belonging. When choice is removed and there is no viable alternative, the internet cannot be branded, like Tolentino says, 'a cheap substitute' for real-life interaction with our communities. Nor can the social internet's 'distortion of scale' be seen as 'psychologically destructive'. This ability to know about everything, to feel omniscient, to hyper-engage, is the very thing that makes the everyday world feel more accessible, lassoing me – and others with disabilities – ever closer to its real possibilities.

The virtual world is not just a flimsy illusion of life sustained by pixels, plugs and electricity. I believe it can be every bit as meaningful as the physical world. But will it ever be treated with the same reverence as reality? An interesting test case is the curious phenomenon of Second Life – a virtual world that allows users to live as an avatar, stepping into a dream body and an aspirational existence from a computer screen. Launched by the San Francisco-based firm

Linden Lab in 2003, the platform was once hyped as 'the future of the internet' with 36 million accounts created at its peak. It sounds to me like a blueprint for Mark Zuckerberg's controversial Metaverse – although Second Life is categorically *not* a game, according to its inventor, Philip Rosedale. His ambition, inspired by a trip to Burning Man festival at the turn of the millennium, was to build a digital wonderland that could facilitate intense connection. A space where anyone could engineer the world into whatever they wished, or needed, it to be. But, for many of the denizens of Second Life, it wasn't simply about strutting around with DD tits, partaking in sordid affairs or gaining supernatural powers. It was the basic things that many people take for granted – walking, running, meeting people, travelling, absolute command over the body – that held so much appeal. Disabled people embraced this new technology, forming around half of the virtual population on Second Life. Most were seduced by the prospect of corporeal abandonment, the ability to shake off the constraints of gravity.

But Second Life has been largely mocked. It was dismissed as 'a consolation prize for people for whom "first life" hasn't quite delivered', according to the writer Leslie Jamison, who interrogates virtual realities in her essay 'Sim Life'. After delving deeper into the demographic of Second Life, Jamison realised that her initial aversion towards the platform testified to her 'own good fortune', her able-bodied privilege and independence. 'When I moved through the real world, I was buffered by my (relative) youth, my (relative) health, and my (relative) freedom,' reflects Jamison. 'Who was I to begrudge those who had found in the reaches of Second Life what they couldn't find offline?' As she met with members and saw the opportunities that Second Life gave to people with disabilities – all the active experiences and multiplicities of being that were blossoming inside their computers – Jamison's respect deepened by the day.

One of the first users Jamison met was Alice, a 57-year-old woman with multiple sclerosis living in Colorado. When her neighbourhood association prohibited her from building a ramp at the front of her house, it became more challenging for Alice to get out and see the world. That's when she created a waterslide-loving avatar on Second Life, spurred on by the chance to do all the things her body could not. Eventually, Alice cultivated a buzzing community on Second Life, bringing together people with different disabilities – from Down's syndrome to PTSD – who trotted around together on an archipelago of virtual islands. Next, Jamison encountered a visually impaired woman while trekking around inside the digital world. Her avatar had a rooftop balcony with a vista overlooking the crashing waves of Cape Serenity which, courtesy of screen magnification, she could see more clearly than any of the real world beyond her computer. Both users told Jamison that they came to Second Life to seek out what their physical lives lacked, 'the sense of things *happening* all around them, and the possibility of being part of that happening'.

Jamison found that these freedoms also extended to caregivers. There was Bridgette, an Atlanta mother working eight-hour days at a call centre in between looking after her severely autistic twins. In her 'second' life, she escaped to a curated paradise, lounging beside the pool in spearmint-green bikinis with glazed doughnuts and stacks of books. 'When I step into that space, I'm afforded the luxury of being selfish . . . It's like a room of my own,' she said, referencing Virginia Woolf. Soon Bridgette's husband got in on the act: he created an avatar so the two of them could finally go on virtual dates together, as their children's special needs made finding babysitters difficult. It was a twenty-first-century romance, a glamorous blonde bombshell and a squat silver robot galloping through cyberspace, while the couple sat together at their laptops in the home study.

To me, Alice and Bridgette encapsulate all the ways in which the internet is not the reductive, corrosive, vampiric force that Tolentino and Carr believe it to be. For the disabled and their caregivers, the internet can be life-giving, a matter of survival. Jamison concluded the metaverse was not all fakery: it was delivering real, tangible improvements to people's lives. And that, as she writes, is 'hardly worth vilifying'. Many cannot resist questioning if digital living is a dangerous act of avoidance, an attempt to lose oneself in a frivolous fantasy by chasing a kind of pseudo-pleasure. But, in the words of Donna J. Haraway, the American philosopher and scholar in technology studies, absolutely not: 'The virtual isn't immaterial. Anyone who thinks it is, is nuts . . . I don't know what planet you are living on.' Virtual realms are not illusions. They are real virtual places, where real virtual events unfold. A virtual football match, for instance, still has a real winner. Just as virtual lives are no less valid or genuine simply because they are produced through technology.

So, if reality can be found in these virtual worlds, can we also form authentic versions of ourselves online? And more importantly, can people transcend their medical conditions by making a home in a virtual body? Behind every avatar a physical person exists. Individuals, like Alice for instance, are achieving real goals, forming real friendships and experiencing real emotional connection. In 2018, a documentary called *Our Digital Selves: My Avatar Is Me!* followed another thirteen disabled people who live as avatars on Second Life. One participant, a former fashion designer who was forced to retire when she was diagnosed with early onset Parkinson's, shuts down her critics: 'People sometimes think it's like, "Oh, you're trying to escape your physical body, you're trying to deny who you are" . . . But this is another part of who I am.' She is right – that's just it.

Technology and the internet have given us permission to express ourselves with an unprecedented degree of freedom, fluidity and experimentation. To access the pluralities of who we are, and showcase them, in ways that were never possible in the offline world. Why should disabled people not capitalise on that? At its core, Second Life is not dissimilar to the many social media sites that exploded in its wake – Instagram, Twitter, Facebook, TikTok and the like. Each platform has commodified our desire to inhabit a selective self. They allow us to construct narratives of our existence. To edit, engineer and define our selfhood. To self-select what to discard, what to keep and what to stitch into our mythos. This is the universal appeal, the very thing that keeps us logging back in.

My friends and I have now been plugged into the net for nearly two decades, steadily evolving and unpacking our personhood inside this ever-changing digital landscape. Among my generation of millennials, it is only natural to project our personality, beliefs and desires through the prisms of the internet. Growing up, many of our earliest explorations of the self were piloted in AOL chatrooms, Hotmail threads, 'about me' sections of Myspace and rambling dispatches on Blogger.com. Where the real world compels us not to stray outside our designated lanes, to live according to the social rules prescribed to our category of body, online spaces can give us all opportunities to explore and reshape our identity without the same boundaries.

For people with disabilities, the chance to cultivate a digital persona that is distanced from stigma and the physical manifestations of sickness may be particularly enticing. However, social commentators often possess a pessimistic outlook, remaining fearful that the virtual world is gradually eroding our sense of self through its charade-like tactics, its deceptive ability to slap a filter over the truth of who we are. It has created what the psychologist Jean Twenge calls a 'narcissism epidemic', where we have positioned ourselves as actors starring in the biopic of our own lives. This pursuit of digital validation is destroying our moral psychology – HTML, they fear, is infiltrating and corrupting our DNA. But, in my view, giving life to parts of your identity that cannot be expressed in the physical world is overwhelmingly positive and liberating. Unless you are intentionally deceiving your networks to scam, exploit or catfish, any expectation that we must not deviate from the person we present to the world is absurd. Full transparency is a myth. We are self-made and filtered entities offline, just like online.

I will admit that social media platforms harbour a dark side. Disabled people can fall prey to body image anxieties in a culture where Facetuning is so rife that it goes undetected; and, on occasion, disabled users have become targets of virulent trolling. There are also instances of censorship by discriminatory algorithms that hide disabled individuals' content but fail to protect them from abuse – a practice known as 'shadow banning'. In 2019, for example, whistleblower reports revealed that TikTok's algorithm had hidden videos featuring disabled people or disability-related hashtags. When the algorithm red-flagged these posts for violating TikTok's 'ugly content policy', it rendered the accounts of disabled users virtually invisible.

But, beyond these injustices, there are new freedoms to be claimed. Social media has been an overwhelmingly productive, empowering outlet for me. I can communicate to a large number of people in huge paragraphs of text, in a way that I would not be able to do speaking offline. It's like having your own slot at the podium in a virtual town square. I can voice myself, my ideas, more fluently and at length, without the physical need to exert muscle power. This doesn't mean I am inauthentic or conducting a performance, simply because the real world doesn't always allow me such expression. I believe, to some extent, I can be even more true to myself when I'm online, without the frustrating physical constraints of my disability. My presence in the virtual world opens up not only who I am, but the potential to be everything that I can imagine myself to be. It does not erode my identity; it fortifies and consolidates it.

This engagement with the digital realm is not about hiding or deluding myself, nor is it about swapping meaningful experiences for cheap, addictive thrills – it's about regaining control and agency. It is an entry into the world, not a 'confining' prison dragging me away from it. Calls for digital detoxes (that decision to disengage from our online spheres, to brb and gtg) and bullish anti-internet discourse are luxuries that fail to reflect the realities of people with disabilities who often rely on these technologies to live, thrive and participate. The shift to virtual living has been transformative. It's more than an addiction, it represents inclusion and prized freedom.

The World Wide Web has opened up life, bringing access to employment, dating, entertainment and services, like online shopping, direct to the individual. Meanwhile, knowledge is no longer sealed inside libraries and educational institutions under the administration of anointed experts, it's a click away. Radical advances in technology may further improve the quality of life for people with disabilities, with developments in virtual reality promising to create fully immersive experiences, such as live concerts. So many aspects of life that were once only accessible to the physically able are now dispersed digitally, beamed to us via Wi-Fi in the air – anyone can reach out and catch them.

'Virtual reality is coming', the *Sunday Times* newspaper boldly proclaimed in early 2022. 'Fully immersive, interactive, computer-generated realities, alternative worlds in which people can touch, taste and smell, are hurtling towards us.' The notion that we could soon be spending eighteen hours living our life in a simulation has gained traction among academics and philosophers too. David Chalmers, co-director of New York University's Center for Mind, Brain and Consciousness, believes that in thirty years' time ordinary people will choose to live the entirety of their lives in virtual environments. In his book, *Reality+*, he explains that the pursuit of physical reality will likely become 'a novelty or a fetish'. Second Life's creator Philip Rosedale agrees, predicting that the real world and all its material trappings will become something of a fusty museum, secondary to these virtual dimensions where our true lives are played out.

If you find this vision daunting, you're not alone. Many think that being severed from the natural world sounds unsatisfactory, dizzying and, frankly, hellish. It is eerily close to E. M. Forster's 1909 dystopian short story 'The Machine Stops', where humanity lives in isolated cells underground, with all bodily and communication needs met by an omnipotent 'machine' that resembles the internet. This prospect of abandoning the physical world seems at once fanciful and futuristic – more like a lab experiment plucked from the Wachowski dosette box. But perhaps Rosedale and Chalmers are onto something – perhaps their theory was more prophetic that we first imagined.

More than ever, we are teetering on the cusp of a collapse between the virtual and real worlds, with Bitcoin bros, Crypto and NFTs now mainstream; derisibly basic. Not to mention we can even purchase 'downloadable' digital wardrobes to parade exclusively online. But this techno-revolution will have more profound implications than how we invest money or flaunt the latest trends. Ultimately, I wonder, could it reframe our perception of disability, by making the limitations of our bodies almost . . . irrelevant?

When we remove the need for muscle strength to move through the world and carry out day-to-day tasks, the human body is made obsolete. The restrictions of being physically disabled dissolve a little. Consider the inaccessibility of old buildings, stairs and clunky public transport. They no longer pose a threat when you are physically situated in a mostly stationary position at home, mentally immersed and darting around inside a computer-generated environment. In studies, individuals with cognitive disabilities, such as autism, have already found that virtual realms offer a safe space and non-threatening surroundings. There is also potential for people with visual impairments to see images more clearly through virtual reality goggles, with the power to magnify and alter the lighting contrast to improve their sight. You are left free to enjoy a greater breadth of experience, to join in, be self-reliant and not face judgement or segregation from the rest of society.

Naturally, we cannot afford to be complacent or lull ourselves into accepting the virtual world as a utopian space, beyond need of introspection or improvement. In fact, I fear that virtual reality could inadvertently increase inequality among disabled people. There is not only a financial cost to accessing virtual realms, but there is no guarantee the tech will be compatible for a full spectrum of medical conditions, resulting in some people's exclusion from life. It could reinforce discriminatory ideas about the comparative worth of different impairments.

I also cannot help but think that, by focusing on these futuristic realms, we risk distracting from advances that could make a difference to disabled people right now, in the physical world. Already, society is failing to face up to current societal problems and tackle pre-existing stigmas. By pinning our hopes on cutting-edge tech or egalitarian virtual worlds as a panacea, are we just designing an elaborate avoidance strategy? Through redirecting the finances and talent back into the world around us, we could revolutionise disabled people's lives in the everyday. When it comes to Second Life inhabitants Alice and Bridgette, for instance, the provision of a ramp and improved access to childcare support for children with special needs may drastically improve their circumstances – allowing them the means to live and enjoy the physical world as much as the virtual.

But it's not that simple. While these problems must be addressed and taken seriously, they risk overlooking the wider philosophical value of technology and what it represents for people with disabilities. There is huge revolutionary potential in technological systems – from virtual reality to innovative materials and machinery. They all possess the power to change how we live our lives and transform our idea of a 'normal' body.

For centuries, disabled people have been viewed as naturally passive and weak individuals. Society believed that it was in their nature to be segregated from society. And when we declare that something is natural, this is equivalent to saying that it's innate and expected. That it is just how things are. It cannot be changed. But what if humans are no longer seen as natural beings, but as constructed entities? As Donna J. Haraway proselytised in her 1985 essay 'A Cyborg Manifesto', modern life has transformed us into hybrids of machine and organism. In short, we are what Haraway calls 'cyborgs' because our relationship to technology has become so inextricable and intimate. Mobile phones are almost appendages, laptops more like phantom limbs. They are part of our anatomy. And, while Haraway's theory rarely engages with disability, cochlear implants, titanium prosthetic legs, and pacemakers synthetically generating heartbeats, are fine illustrations of humanity's fusion with machines.

Now here's where things get interesting. When humans are no longer regarded as natural entities, this changes everything. We may find ourselves in a world where long-held assumptions about what is 'natural' can be disputed and thrown into doubt. A world that could open up new possibilities for marginalised groups, as we move away from the idea that identities and power dynamics are preordained or dictated by nature. Haraway's framework should make us optimistic about the emancipatory possibilities of the technological era. Perhaps everything from smart clothing to VR headsets could eradicate inequality offline and deliver fresh opportunities for disabled people?

Recently, I read about a group of schoolgirls in London who designed a real-time sign-language translator, inspired by their friend Amy who is deaf. The eleven to sixteen-year-olds successfully coded an app, powered by artificial intelligence, that can interpret British Sign Language (BSL) and translate it into spoken English as well as the reverse, translating spoken English into BSL videos. In essence, a technological device (a phone held in your palm) takes on the anatomical function of a human ear and voice. They hoped that, firstly, it would prove invaluable in daily tasks such as ordering food at a restaurant. But, beyond that, their tool aims to level up society, securing success for people with hearing loss in life-changing scenarios like job interviews. It instantly reminded me of another app: Be My Eyes. Here real-life volunteers are paired up with visually impaired people who need immediate assistance with an everyday task – whether that's reading aloud cooking instructions on a food packet, describing the specific colour of a dress or even completing lateral flow tests. It's all delivered via mobile phones and tablets. Created by Hans Jorgen Wiberg in 2015, Be My Eyes was hit with an influx of over 5.7 million volunteers, far outnumbering the 395,000 visually impaired people using it. Both apps show the empowerment, allyship and radical possibilities that open up when the impaired body becomes enmeshed with technology.

And it doesn't stop there. Bionic innovations like powered exoskeletons reveal what the future might look like when we physically attach digital devices onto the human body. FuseProject's Seismic Powered Suit, for instance, is a wearable technology which augments the body with cyborg-like abilities – amplifying the strength and endurance of the user with electric impulses that replicate muscle power. This could enable individuals who cannot walk or are paralysed to navigate their homes and cities with greater ease. When it comes to therapeutics, Dutch designer Pauline Van Dongen has prototyped 'smart' knitwear that can be worn next to the skin. Her 'Vigour Cardigan' monitors the wearer's biometrics through sensors in the yarn that aid physiotherapy treatment, whereas her 'Mysa' sweater guides breathing exercises through a vibration pattern along the wearer's spinal cord. In a similar vein, a biotech company, Algalife, has pioneered a new fabric that releases antioxidants and vitamins directly into the skin. This technology could disrupt rigid classifications and push us beyond hierarchal divisions. If everyone's life is supported or optimised by technology, there will be less basis to segregate those with disabilities. This is cyborgisation in action.

While these attention-grabbing innovations belong to a new age of assistive technology, it is an unsung fact that some of the greatest technological inventions of our time were originally aimed at enhancing the lives of disabled people. These assistive technologies went on to be embraced and co-opted by the mainstream. Touchscreens on iPhones and closed-caption subtitles on videos, for instance, were first invented to address the physical needs of disabled communities but have since been universally welcomed. This phenomenon is referred to as the 'curb-cut effect', whereby disability-friendly design features are ultimately appreciated and adopted by the majority. Perhaps physical impairments are the rocket fuel of innovation? Disability certainly forces you to become a lifehacker, to think creatively and find ways to make your surroundings more accessible.

Game-changing technological advances have often arisen out of constraint. It is inscribed in our mythology with the Greek figure of Hephaestus, the God of invention, who was born with curved feet, a congenital impairment. In Homer's *Iliad*, Hephaestus is depicted as a gifted artisan revered for his creativity, 'limping' around his workshop on 'shrunken legs'. Often, he is surrounded by an assembly of disabled figures who aid him in his work – crafting everything from automatic gates for Heaven, to driverless carts and a voice-activated bellow. Think of these as ancient Greek prototypes for the Tesla and Amazon Alexa, Alexandria being the Silicon Valley of its time. Hephaestus set up his workshop to accommodate disability, with assistive technology and mechanical automatons or robots, to help move heavy objects. These myths represent some of the earliest writings relating to disability, instituting an ancient correlation between impairment and innovation.

But despite this tradition of disabled individuals pioneering innovative solutions for themselves, their contributions are often eclipsed, with society failing to see physical limitations as synonymous with acts of self-sufficiency or creative genius. It is not widely known, for example, that the crucial design function of the iPhone – what is arguably the most influential product of the twenty-first century so far – was not conceived by Steve Jobs and Apple, but by a small independent company called FingerWorks in Delaware. In 1998, FingerWorks was established by a man with multiple sclerosis called Wayne Westerman, who needed another means to input text into his computer that was not a keyboard. The touch interface he created was quick, precise and responsive to multiple fingers. It dissolved the clunky barriers of human-computer interaction in a way that hadn't been seen before. The FingerWorks touchpad instantly attracted the attention of Apple technicians in the user testing room, who quickly integrated the same technology into a mobile-phone prototype. The first time Steve Jobs saw the demo in action, he was speechless, blown away by it. Apple went on to purchase FingerWorks, employing the whole team to develop their new top-secret project – what was unveiled as the original iPhone in 2007. Today touchscreens are seamlessly integrated into our everyday lives. They are ubiquitous; everyone uses them. When we extend our lens of inclusion in design processes, we often end up creating better technologies for all.

However, a failure to do this means that we risk designing technology that is inaccessible to some disabled people. In 1981 – a world untouched by the tentacles of the internet – Steve Jobs claimed that computers would become like a 'bicycle for the mind'. Although humans lacked the natural speed, power and mobility of other species, 'we're tool builders,' Jobs said, 'and that's what a computer is to me . . . it's the most remarkable tool that we've ever come up with, and it's the equivalent of a bicycle for our minds'. It is a salient metaphor, reflecting how human innovation can allow us to transcend some of our mortal limits: to ride further, faster and more efficiently by creating ingenious solutions that will overcome any physical shortcomings. But, put simply, not everyone can ride a bike. When a diversity of abilities is not considered in creating new technologies, then you have a problem. What is designed to improve people's lives, to make so many parts of life more efficient, can end up doing the opposite: proliferating exclusion.

Most technology alone cannot yet predict if the person interacting with it has a disability, which carries dangerous implications. Take driverless cars. They rely on intricate algorithms and data to learn what pedestrians look like – but if the training data doesn't have an expansive sense of the human body, including people who use wheelchairs, the vehicles risk bumping into them or running them down. Human variation must be accommodated at every stage of the product design and software programming. Numbers and equations are not sentient beings. We are drawn to their precision and neutrality, but they fail to understand the unruliness of the real world. Unless we tell them. Digital inclusion is fast becoming a rising concern in a society where almost every facet of life is moving online. When new gadgets and software are built without a deep, intuitive understanding of how they will be experienced by people who do not possess 'normal' abilities, we preside over a digital landscape that risks disenfranchising or endangering scores of people.

A simple example here is a CAPTCHA test – those online challenges used to determine whether you, the computer user, are man or machine. Perhaps you are asked to transcribe a visually distorted code, listen to a garbled recording or pick out all the fire hydrants in a blurry grid of images. Suddenly you are Turing cracking the Enigma, with a nerve-wracking pause to find out whether you can pass go. Now, consider the experience of a visually impaired person. Screen readers (software that converts text and image content into speech or Braille output) and other assistive technology tools cannot interpret a CAPTCHA – which is, by design, meant to be unreadable by machines. Since websites use CAPTCHAs as virtual gatekeepers at every login or registration process, a failed test will completely block access to vital online services. This is clear discrimination. In a study of homepages for the top million websites, over 50 million separate accessibility errors were detected – an average of 50.8 errors per homepage. The most common issues were low colour contrast between text and backgrounds, navigation links that are poorly coded and therefore undetectable to screen readers, and imagery with missing 'alt text', a short textual description of what an image conveys. These are the basic tenets of accessible web design, and yet they are continually bypassed.

While virtual worlds offer enormous benefits for disabled people, they throw up all manner of ethical considerations. In the wild west of cyberspace, whose duty is it to uphold equal rights? How can we ensure that technology is safe and effective for all? Do we still have moral obligations to virtual humans? When tech companies and stakeholders lose sight of these responsibilities, failing to eliminate access barriers, it can magnify inequalities among disabled people. Technology has given us a power that was once unimaginable – but it does not dictate how to use that power in a way that is just and fair. With a great deal to gain in the digital age, people with disabilities must be represented at the cutting edge of new developments, or there is a risk that they will be left behind and marginalised further.

So how will technology reshape the future of humanity? That is perhaps the most tantalising question of the day – and one that might soon hold the key to boosting disability equality. But we are posing it all wrong. Technology is too often seen as an autonomous, deterministic force that controls the direction of our society. Whether that's world domination, the end of civilisation, or the birth of an evil robotic dictatorship, we are powerless to resist its path. There is no going back. This is especially evident in how, over the past decade, the internet has gained the reputation of quicksand. The way it changes its stickiness in response to stress or vibration, swallowing you up and making it impossible to escape. Despite our alarmist cultural awareness of the dangers, no one really knows how to release themselves from its pull, to put the advice into action, to evade the trap. Right now, we are presented as hostages, surrendering ourselves to a fate increasingly submerged by screens, a life mediated by the cold hands of tech.

But technology is not the captor, nor the active agent in our story. It is a human construct, moulded by society's interests, values and choices. Theoretically, this gives us infinite opportunities to decide our future, to exploit human ingenuity and self-select where we want to go. New technologies create new realities. When we harness scientific breakthroughs to find the most promising, life-changing applications for disabled people, that's when the digital world becomes a crucible of positive change.

From the dawn of the millennium, that night spent prophesying the future, I have wanted to be swept away by the electrifying advances in technology. The twenty-first century has so far fallen short of those lofty, nocturnal visions of flying cars and teleporters – but it has given me more than I ever could have predicted. Every day my life is enriched by the innovations of humanity. Connection, self-expression, laughter and learning, all propped up by a click and a scroll. Technology is our route to progress, the ability to reprogram the conditions of our reality, blasting what was seemingly impossible into new avenues of possibility. And so, we must ask ourselves, what reality do we want to see? What will it take for technology to be an equaliser? What changes do we want to cultivate? Imagine the future that awaits us, imagine what will be achieved.

# The Other Glass Ceiling

My formative ideas of ambition and success were imparted by a steady roster of babysitters – Friday nights spent cradling goblets of hot chocolate, awestruck by their impassioned chronicles of the working world. Firstly, it was our aspiring costume designer. She had spent a long summer working on film sets, traversing the sandy humps of the Sahara Desert, chasing actors with tape measures and lint rollers. I was wide-eyed at her talents, the cut and thrust of it all. Her hands gesticulating wildly as she described the residual pangs of repetitive strain injury from cataloguing 20,000 antique buttons. Next, it was the first-year junior doctor. She beamed over her copy of Guyton's textbook of medical physiology, graffitied with an industrious rainbow of Stabilo Boss, its spine buckling under the weight of Post-its. Her glasses were resting on the bridge of her nose as she cradled a calculator tapping out all kinds of mind-bending scientific equations. Surely she was decoding the origins of human life? I had no doubt with this girl. In exchange for intel about a teacher who allegedly kept a secret stash of gin in the school supply cupboard, she regaled us with gory tales about roadside resuscitations, botched appendix removals and a C-section delivery of a baby with hair resembling Cher's eighties rocker mullet. Lastly, it was our glamorous half-Peruvian babysitter. She gossiped about her time spent trotting along the Avenue des Champs-Élysées for an internship at L'Oréal, as we tussled with the crimping irons, revved up the BaByliss Crazy Braid, and wrestled our feet into foam toe separators, buffed and primed for their glitter pedicure. Every tale was as intoxicating and heady as the formaldehyde in a single slick of that cobalt nail varnish. I wanted in.

But, unsurprisingly, my first sniff of the labour market was far from the plummy visions I had let run wild in my head since those nights drunk on hot chocolate and the fumes of Claire's Accessories' finest bottled lacquer. With an entire week set aside for a work experience placement of our choosing, I thought to myself, let's give doctoring a go. Walking through a warren of aseptic-smelling hospital corridors, it felt disconcerting to be back several months after an initial discharge from intensive care. Could I make it on the other side?

The night before I had been issued a grave warning from my older sister – something about an impromptu interview or workplace competency test? As ever, the sisterhood extended to stoking rabid fear, but fell short of delivering any solid, practical advice. From what I could tell, there were unforeseen hoops to jump through when my sister started hospital-based work experience two years earlier. I gawped in horror at her account of being whisked off by a short pigtailed man for an informal tête-à-tête. She found herself being asked to critique a series of patient artworks and conjure up credible narratives about the painter's underlying mental state. These were not the legible ink blots typically associated with a Rorschach test, but rather incoherent, crusty blotches of poster paint. The man – a healthcare assistant who moonlighted as an amateur art therapist – was in raptures, pigtail whipping in the air as he gestured back and forth to aggressive patches of red and eccentric painterly flourishes. Did it bespeak a repressed history of something, brewing deep in the subconscious? Or was it indicative of a deep-rooted narcissism? Christ, it sounded horrific.

I had seemingly passed my competency test – well, I'd heard nothing to the contrary – and by lunchtime, I was firmly ensconced at the coalface, ferreting around the staff changing rooms for a pair of surgical clogs and scrubs that weren't cut to bariatric proportions. The patient, meanwhile, was pumped with anaesthetic in the adjacent operating theatre ready for a minor procedure. As I crossed into that bleached room, the laminar air-flow system was dialled up to a terrifying rate, ripping like a tornado through the ceiling vents and dragging on the swing doors. All the focus in the theatre bounced between a flayed-out knee that was peepholing through a blue paper drape on the operating table, a retractable video monitor, and unconfirmed sightings of a box of Milk Tray back in the staff coffee room. It was a fascinating insight into the fragility of human life, in all its forms. However, before the patient could be roused from his arthroscopy, I was summonsed back onto the ward to chaperone an elderly woman during her occupational therapy appointment.

The lady, with hips like Hobnob biscuits, had just begun describing her day-to-day care needs, when she was shepherded towards a wet room for a showering assessment. Not yet able to excuse myself under the pretence of grabbing a fresh supply of towels, three of us became wedged in the bathroom, a 2-metre-squared slip 'n' slide. The humidity was rising, fast. The herbal aromas exuding from a bar of Pears soap were making the eyes water, the throat scratchy.

It was a scene that had all the Hitchcockian trappings – horror, suspense, nudity and the distant shrieks from a neighbouring hospital bay.

Amid these eye-opening exploits, I saw what it meant to be part of a collective force for good, and that bodies working together were how you healed the world. But my life's work was not located in that muggy wet room. The following year, my search for a vocation led me to a volunteering job at a hospice charity. The instant I entered the inconspicuous office block – mission control for the retail and marketing department – a curly haired receptionist pounced on me, scurrying me over to an empty desk. She set down a pile of fifty rumpled envelopes and delivered my first assignment: to peel off the used stamps for 'repurposing'. I tried to hide my shock at what I was being asked to do, rationalising that the illicit deed was for a charitable cause – for the greater good? During my hour spent tearing around raggedy stamps, the painstaking process of pulling the remnants of fuzzy white envelope from its scalloped edges, I was like a philatelic Robin Hood.

Once I had proven my worth (and my discretion), I was called over into a small conference room by a whippet-like man. His every inch was telling me 'head honcho' – from his crochet tie down to his box-fresh Reeboks and Garmin pedometer. In one brisk move, he magicked a pen out of his breast pocket and began laying out some ambitious plans for an inaugural staff newsletter. A place where, say, a notice of the WI county bake sale could find harmony with a full uncensored account of when Brian, an unsuspecting 78-year-old volunteer, had to process an eighteenth-century 'thong', a threadbare bustier and a bedraggled garter found in a forgotten donation sack (a thing no man on beta blockers

should be asked to do). I was sold. In those weeks of bringing together the editorial vision – the thrill of designing layouts, selecting imagery, writing and editing short articles – I
had found it. This was it.

In the intervening years, I honed and refined my
career ambitions. As an aspiring fashion journalist, I
wanted to work in magazines – capturing the zeitgeist
across style, culture, film, photography and incisive writing. It is everything I love. But, as my time to enter the
job market drew closer, I grew apprehensive, disillusioned
even, about the unnavigable reality that awaited me in the
working world. The likelihood of a role in the fashion
industry – where disability was expunged from editorial
images and, as far as I could tell, still invisible behind the
scenes – felt like it was slipping away from me. I was also
becoming increasingly despondent about the wider picture
for people with disabilities on the quest for employment
and purpose.

'Everyone has the right to work, to free choice of employment, to just and favourable conditions of work and to
protection against unemployment,' according to the United
Nations Universal Declaration of Human Rights, 1948. The
Right to Work forms one of the thirty protected freedoms
set out in this seminal text in the history of civil rights. But,
as it stands, the competitive, productivity-fuelled nature of
the workplace has created a climate of discrimination for
people with disabilities.

While there are currently around 8.3 million disabled
people of working age in the UK, only 4.4 million are in
work. This gross discrepancy comes at a time when diversity
is a concept that, quite rightly, holds enormous clout in the
workplace. It has become not only a corporate buzzword

and the basis of ethical practice, but a proven strategy to enhance the productivity of a workforce; inclusive teams are more effective and outperform their peers by 80 per cent, according to research by Deloitte. And yet disabled people are demonstrably excluded from the diversity drive, frozen out of the world of work.

The labour market remains a cold, perfunctory domain where the dark myths surrounding disability are felt most severely. Negative social biases are denying people jobs, limiting the trajectory of lives and opportunities. Financial well-being, the vital protections that come with securing a payslip, cannot be expected; just as the promise of self-fulfillment that is typically acquired through one's professional persona, can feel excruciatingly out of reach.

The prospect of not having a steady stream of income is ruinous, as life costs more if you're disabled. On average, people with disabilities face extra costs of £583 a month due to add-on bills like regular taxis, heating or medical supplies that are necessitated by certain health conditions. This means that a stable job, in addition to state benefits, is the only protective measure against an increased threat of poverty. In other countries where the safety net of free, publicly funded healthcare is removed, a paid job becomes ever more a matter of survival – it is life support in the form of employer-sponsored medical insurance.

This financial instability is currently having a disproportionate effect on the welfare and security of people with disabilities. Seven million people in poverty are either disabled or live with a disabled person – that represents nearly half of everyone in poverty, according to a Joseph Rowntree research report. This comes at a time when the disability pay gap is not improving. Disabled workers consistently earn an average of £2.10 less an hour, or 20 per cent, compared to non-disabled staff in the UK. They are also over-represented in less skilled, part-time work with fewer opportunities for promotion – evidenced by the fact that no executives or senior managers have a disclosed disability at any of the FTSE 100 companies, according to a 2021 report.

While limited income and professional prospects are leaving disabled people exceptionally vulnerable and inhibiting quality of life, it is a moral imperative to ensure everyone has access to work. This social and economic exclusion is not just harmful to individuals on a domestic level. It also restricts wider economies with wasted human capital, reduced numbers of taxpayers and an increase in benefit claimants. With two in five people of working age predicted to have a chronic or fluctuating condition by 2030, it can no longer be dismissed as a peripheral issue.

As I began to contemplate the launch of my own career, I was tiptoeing the scope and scale of disability inequality for the first time. In the exhilarating leap from an education system, where people are invested in you, to the daunting, competitive world of employment, I saw injustice slithering across society like a viper. How come, after decades of a consistent disability employment gap, were so few people challenging it, not least acknowledging the desperate need for change? I ruminated these ideas as if they were chewing gum – that constant internal tussle, the round and sticky dimensions of futility, the fade to blandness as the freshness of hope withers away. My chance of succeeding, of building a fulfilling career, felt ever more distant in an environment that irrationally casts disabled bodies as unproductive, burdensome even.

More than anything, I wanted to know what it would be like to feel free and unimpeded. To effortlessly determine my own direction, success, failures, triumphs. I hated the fact that my physical health was going to impact, and likely limit, my ambitions. For years, I'd fought hard for that not to be the case. I suppose the symbolic image of scaling a career ladder isn't exactly disability-friendly, is it? Success would be an act of defiance – confronting the capitalist paradigm which favours employees who are built quick, mobile and robotically efficient. It was my job to create new ways of working and forge a place inside an industry that wasn't expecting me. I had faith I'd get there, but no idea how or how long it would take.

It was time up, pens down on my final exam in Oxford. The wimpish antics of Troilus, his capricious Criseyde and the like, were shuttered away into a cerebral self-storage unit. Fear dissolved like the ink on my stained fingers. Everything felt lighter as I could see for the first time the entire anatomy of summer – of sunbaskers and confettied magnolia – that had been quietly choreographed and laid out around me.

As the days raced on, however, the spell was wearing off. As bumbagged tourists infiltrated the cobbled streets, I was growing conscious that my student existence had reached its expiration date, wilting like the corner-shop carnations that once adorned lapels of black academic robes. It seemed I was inhabiting an in-between space, hovering over the starting blocks from where the rest of my life was stretched out. But instead of being a bright, knowable horizon, like the news of job offers and postgrad courses that rung around the quads, it was a haze. The rumbling question of 'What next?' became ear-piercing. I knew I had to pack up my life here and design another identity. Something, anything, to slip into.

In reality, I was far from alone in my occupational angst. This prompted me to wonder: was my nervousness wholly related to my disability, or simply a fragment of the universal millennial experience? It was hard to pinpoint where my sense of despondency intersected, and deviated, from that of my friends. The pressure to fall into a dream career doesn't discriminate on the basis of disability; the search for purpose and meaning being a collective struggle that we were all feeling. As Oren Cass, author of *The Once and Future Worker*, explains, 'We've created this idea that the meaning of life should be found in work. We tell young people that their work should be their passion. "Don't give up until you find a job that you love!" we say. "You should be changing the world!" we tell them. That is the message in commencement addresses, in pop culture, and frankly, in media.' Like a stranglehold, the message is taut and suffocating, especially if, like me, you found yourself swimming downstream in the effluence of Oxford graduates towards a competitive talent pool. When our working lives are such an intimate reflection of who we are, what we represent, feeling anything other than happiness and fulfilment impinges on our self-worth. The first years of a career are like working out how to live and how to be content – as if it were something tangible that we could hold onto.

This cultural tendency to conflate employment status with an empowered self, is particularly rife among my generation. Without even realising it, our occupation is made a mirror of our character, worth and standing. That calling card, 'What do you do?', is a catch-all — four monosyllabic words made to constitute an entire personality assessment under the candlelit glare of the dinner party milieu. 'The underlying question suggests, "Who are you?"' as Dustin Galer, a disability and workplace theorist, explains, '[and] serves to ascribe social identity and value to an individual in order to situate the person within certain sociopolitical structures.' When the purest form of self-expression is what we do for a living, this harbours complications for disabled people who are twice as likely to be unemployed, or unable to pursue their dream career.

Work should provide an ideal opportunity for disabled people to assert their identity in the public sphere. To seek freedom and fulfil a desire for economic independence. Because, as much as capitalism works against us, people with disabilities often bank on the attainment of neoliberal ideals – if you can climb to the top and claim autonomy, you will gain social credibility and shake off negative assumptions about your value. 'Work affords people with disabilities a sense of status that is otherwise impossible to attain,' as Galer elaborates. 'Many conceptualize their job in terms of a personal success in overcoming low expectations of their potential. Work is seen as confirming to themselves *and* others that they possessed a complex and multifaceted identity beyond the bounds of disability.' Successful assimilation into the professional world is indeed critical to the disabled experience — it strikes at the heart of questions of dependency, independence and autonomy. But, right now, systemic barriers in the jobs market mean that the social and financial benefits of employment often remain unclaimed by people with disabilities.

Fired up with this existential angst, I sat at the desk in my college room, historical re-enactment society marching past the window, eclipsing the sun with their clanging shields, lances and metal-headed maces, gauntlets punching the air. I was positioned exactly where I had strived to be, with the eager readiness and rubber-stamped qualifications to set me on my chosen career path, and now, the practical realities of it were becoming harder to dismiss. I had been powered by that cultural ideal of 'having the world at my feet'. But – for me, at least – it felt like a myth. I had to face up to the fear that my next steps were never going to align with the fantasy I had fleshed out in my head. In doing so, I didn't experience the defeat I had desperately feared, but felt a new wave of determination. The privileges of health are not guaranteed – I'd always known that – so I would have to find ways to mitigate the constraints of my disability. To create a place for myself inside an industry that wasn't geared up to accommodate me.

When the news arrived in my inbox that I had secured a journalism internship, one I had applied for several months earlier, with the fashion team at a national newspaper, it threw me a lifeline. However, relief was now rising into terror as all the practical challenges swirled around my head – how would I navigate the streets of London? What was the best way to negotiate a flexible working schedule? Would the offer immediately be rescinded when they learned about my disability?

I spent hours ruminating over what to say, how to phrase it, how to package up my disability in a 'palatable' way, as problematic as that sounds. I felt an obligation to mediate and apologise for my disability. A tentative prelude of 'Sorry for the inconvenience but . . .' and some top notes of 'No worries if not!' Surely, this is a flagrant violation of the feminist code? Exposing all the symptoms of imposter syndrome, and little self-assurance. A girl boss would never. Leading up to that point, everything I had read about navigating the working world as a millennial woman was about 'leaning in', being 'fierce' and 'power dressing'. Nothing about this scenario was in accordance with the playbook. Where did disability fit in? As women we're always told to take up space, but this is what happens when you cannot physically access those spaces – you must wrangle your way through inaccessible doors first and express heartfelt gratitude upon your entry. I thought that by leading with an apology, they would perhaps be less likely to ghost me. But this can set a harmful precedent, reinforcing how my body is the problem, not the exclusionary physical and social barriers that fail to accommodate disability. People with disabilities often require some degree of assistance and allowances but the internal need to feel grateful for these concessions creates a hierarchy – an imbalance of power that places you in a position of dependency from which it's impossible to escape.

The burden lies with the disabled person to constantly trailblaze and push for accommodations in the workplace – fighting through a thicket of red tape. In my view, people with disabilities should no longer be seen as a surprise to employers, but as a welcome share of the recruitment landscape. To encourage disabled people to succeed, and mitigate obstacles before they arise, we need accessible measures in place by default. This way the onus isn't placed on the individual to explain intimate details and barter away, just to gain their right to equal opportunities.

Reminding myself of this, I typed out a confident and expectant reply to the newspaper. Email sent; its familiar swoosh given an aggressive underscore today, feeling more akin to a gut punch. I tied up my hair, slipped the kettle on, and tried to distract myself from imagining its receipt in the London office. Was it Miranda Priestly on the other end? God forbid I'd pulled her away from those cerulean knits. I was just coming round to the fact that I probably wouldn't be hearing back that business week, perhaps at all, when something pinged into my inbox, triggering a surge of adrenaline.

Loins girded, nervous about what the reaction might be, I clicked open and was relieved to find a voice of encouragement, warmth and receptiveness. It was clearly unchartered territory for us both, but it seemed like there was an openness to making things work. Too often, it's our fear of rejection that stops us from pushing for opportunities and taking risks – a universal experience that is intensified in the face of disability. But the reality is that if you reach out in a proactive and honest manner, it will likely be reciprocated with kindness and willing. Next steps secured, I glanced up to a handwritten notecard from my friend – it featured a sashimi roll with a devilish glint in his eye, speech-bubbling the words 'they see me rolling' – and thought to myself, this might just work out.

Dawn rolls over London with a calming predictability. Beyond each masked window the amber hues of sunrise illuminate the summer skies – a glow that lingers, tracing and teasing the blackened silhouette of an unconscious city. As the great fog disbands across the metropolis, the air is replenished by aromas of roasting coffee, a baker's dozen of Pret vegan croissants and the faithful awakening of its inhabitants. Yet today, this confident synchrony is broken as my scooter wheels hit the pavement, picking up speed in the glinting sun, wisps of my hair flowing in the breeze.

I am dressed in leather trousers and a green silk pussy-bow blouse, navigating in between a posse of bare-bellied, Cockney roadworkers bellowing out some fruity dialect. My outfit is intended as a modern riff on Melanie Griffith's iconic *Working Girl* wardrobe – but if anything tells me I'm not striding off the Staten Island Ferry into the electric rush of Manhattan, it's my scooter lumbering over an errant pot-hole. As I pass some Tube station steps, a hot metallic smell slashes through the upwind, making my stomach flip just as I'm forced to swerve what looks to be a pigeon's colonic splattered all over the concrete. I'm struck by the glamour of it all. Intuitively, I reach forward to ensure my laptop isn't making good on its promise to jump out of the scooter basket when I spot a miniature dachshund waggling its butt perilously close to my wheels. Its feet, as tiny and squidgy as warm chocolate buttons, must be avoided at all costs. I am a 3-centimetre tread depth away from becoming a viral *Daily Mail* headline: 'Self-obsessed Fashion Intern Mows Down Adored Sausage Dog, Peppa, 2, in Mobility Scooter Rampage'. Before I'm forced to make an emergency stop, Peppa's leash is retracted, with the ferocity of a bungee cord, by a tall man in a bow tie, forcing her to let out a small yelp before she resumes her swagger towards the zebra crossing. Her path heralded by the low thrumming of two stalled double deckers and the fury of halting traffic.

This was my shot: could I make the terrifying leap from the cotton-wool-lined halls of education to tread the competitive minefields of the working world? After years of livestreaming Fashion Week from my sofa, inhaling the inky smell of glossy magazines and casting judicial verdict on the new season catwalks, my spectator interest in fashion was becoming a reality – and a profession. A large part of me felt exhilarated by the prospect, the possibilities unfolding before my future self. While people with disabilities are often steered away from the careers they dream of, simply because the obstacles appear intractable, this felt bold.

Pop culture's mythologisation of fashion industry personalities as equal parts ferocious and farcical filled me with trepidation. Research told me this was an inflated conspiracy – that I was unlikely to find myself among the next generation of Bolly-guzzling Patsy Stones, with an Eddie Monsoon screeching from inside the fashion cupboard that she'd exhumed what looked to be a 'Lacroix, sweetie! Lacroix.' But still, I had been privy to some mortifying reports of brass-necked saboteurs masquerading as smiley, glossy-haired interns. Wolves dressed in Bottega Veneta shearling biker jackets. A family friend, while chatting with a fellow intern between munches of cream cheese bagel during one lunch break, flippantly disclosed that she was no longer sure if her heart lay in PR. Three hours later, she was hauled up to see the manager. She lacked the ambition, commitment and loyalty required of their staff. Her position was untenable, she was to clear her desk and be out by EOP. The intern (informant) – who was failing to conceal her mischievous smirk from behind an Apple desktop – would escort her out the premises. I was anticipating the worst.

Exclusion and prejudice were part of the mythos of fashion, but I had reason to be fearful beyond the wicked ruses of cut-throat fashion assistants. It was startling how far the image of my commute via mobility scooter strayed from our cultural imagination of what a fashion intern should look like – cool, nonchalant and dressed to kill. I cannot deny that it was internally frustrating. Where there is an expectation that interns must be both telepathic and balletic, with an almost uncanny reflex to hop up and give unprompted gestures of support, I knew it would be hard to prove myself. Or reach 'indispensable' status by dogsbodying myself – developing an umbilical tie to the clothes steamer, while dispensing cups of tea at a rate that would flabbergast even Mrs Tiggy-Winkle. I felt apprehensive not knowing how people may respond, and how my success could be derailed by a lack of understanding or poor accessibility in the office.

Though if my participation meant getting dropped off in London by my parents, who could carry my height-adjustable desk chair to use in the office, I happily took it. The reality is this is a necessary part of my success, holding my nerve even when vulnerability flays me open and leaves me exposed. Sure, it was slightly unconventional but there were only two options here: persist despite the challenges, discomfort and looking less than cool, or give up and never try. The latter was unthinkable, and this made it simpler.

I was finally at the skyscraping London headquarters of a national newspaper, gazing up at its imposing glass façade which appeared like liquid, white sunlight and cloud dancing across its undulating surface. Inside, the foyer boasted the dimensions of an airport terminal, flanked by metal detectors and armed security guards, reminders of a recent spate of terror attacks. After procuring an ID badge and surviving a series of fruitless attempts to ram my scooter through a barricade of turnstiles, I was certified to head upstairs to the newsroom. Chassis dented, though still intact.

The lift system, the likes of which I had never encountered in my waking life, was initially confounding. There were no call buttons. Was this some kind of eccentric initiation challenge? I took a suspicious glance up to locate a flashing CCTV camera rigged up to a wall somewhere. It was surely doing zigzags on me, anticipating a 'gotcha' moment. It now appeared all carriages were being summoned from a central touchscreen panel. I scooted over for closer inspection. Select floor number, wait to be assigned your designated ride, and then go over to wait beside one of the eight lifts. It promised optimal traffic flow and shorter passenger wait times – simple, intuitive, efficient. By scooter, however, what is a most admirable concept falls down. Like the devil you had to outwit, I found myself driving up to code in my floor number, countdown on, racing back around to reach my lift. If the carriage was full, the process had to be repeated from the start, condemned to eternity. To complicate matters, I was having to execute three-point turns on glossy, polished floor, between dozens of suited journalists balancing trays of oat milk latte and stacks of the day's newspapers. All while trying to keep the hypersonic squeaks of my bootcut leather trousers down to an inaudible degree and not run over any brogues. I could not slip up.

I drove out of the lift only to be met with locked glass double doors. The Houdinian feat of getting off the scooter to swipe my ID badge and authenticate access, then trying to yank open the heavy door, rush back to the scooter, still holding the door open enough to wedge myself through the crack, seemed ambitious – if not physically impossible.

Realising I was a mere whisker away from a workplace incident claim, I decided to wait it out, smiling, floundering, and nervously hoping someone else would arrive and I could dash through behind them. By the end of the first week, I had my routine fine-tuned and slick: the lifts no longer feeling like a HIIT workout class and patience being a necessary virtue in getting through those damn doors. It reached a point where someone would pre-emptively spot me by the doors and scramble from behind their desk to swoop in. Or, another time, a girl frantically waved from the closing lift doors, shouting to her friend who was wearing headphones to make sure she'd seen me. But on other occasions I'd wait there, static, for several minutes.

As an intern or new recruit in the workplace, you aspire to appear unflinchingly cool. To resist showing weakness and be effortlessly confident, capable, independent. Our culture tells us that these are the virtues that yield success. We must harness and perform them at all costs, especially in the realm of fashion, an industry defined by beguiling surfaces, exteriority and aesthetic value. But having a disability disrupts this pursuit. The dynamic shifts when I'm reliant on Good Samaritanism just so I can enter a workplace and seeking permission for reasonable adjustments. It places me in a position of vulnerability from which there is no elective escape. I understand what it's like to be exposed, to be hyper-visible with my physical limitations seen, if not always on show. This state of being lies in contradiction with everything we know about the working world – a sphere where taboo is cloaked up and shuttled under the carpet. To get ahead, you must blend in. To be seen as a vital part of the workforce, you must not betray any sign of illness and frailty to your colleagues or boss. What lies beneath the surface is forbidden, stamped on. An inclusion study by Deloitte found that 62 per cent of all employees (disabled and non-disabled) engage in a practice known as 'covering', the phenomenon whereby individuals must actively control their image, altering their self-presentation and mannerisms to blend in with the mainstream. Often, people with disabilities are unable to conceal themselves or seamlessly imitate the customs and vernacular of a workplace – impression-management becoming a tortuous endeavour. While conformity remains a commodity at work, one that can secure promotion, career advancement and financial reward, it will unjustly hinder disabled people's careers.

We are made to believe success in work is dependent on this oppressive, unspoken need to put people at ease by blotting out signs of weakness or disablement. But in my view, vulnerabilities are the closest thing we have to showing our true selves, to tearing down the mask. When I refuse to conceal my own vulnerability is when I feel most connected to people. It puts me in a state of mind where I feel I have nothing to lose. A state of mind that has previously borne out my success. I'm not afraid to ask for help, which has expanded my ability to act with maturity, assertiveness and self-possession, even within intimidating scenarios. We need to recognise that these are commanding, innately human qualities that will benefit any workforce – leading to increased productivity and collaboration, igniting people's empathy processes along the way.

Going back to that first day of my internship, however, I still had to find my new office desk. In a far-flung corner of the newsroom lay the spiritual home of the fashion editorial department, or 'fashion desk' as it was known to insiders. As I drew up closer, I could smell thick wafts of tuberose and white jasmine atomised in the air (its expressive top notes betraying itself to any self-respecting beauty nerd as Gucci Bloom Eau de Parfum). A dozen white gloss desks were lined up in blocks and configured around expansive cityscape views. Their surfaces strewn with magazine proofs still scorching from the copier, as well as annotated flat plans awaiting sign-off. Then, from a gathering of possibly the most stylish women I'd seen in my life – a jangling haze of sculptural pearl earrings, toile de Jouy dresses, cream suede boots, and seventies geometric-print skirts – I was greeted with enthusiastic, inviting faces.

After a collective rush to find me convenient desk space and somewhere to park up my scooter, I exhaled in relief. 'This is great – it drives so smoothly,' one raven-haired beauty assistant said to me as I reversed around a filing cabinet, her kohl-lined eyes glancing at my scooter while she pushed aside crates of mascara samples branded 'highly classified'. The instant my desk chair was positioned in place, I was set to work writing round-ups of the day's breaking fashion news and transcribing profile interviews, typing out dizzying reams of journalistic chatter. Unexpectedly, my Mavis Beacon touch-typing came full circle – Mavis's pacifying tones once again became gospel, guiding me as I rippled my fingers across the keyboard. I typed away, as a fellow intern on my left was tethered to the phone, trying – with a level of chutzpah usually reserved for military personnel – to track down high-resolution images of face oils from a PR director. Next on the agenda was researching bra size inequality (who knew?), scouring the net for sources to comment on Madonna's sixtieth birthday, sourcing twenty neon-pink Perspex boxes to be shipped overnight for a photo shoot the next day and compiling edits of stylish workwear.

However insurmountable these opportunities look from the outside, I quickly learned that one of the most valuable attributes to gaining recognition is a quiet power. I had to swallow a creeping sense of demoralisation that I couldn't assist in ways I wanted to, but I ensured my contributions were always valuable; actively emphasising my creative ideas and research abilities, rather than my difficulties with physical tasks. You earn equal credibility by showing commitment, a positive attitude and lifting the team without conditions – but this takes time, creativity and persistence.

Over the course of the next year, and several magazine internships later, I started to recognise how I could use my perspective to raise issues relating to disability in this rapidly evolving industry. Perhaps especially in fashion, an industry where people who had historically been othered could start to see themselves. I wanted to be part of that groundswell, to cultivate a more inclusive future through the lens of mass media. As an intern, I had the chance to write a handful of feature articles for each publication – one commission being a personal, memoir-style essay about fashion and disability. Initially, I wasn't sure if I could do it, having never attempted to capture the nuances of myself in words before, not least on the pages of a magazine scrutinised by a million readers. I feared putting myself out there to be judged, or even admired, as someone with a disability at a time when media portrayals of disabilities were far removed from how I saw myself. There was, and still is, an editorial desire to churn out a sob story. To sentimentalise disability in a way that will shock or psychologically jolt readers as they take a bleary-eyed sip from their morning coffee. Geared up for clicks and shareability, these stories fail to capture the real human behind the tale – at worst, they rehash deleterious myths about disability. But I didn't have to obey the social scripts that came before me. This was my moment to positively reshape the cultural narrative, stretching the powers of language and storytelling into new alignments, revealing what was once unseen. For the first time, I saw a new opportunity awaiting me – and I took it.

When the published issue landed on my doorstep, nestled inside the morning papers, I scanned across the words once scrawled across my reporter's notepad. Within hours, I was receiving a flood of messages on social media about the piece – how it was a breath of fresh air, how it gave a positive insight into a perspective rarely spoken about. That day I knew that I was onto something. The truth is, when handled in a way that is sensitive and authentic, disability is a subject that resonates deeply. It touches on universal human experiences, from vulnerability and freedom to self-image and determination. We've just been afraid to tap into it.

But as much as it felt like I was finally making a small imprint, the day-to-day working reality was tough. With no opportunities for part-time, flexible work in a permanent position – a fact that was made clear to me during my internships – the only real way that I could contribute meaningfully, grow my platform and have earning potential in my chosen industry, was through freelance work. It wasn't the job I had envisioned – it was unreliable, insular and non-existent at times. A fact that was frustrating when I was hungry for professional responsibilities.

Frustration forced me to think creatively: I built my own blog, took on research jobs in investigative journalism, threw myself into the activism side of fashion by working with a parliamentary group in Westminster, in between writing freelance articles. Lately, I have reached professional mile-stones I hardly thought possible. But my career is still a work in progress. It has felt like a punishingly slow start, watching my peers rise up the ranks, aware that I have talent and desirable skills, just not packaged up in any conventional, linear form.

As I began to develop my voice as an activist, I was beginning to see the depth of disability inequality for the first time. In this arena of change-making, my pursuit of a career folded in on itself. It became self-reflexive, as I was now witnessing the agonising injustices of disabled employment reflected onto my own story. I started to recognise my individual responsibility to change the system, to carve out a new way of existence that didn't subscribe to ableist norms.

Hiring methods, often hostile and inaccessible, are the first stumbling block for disabled people eager to launch themselves into the job market. Like an investigatory biopsy, employment gap data points to the obstacles metastasising in the system: almost a quarter of UK employers reveal they would be less likely to hire someone with a disability. Although the decision to disclose one's disability on a job application is, by law, a personal prerogative, it remains a contentious issue. Many fear that being open and forthright about their condition is a fool's errand, a sure-fire way to rack up a slew of instant rejection letters. Others rationalise that it can act as a kind of vetting process of itself. If future employers are so close-minded and unwilling to see past disability, this speaks volumes; they are unlikely to have an inclusive working culture or infrastructure that can offer support down the line. Ultimately, neither strategy can provide absolute protection from discrimination, with the UK-based charity Leonard Cheshire reporting that almost one in five (17 per cent) of disabled applicants have had a job offer rescinded by their employer because of their disability.

In 2021, a *Financial Times* article, 'I was shocked when the interviewer ghosted me', drew attention to how disabled job seekers have been fettered by negative bias for years. When Shani Dhanda, 33, an entrepreneur with osteogenesis imperfecta, left school aged sixteen, she made the conscious decision to flag her disability on job applications. 'I had one sentence in my covering letter that said I have a condition but specified that I don't need any adjustments,' Dhanda said. After applying for more than a hundred jobs, however, she failed to get a single interview. Dhanda then changed tack, retracting all mention of her condition from her CV – and suddenly she was offered an interview that resulted in a job offer. When employers read that a candidate has a disability, they often make unfounded assumptions. Even before meeting the individual, it is assumed they are unable to deliver the work or cope with the strenuous demands of the workplace. This is perhaps inevitable in a results-based, profit-making system that prioritises growth and prosperity over employee welfare. James Taylor, strategy director for the disability equality charity Scope, explains, 'The perception among some employers is that hiring disabled people is expensive and risky. There are some quite outdated underlying attitudes about what disabled people can – or can't – do.' To really stand out, it seems that your talents and skill set must outshine other able-bodied applicants – to the extent that what you bring to a workplace, your intrinsic value, outweighs any perceived risk or liability on account of your disability.

But in our rapidly evolving digital era, it's not just human bias we need to keep in check. Interview invites and selection processes are increasingly determined by computer-based systems, soulless algorithms built on ableist measures of achievement. In most cases the computer will model the 'ideal' employee on a company's previous hires. Given that disabled people have long been excluded from the workforce, this perfect archetype will almost always be based on able-bodied workers. Even if the system was able to generate reference points that might account for outliers, the way each disability presents itself can vary from person to person. For instance, two applicants with autism will likely have very different strengths and difficulties. So, in their current state, these machines lack the sophistication and empathy to make such nuanced distinctions. As an accelerationist nightmare, it allows discrimination to breed furiously, and go unchecked. Consequently, these AI-powered hiring tools do not offer a progressive future, rather they perpetuate the long-standing exclusion of candidates with disabilities.

Speaking to *MIT Technology Review*, Roland Behm, a lawyer and advocate for people with behavioural health issues, explains that AI companies and employers are not deliberately screening out disabled people. They just 'haven't spent the time and effort necessary to understand the systems that are making what for many people are life-changing decisions: Am I going to be hired or not? Can I support my family or not?' Alarmingly, these hiring procedures also thwart discrimination litigation processes as there is no ability to find out whether the algorithm rejected someone due to their disability or another reason, like a lack of relevant experience. This is called the 'black box' problem where these AI processes are impenetrable to humans. Even the people who design them cannot decipher how data variables are being combined to make judgements. Candidates are suddenly left without a clear explanation for hiring decisions and cannot easily launch a discrimination lawsuit.

Governed by a ratio of profit margins to labour costs, many employers currently fail to see the potential in anyone considered a liability, punt or a gamble. Instead, they remain blindsided by false perceptions of what disabled people can and cannot do, without giving us the opportunity to prove all we're capable of. Flexible jobs and accessible working practices are often disregarded in a system that demands near-relentless stamina and competitive presence. It's the very question of who can clock in earliest, as the thick fog engulfs street lamps, then clock out under the watchful gaze of moonlight. In most workplaces, it seems that the productivity of bodies is ranked like an arcade game. Imaginary leaderboards, with their red digits lit up high, are broadcast to the workforce. High scores will earn you ticker-tape rewards, to be cashed in for perks and promotion. Perhaps a coveted spot on that upper rung of the career ladder. Strike the bullseye – ding-ding-ding! – and gain instant entry into the next level where an even higher pace is enforced, and a ferocious output demanded.

Modern work culture is fixated on ideals of speed, efficiency and productivity – the holy trifecta of bankability. It seems the twenty-first century flicked us into acceleration mode. Life is now propelled by the pressure to work harder, faster, better, stronger. As we tear along, ascending to the cloud-dappled stratosphere in our ruthless pursuit of productivity, people with disabilities are unjustly left behind – wanting to take off, yet remaining static at ground level.

The breakneck pace of our current labour market – which cannot compute any different velocities or trajectories – is a prime example of how the conditions of modern life are built in opposition to disability. It wasn't something that I could pinpoint until I read about what the sociologist John Tomlinson calls our 24/7 'culture of speed'. In his 2007 book of the same name, Tomlinson outlines how immediacy and endless production have become the defining characteristics of today's society. 'Acceleration rather than deceleration has been the constant leitmotiv of cultural modernity,' he writes. This insatiable need to be active – the sense that activity is, in fact, an end goal in itself – has come to regulate our everyday experience. Perhaps this is an inevitable outcome of the rapidly advancing technology in recent decades. We live on-demand lifestyles, immediacy hooked up to our veins in breaking news flashes, iPhone photography, Amazon Prime parcels and looping social media feeds. These frenetic conditions have all conspired to instil 'assumptions and expectations of effortlessness, ubiquity and endless delivery in a fast-paced, technologically-replete and telemediated world'. There is no time to pause or slow down. There is no break point.

Nothing is untouched by our compulsive need to move at full throttle. We've reached the point where it has become embedded in the public psyche, shaping our perceptions of community, family life and relationships. Even our own identity and value. As the author Robert Hassan puts it in *The Empire of Speed*, 'We have never experienced such a world where rapidity – *speed* – is at the very core of our collective and individual experience.' Millennials, especially, have grown up with an intuitive understanding that speed equals success. To be a mover and shaker, a powerhouse or juggernaut, you must possess a preternatural quickness and agility. The Forbes 30 Under 30 List, released annually since 2011, is further proof of how society has come to view speed as the definitive mark of talent, distinction and merit. To rank on these lists, you must catapult yourself to the top of your field in a rapid timeline. Your competition is not only your peers, but the tyrannical tick of the clock.

Speed requires not only physical strength and athleticism, but endurance and stamina. It's the ability to exert the body against gravity. To perform sharp, precise movements. To hustle and slay. Anyone missing these core attributes is put dangerously out of sync with the ever-increasing pace of work – and, by extension, life. Read any magazine profile on a Silicon Valley CEO (the modern pin-ups of instant success), you'll learn that turbo-charging your career demands robust physical and mental health. To get ahead requires an unceasing cycle of mindfulness apps, HIIT workout schedules and expensive superfoods. When this is the case, people with disabilities and chronic illnesses will never start out on an equal footing. For me, it's a race of which I must opt out.

So why did we buy into this warped idea that accomplishing things in haste gives success its seductive edge? How did we become so consumed by the thinking that impatience is an essential ingredient in the pursuit of our professional goals? Urgency does not make achievement more valuable or inspiring. Besides, the evidence shows that it is self-defeating to have your career fast-tracked. Research by Charles Duhigg, journalist and author of *Smarter Faster Better*, confirms that people who are dealt early setbacks are ultimately poised for greater success because they have a personal history of failure, an accumulated wisdom of what it means to struggle. That rare, overlooked species of the late bloomer has highly developed levels of persistence and resilience. Being able to adapt and change to your circumstances? Well, those are fundamentally employable traits.

Our culture's obsession with early achievement will likely breed frustration, panic and disappointment. This glamorisation of overworking, the rapid-fire pursuit of success, is ultimately making it harder to find fulfilment, to reach that all-elusive state of happiness. 'A 24/7 world is a disenchanted one,' Jonathan Crary warns in *24/7: Late Capitalism and the Ends of Sleep*, his scathing critique of the disastrous consequences of the open-ended, continuous activity that defines twenty-first-century capitalism. By pushing human life into duration without breaks, we eradicate 'shadows and obscurity', the possibilities of 'alternate temporalities'. It is, he writes, 'a world identical to itself' – one where diversity and alternative modes of existence are unable to thrive.

John Tomlinson does not apply his original framework to disability – or detail how our 'culture of speed' may carry further negative implications for people who aren't able-bodied. Yet it feels like an illuminating explanation as to why the labour market and working practices can be so hostile to disabled individuals. When immediacy is our most powerful commodity, disability becomes a problem. It imposes its own speed where slowness may be enforced by the body at any point. Or, as the writer Ellen Samuels puts it, disability and illness have the power to 'extract us from linear, progressive time with its normative life stages and cast us into a wormhole of backward and forward acceleration, jerky stops and starts, tedious intervals and abrupt endings . . .

It forces us to take breaks, even when we don't want to, even when we want to keep going, to move ahead.'

Disability is an existence determined by the subjective rhythms of the body. Disabled bodies don't always comply with objective, universal timelines set forth by society's master clock. They may violate fixed ideas about how much time or energy a specific task should take, they may be incompatible with a standard nine-to-five job, and they may suddenly rip up the five-year plan glued on the back page of a colour-coded bullet journal. This sense of desynchronisation that characterises the disabled experience often remains undetectable. But in the workplace – which is anchored by notions of time, speed and productivity – it becomes increasingly difficult to hide. Even the act of being initiated into a workforce requires a CV with a perfect, unbroken chronology. To exist outside of the punishing clock of the labour market means you are easily mistaken as dysfunctional. Red-flagged as underproductive. In an ever-accelerating world, where the speed of productivity can never be fast enough, people with disabilities are under threat.

Not having full control of my health means that I contend with the reality that, at times, my life doesn't run along a linear trajectory, or at one controllable pace. I must accept the infuriating fact that my body has a monopoly over my career prospects. So, what does it feel like to be positioned against the grain of time? In the context of work and study, frustratingly, I cannot work for eight-hour stretches. I'll arrive at least fifteen minutes earlier than everyone else, never knowing how long a particular journey will take me or whether I'll encounter unforeseen obstacles like 'out-of-order' lifts and locked side doors. I'm the one who will be held accountable, so I must anticipate the worst – a mindset that is draining, yet so instinctive I don't think about it anymore. Taking out insurance in the form of my own time is the only way I can gain control over the stress and unpredictability. But often there is no return on my investment; it simply amounts to wasted time. Hours spent waiting around or resting up that others can fill with more satisfying tasks. This is a sacrifice and a commitment. The price I must pay to succeed.

Lost time is not confined to these everyday rituals. It's the blank spaces, lacunas and abridgements that perforate my entire lifetime. It's the grief for experiences I've missed and cannot go back and repeat. It's the periods of time snatched by illness and hospitalisation. It's being required to work in double speed to catch up, missing out on yet more and more experiences. As professor and author Alison Kafer explains, the way disabled people experience time is in flex, 'not just expanded but exploded; it requires re-imagining our notions of what can and should happen in time, or recognizing how expectations of "how long things take" are based on very particular minds and bodies'.

Modern society is infatuated with time. As the most used noun in the English language, entire working lives are disciplined, paced and corralled by the hands of time. But we must remind ourselves that clock time is man-made. It is regularly bent and altered to fit political and social agendas that benefit some, ostracise others. When human activity is strictly regulated by the clock, it inhibits us from a true understanding of our own body and environment. In fact, there is a growing distrust in the long-held supremacy of corporate culture, its infliction of a strict five-day, forty-hour working week. The alluring prospect of a shorter four-day week is instead gaining traction across the globe, flirting with the white-collared establishment. In Iceland, for instance, a pilot study demonstrated that working fewer hours can indeed make a country more productive. Over a period of four years, a group of over 2,500 employees logged fewer hours without a pay cut and experienced positive results – from overall enhancements in productivity and well-being to a reduction in stress levels.

In *Can't Even,* the journalist Anne Helen Petersen interrogates our infatuation with time and productivity, rebuking the forces that have pushed an entire generation towards the edges of work addiction. Burnout, a symptom of our obsession with productivity, is now our default setting. 'It's not limited to workers in acutely high-stress environments,' argues Peterson, 'and it's not a temporary affliction: It's the millennial condition. It's our base temperature. It's our background music. It's the way things are. It's our lives.' As one of the greatest issues that currently disfigures our experience of modern life, we require an urgent antidote. A deceleration device, stat.

Paradoxically, the way many disabled people exist, listening to the cadences of the body, can deepen our understanding of productivity within a culture that tells us to push ourselves beyond our limits and block out internal warning signs in frantic pursuit of just 'getting a job done'. Instead, it gives time an organic and humane dimension, telling us to be more present. It implores us to slow down and reflect, rather than always mindlessly moving forward; to adopt our own liberatory pace attuned to our physical and mental state; to fall back in sync with ourselves, not the external, mechanical routines of society. This individualised approach, with its power and possibilities, will naturally yield more fulfilling, productive outcomes. And, in turn, offer up a blueprint for a new best working practice where timelines are flexible and self-defined. To many businesses the logic remains: more hours worked, more tasks accomplished, maximum profit gained. But this fails to recognise the value of increased employee health, well-being, work/life balance, motivation and retention levels – which all translate into an uptick in revenue.

In Joan Didion's 1968 essay 'In Bed', she writes of the debilitating migraines that consigned her to bed for up to five times a month. This was not an opportunity to work and write; instead it offered something more metaphysical – a kind of spiritual reset that ultimately enhanced her productivity. 'Right there is the usefulness of migraine, there in that imposed yoga,' she writes. 'For when the pain recedes, ten or twelve hours later, everything goes with it, all the hidden resentments, all the vain anxieties. The migraine has acted as a circuit breaker, and the fuses have emerged intact. There is a pleasant convalescent euphoria. I open the windows and feel the air, eat gratefully, sleep well. I notice the particular nature of a flower in a glass on the stair landing. I count my blessings.' There's a pervasive feeling that we are not permitted to pause, switch off or take time out. But here, Didion's act of submitting to her body, of offering it what it needs, gave her opportunity to restart and re-engage with her surroundings. This clarity of vision was, arguably, essential for the creation of her literary works and mastery of her field.

It's clear to me that people with disabilities deserve greater consideration when it comes to securing and maintaining employment. But this requires time, space and reflection – qualities that are incompatible with the current speed of existence. Our pedal-to-the-metal mentality doesn't afford any intervals to stop and develop the infrastructure needed to support new ways of working. Making jobs accessible – and by this, I mean tailoring roles to fit the skill set and abilities of each disabled individual – should be considered obligatory on the part of employers. By not doing so, we are wasting the diverse potential of generations of disabled people, while needlessly placing society at a disadvantage.

A decade ago, just as millennials were filtering into the workforce, a new type of career was starting to emerge – a kind of shadow labour market with a revised definition of productivity. A job was rebranded from a fixed, stable occupation with clearly defined workspaces, responsibilities and trajectories, to a rapidly evolving, self-governable, nomadic entity where its only requirement was a functioning Wi-Fi code. As the author Emma Gannon describes in *The Multi-Hyphen Method*, our professional selves were becoming an infinite succession of hyphens. The parameters of work had exploded: jobs could now be multiplied up to reflect where your interests lay or who you wanted to be at any given moment. Finding employment, Gannon explains, was suddenly more akin to 'choosing a lifestyle'. This involved curating a portfolio of roles where you could move from, say, digital strategist, to freelance accountant, to stand-up comedian in the space of a week. You might even throw in a side hustle selling hand-knitted pet costumes on Etsy – your options, infinite.

Far from a display of fickleness or an evasion of responsibility, the Multi-Hyphen Method was about 'taking some power back into our own hands'. When you consider how the mainstream labour market is built for able-bodied workers, this reclamation of power, the chance to topple hostile hierarchies, becomes not just enticing, but revolutionary. In Gannon's model, the career ladder is self-constructed, which means the worker gains greater autonomy and the need for constant external appraisal is removed. In the pick-and-mix labour economy, you 'leapfrog over old barriers'. It is no longer about bending to corporate structures, seeking permission from HR or hoop jumping. You can control your work schedule and create an individualised, disability-accessible workspace. And, for disabled people, this new way of working is an invaluable prospect, offering up the chance to design a bespoke career.

Here independence and innovation replace red tape and servility. This shift has given a lifeline to workers with disabilities like myself and 26-year-old Ione Gamble. As the founder and editor-in-chief of the multi-platform zine *Polyester*, Gamble illustrates the power of making your own opportunities and calibrating your working habits to the nuanced rhythms of the body. Since being diagnosed at nineteen with Crohn's disease, an incurable autoimmune condition, she has faced long spells of bed rest. Bringing the boardroom to her bedroom, Gamble suddenly found herself editing print issues of her zine, dialling in on video calls ('always filmed from the chest up, as to not reveal the duvet straddling my waist', she adds) and filing countless articles, all from her bed. 'It may not be the Instagram-ready workspace most now associate with femme entrepreneurship,' she writes in an essay for *VICE*, 'but I've built a fledgling business and inclusive community from between cotton sheets.' This DIY mentality is encapsulated in the 'cut and stick' pages of *Polyester*. As a love note to the margins, her zine revolts against the unrealistic social expectations peddled by mainstream media, instead offering the seductive alternative of unapologetic selfhood.

There's no denying that adversity breeds creativity. But to an outsider, these unconventional working methods may be shrouded in pity, idleness, secrecy or shame – and frankly, just deemed a bit odd. We often forget that there is no single, valid way to achieve an assignment. It's the results and outcomes that count, not the means of getting there. When we open up the possibilities of what work can look like, magical and unexpected things can happen. Ione Gamble's story belongs to a line of creative histories that were borne and sealed in the bedroom. Famously, Frida Kahlo used an adapted wooden easel and ceiling mirror to paint self-portraits lying supine in bed, following the severe bus accident that left her with a fractured spine and other traumatic injuries. The transcendent nineteenth-century poet Emily Dickinson, who experienced a host of medical ailments, including lupus, Bright's disease, tuberculosis, epilepsy and psychosis, reputedly wrote every one of her 1,800 poems from her second-floor bedroom in Amherst, Massachusetts. In fact, many creative minds have elected to write from beneath the sheets, from Phoebe Waller-Bridge to Marcel Proust and Edith Wharton. As Gamble attests, just because her career has bloomed from inside the four walls of a bedroom, it 'doesn't mean my achievements aren't valid. Chronic illness has taught me to be kinder to myself, and stop relentlessly focusing on the arbitrary career goals of myself and my peers.'

For a long time, there was an element of luxury, privilege even, that came with having such a loosely defined, self-governable job. It demanded a perilous trade-off: the security of a regular payslip was lost, as flexible, autonomous working patterns were gained. For the vast majority of disabled people, the prospect of not having a steady stream of income, a pension pot or other employee benefits made freelance work too risky, too economically volatile. Many of its freedoms were likely reserved for the younger, more educated and affluent minority. But could Covid-19 change this? Will a global pandemic – which has torn open the entire employment landscape – bring flexible work opportunities to every disabled person?

At first, there was timorous optimism that the shift to remote jobs and hybrid working practices would improve access to the labour market. Optimism even turned to tangible progress, when the Trades Union Congress reported that over half of disabled employees were working from home during the pandemic. Before that point, only around 13 per cent were permitted to do so – despite it being the most sought-after workplace adjustment. The appeal is self-evident if you consider how employees are no longer forced to make arduous commutes or navigate inaccessible office buildings. Obstacles that once impeded the disabled workforce appeared to be disintegrating, overnight. But is a remote, digital work culture really a magic bullet when it comes to wiping out the disability employment gap? Or are these instantaneous gains diverting our gaze from the knottiness that lurks beneath the surface?

In the first year of the pandemic, the proportion of employers who said their organisation employs disabled staff fell to 33 per cent – a 16 per cent drop from 2018, when it was recorded as 49 per cent. This data points to the fact that something is clearly amiss. By focusing on the physical environment, we perhaps overlook the ableist structures of a workplace that extend way beyond the building itself.

And, in turn, ignore both the social isolation and reduction in support that may arise under the fair-weather guises of 'remote working'.

It has transpired that disabled workers' rights are being neglected, with allowances failing to keep pace with rapid changes in the modern jobs market. Almost half of those who requested reasonable adjustments did not receive the provisions they needed to carry out their role effectively during the pandemic. Meanwhile, a 2020 report by Citizens Advice found that 48 per cent of those who had been shielding (because they are extremely vulnerable due to health conditions) were facing redundancy. In the long term, Covid-19 could deprioritise workplace access and leave disabled people at increased risk of unemployment during a time of economic downturn. To frame the pandemic as a fix-all for disability employment rights is merely a procrastination on the legal and grassroots actions that must be enacted, right now.

As the data has revealed, an arsenal of measures is still needed to tackle the persistent barriers in the labour market and close the disability employment gap. First, a robust legal framework can provide much-needed armament for disabled job seekers and employees. The passing of the Equality Act 2010 has enshrined many vital protections in law – from the principle of 'reasonable adjustment' which was instrumental in the creation of disability accessible workplaces, to the authorisation of positive discrimination. The latter means it is entirely legal for employers to treat disabled applicants more favourably in the recruitment process when they are pitted against an able-bodied person who is equally qualified for the role. In other words, positive discrimination refers to the preferential treatment of disabled individuals to remove any disadvantage that they may be facing. Unlike race, age, religion or sexual orientation, disability is the only protected characteristic where this process is permitted. But without the impetus, urgency or desire to attract disabled employees, this law is redundant. If it is never enacted, it will clearly have limited reach in achieving equity in the labour market.

For all its positives, the Equality Act 2010 legislation is also marred by the fact that the onus is placed solely on the individual. If a disabled person believes themself to be a victim of employment discrimination, it's up to them to launch their own litigation proceedings and prove their case. Proceedings that are not only time-consuming and emotionally demanding, but expensive to carry through. This element of self-regulation, an individual responsibility for action, is a relatively new development – and one that, in my view, represents a backwards step. As the government wants to avoid meddling in the labour market, there is currently no legal obligation for employers to hire people with disabilities or adopt certain standards to support them in the workplace. If employers are proven to be discriminating against people with disabilities, there is only one potential penalty to pay: compensation to the victim. Without an impartial governing body to hold employers to account, discrimination can be hushed up, liable to occur again and again.

Government-enforced disability quotas, whereby employers are legally obliged to recruit a set percentage of disabled workers, offer some potential. In the past, government sanctions were in place to ensure that disabled people were represented in the workforce. But they failed to achieve their aims due to a lack of employer cooperation. And so, with the repeal of the original Disabled Persons Act 1944 in the UK, the duty for securing employment for disabled people shifted from the state to the individual. In today's society, quotas remain inherently controversial. To many, disability quotas, recruitment drives and affirmative action imply disabled people are incapable of securing work independently and require special treatment – fuelling, rather than mitigating, negative stereotypes about disability. Wherever policymaking is designed to tackle the under-representation of disabled people, remedying the effects of historic discrimination, there will be some pushback – with accusations of empty values and tokenistic posturing seeping through the veneer of positive change. But I believe that with proper, more rigorous monitoring, a similar system holds huge potential, especially if fines could be levied on companies who fail to meet the agreed threshold.

Anti-discrimination legislation, however, cannot fix the problem alone, no matter how rigorous it is. Practical and financial support must be offered to people with disabilities as they navigate the world of work. Known as the 'government's best-kept secret', Access to Work is a state-funded employment support programme which has been instrumental in facilitating inclusivity in the workforce. With its offer to cover any additional costs of employing disabled people – such as funding for personal assistants, sign language interpreters, equipment, building adaptations or travel expenses – it heralded a revolution for disability civil rights when it was launched in 1994. Three decades on, however, the scheme is hindered by a lack of awareness and publicity; it remains purely coincidental as to whether employer or employee have heard of it. All too predictably, the programme has also been beset by bureaucracy and stickiness in recent years. Frequent reassessments, caps on funding, repetitive form filling, tighter eligibility criteria and an underlying perception by applicants that they are under suspicion, are among some of the rigorous hurdles. Marsha De Cordova, the ex-Labour minister for disabled people (who has herself benefitted from Access to Work as she is registered blind), claimed the scheme had been left 'unworkable for so many of us' due to 'severe cuts' and 'poor policy'. Case in point: if an employee works part time, they cannot continue using the funded equipment outside of working hours. This means wheelchairs are senselessly shut away in office cupboards at the end of shifts, and the user must find another wheelchair to travel to and from work. Without consistent, reliable support, the fate of disabled workers is at the discretion of others – leaving many needlessly unemployed.

How non-disabled colleagues react to what might be seen as 'preferential' treatment is another complicating factor in the application of the Access to Work scheme. This is a major factor in whether disabled people are accepted in the workforce, according to management scholar Mary McLaughlin and colleagues. If flexible accommodations are perceived as unfair or unnecessary, it will likely breed resentment. This is especially true when such allowances (like reduced hours, sick leave or an exchange of job duties) require employee cooperation. Favouritism, the act of moving the goalposts on account of disability, is seen as an affront in a world where there are limited opportunities. This phenomenon is called reverse ableism, a symbolic queue jump where disabled people are seen to be awarded special perks and favourable status. The negativity and friction conspire to make the disabled person feel socially isolated and vulnerable – at the mercy of whether colleagues believe the additional support is justified.

Other initiatives that provide practical support for disabled people embarking on the career ladder include sheltered employment and vocational training schemes, where disabled individuals get support and assistance on the job. To some, these schemes represent paternalist attitudes towards disability and work – segregated employment being a relic of the Second World War where it was an urgent response to the increased numbers of disabled people trying to enter the labour market. But, for others, this style of employment holds value when it's used as a temporary stepping stone on the route to mainstream employment. For a modern-day vision of what sheltered employment can achieve, just look to the sustainable beauty company BECO, which boasts an 80 per cent blind or disabled workforce. With a stamp of approval from the likes of British *Vogue* and *Harper's Bazaar*, the company pride themselves on always seeing workability not disability. The brand is run by Clarity & Co., an East London charity and social enterprise founded in 1854 to provide employment to disabled people – its past supporters and patrons range from Charles Dickens to Queen Victoria. Nearly two centuries on, the mission remains the same. 'We only focus on what our staff "can" do, not what they "can't",' said Diane Cheung, Clarity & Co.'s marketing manager from their East London factory, 'so naturally everyone is encouraged to try out different roles in the organisation including fulfilment, customer services, in the lab, on the shop floor or in marketing and sales.' This positive spirit sweeps over their beauty factories, where the atmosphere is one of community, joy and the professional satisfaction of a job well done. I believe this shows the instant power and simplicity of social enterprise. In fact, if all UK households switched to using BECO soap in their bathrooms, it would create nearly 45,000 new jobs for people with disabilities, with every bottle sold creating one hour of employment. Closing the disability employment gap becomes as easy as washing your hands.

When BECO hire someone, they provide them with not just a salary, but new skills and confidence in the process. Workers are offered advice on their CVs, interview preparation and support when liaising with employment agencies. A job at BECO is merely a stepping stone on the route to mainstream employment. Their 'Steal Our Staff' campaign, for instance, saw photos of their much-loved employees adorning the product packaging, along with a mini-CV, encouraging others to snap them up and bring them into the labour market – from the Honey Blossom foaming handwash starring Shane, the soap miller, who is 'allergic to desk jobs', to the Wild Berries organic soap bar presenting Ozzie, assistant team leader, who has grand 'ambitions to work in a zoo'.

But in January 2020, an unexpected scandal rocked the company, after it tumbled into administration. News emerged that, following a takeover, disabled workers had allegedly been denied £200,000 in wages by the new owner. Despite accepting money from the government's job retention scheme during the Covid-19 pandemic, he had failed to pay staff. A fact that he denied. For BECO's loyal employees, the sudden loss of income in a period of huge economic instability was devastating. This was compounded by the fact that many were unable to claim other support, such as universal credit, because they had been formally receiving payslips. Twenty-seven employees were also forced to launch employment tribunal cases after they discovered unauthorised deductions in their wages, leading parliament to call for an urgent inquiry.

Social enterprises, like Clarity & Co., give life-changing opportunities to disabled workers who have been shut out of the labour market. But just as it has potential to rewire the system, it also accentuates the historic frailties and shortcomings. Larger organisations may be better placed to offer disability employment schemes, with the economic resources to mitigate any unforeseen friction or financial turmoil. Look at the success of the multi-billion-dollar beauty retailer, Sephora, which has a long history of employing people with disabilities in their distribution centres. The results, backed by years of data, are clear: a higher productivity rate, a lower absentee rate and extremely high levels of reliability. In the US, Sephora has even rolled out a recruiting programme targeting people with disabilities, who now represent 9 per cent of their workforce. This ethos should offer a blueprint for employers – a testament to the commercial value of championing disability representation in the mainstream jobs market.

However, incentives for disability representation in the workplace extend far beyond profit-making. When a disabled person is excluded from the workforce, employers miss out on the resilience and ingenuity that is prevalent among people with disabilities. All those problem-solving skills, accumulated while navigating day-to-day life, remain untapped. As Al Etmanski elucidates in *The Power of Disability*, 'People with disabilities wake up every day to a world not designed for them. They are constantly inventing themselves out of adverse circumstances. They are the original hackers.' I realise, for instance, that my disability has enabled me to become a more creative, empathetic thinker, expanding my mind through an innate capacity to analyse issues and seek solutions. The belief that disablement is synonymous with being underproductive should really be consigned to history.

More specifically, I believe employers are overlooking the value of empathy and compassion in the workplace – qualities that should lie at the core of all professions. I had this discussion with a friend recently, who is working as a junior doctor in paediatrics. Vocational careers like medicine and law, which are sewn into the very fabric of civic life, have their own inflexible standards of practice. These professional pipelines place you under constant appraisal and microscopic scrutiny. They demand physical compliance in the form of reaching set goalposts on a breakneck, immovable schedule. The feat of obtaining such a role therefore requires enormous tenacity and resolve. My friend describes to me how all trainees are required to undergo regular appraisals to prove their achievements to a panel who will decide whether each doctor's progress is satisfactory. But the necessary forms for these formal reviews contain some discriminatory assumptions – like a combined box to highlight whether there are concerns over a doctor's 'health or probity'. By lumping them together, it insinuates that health problems are automatically linked to issues of morality and decency. A sense that, by association, your integrity, openness and honesty is under suspicion which is incredibly stigmatising for people with disabilities.

However, this emphasis on immaculate health fails to account for the unique knowledge that my friend has acquired while being a patient. Her insights into what it's like staying in hospital enable her to form deeper connections with her patients, quickly build rapport and be more relatable – all of which ultimately improve clinical care. 'To fully understand our patients, we ideally need to have shared experience with them,' she says. 'It means I can be a better advocate for them. Having doctors of diverse backgrounds and abilities is crucial because it shows the next generation what is achievable despite adversity. An innate understanding of disability is also vital – it means that kind actions are intuitive rather than reactive.' She described a time when she treated a young woman in clinic who had a hearing impairment as a child, how they instantly bonded over their experiences of accessing healthcare during childhood. 'She felt I could empathise with her and so she fully opened up about her worries, finding me non-judgmental and understanding. Towards the end she got quite tearful, saying she felt inspired by what I'd achieved, that I had made her day.'

By erecting hurdles that make it harder for people with disabilities to join the workforce, organisations close themselves off from these unique skills. But perhaps we lose out on something even greater – a sense of care for ourselves, our jobs, and each other? The solutions I have outlined, from practical support to vocational training schemes, show how we can make reparations. Once we begin to nurture all the talents that lie outside of a 'tick-box' pro forma, disabled people will not be passed over, nor pulled away from their ideal careers.

My chance of having a conventional career is likely behind me. But I think I've found something more personal, more suited to me. It's taken me years to realise that in searching for a career, a purpose, I've been searching for myself. As a writer and disability activist, I still struggle to reconcile the fact that most of my professional identity has so far been inseparable from my disability, a facet of myself that I'm only beginning to comprehend. There is an element of risk in cultivating a career that is tied to your minority status. The pervasive fear of tokenism, a suspicion that you are being employed to fulfil a quota or role because of your perceived uniqueness, not your talent. It also requires an immense degree of courage and psychological endurance to be truly yourself. There is no room to hide – the luxury of making your disability unseen and escaping the stigmatising gaze is stripped from you. Work becomes an extension of all your uncertainties and existential concerns. It's exhausting, and hard to detach yourself from a place that is borne out of the darkest struggles.

In reality, the emotional burden is met with a big reward. As you turn yourself inside out, an enforced sense of discomfort pulsating through your core, something clicks. In the most intense moments of exposure lies an enhanced understanding of identity. The most fulfilling aspect of my work has been trying to reach out and capture it, to translate it into words. I now realise that I am incredibly fortunate to feel purposeful in my work, which I have built up, slowly and independently, from an open laptop. Interrogating the politics of disability, telling the most complex human truths and opening up space for others to share their experiences too, is personal and invigorating. It has given me something I never knew I wanted. A fire inside me, an unexpected passion and drive that many of my peers are yet to find. The objective of my work is to push society towards a place where disability is not a fringe subject, buried in the shadows, but a normal and accepted part of life where it no longer has to limit you. I don't exempt myself from that vision. Ultimately, I know my talents extend beyond this one aspect of myself. I am torn between not wanting disability to define me and the intoxicating appeal of making a positive social impact, which time and time again offers invitation for catharsis and self-discovery.

While I've been writing this – picking apart tiny fragments of myself, holding them up to the chinks of passing light for closer, sometimes painful, inspection – I'm beginning to realise that it has changed my life. At times it's imperceptible: my body unchanged, in the same way that my physical surroundings have remained constant, during a year of isolation imposed by a pandemic that still rages on. Yet, something is different. In the process of writing my story, fighting for justice and clawing a more inclusive future into being, I've rediscovered myself in these pages. From the precipices of rage to the surge and swell of empowerment, back down to those gleeful moments where I've laughed myself to the verge of exhaustion, I've felt completely alive. The perception of who I am, a new knowledge of the social conditions that have shaped it, is sharper. There are not many jobs you can say that about. I've long believed my career was afflicted by compromise and disruption in the sense that I was torn from the path I wanted to take – the path I was 'meant' to take. And yet, in being shut out from a world of opportunity and stripped of choice, in the embers of self-immolation, I might be finding everything I once sought. Writing this book, seeing what I've created, reasserting who I am, has told me – maybe this was it all along?

# Acknowledgements

Undeniably, this book would not be what it is without my elder sister, Sophie Jackson – her wisdom, support and encouragement lines every word. Since I began the writing process, she has given pep talks on demand and read over my early drafts, delivering her brutally honest verdicts – I was very grateful for that 'constructive' feedback, even when it wasn't always graciously received. Naturally, her role was also pivotal when it came to recollecting some of my more mortifying moments (refer to page 119). She delighted in the schadenfreude of it all, piling on more and more hilarious, wince-inducing details about my past self than was frankly necessary given the word count of each essay. But, when I faltered or gleaned the enormity of the task before me, it was her positivity – or those uncompromising words 'just get on with it' – that recharged me.

To my parents, Mark and Christine Jackson, I am endlessly grateful for their support, optimism and cosmic generosity. This book is not a product of the years writing it, but a lifetime of experience – joy, courage and collective resilience against struggle – that is contained in its pages. That is their handiwork.

To my friends and closest allies who have cheered me on from afar while I've been shielding, expressing utmost confidence and excitement at what I was creating despite having little to no evidence of its quality.

And, of course, an enormous thank you to my editor Elena Roberts at Cornerstone, who first saw potential in this book when it was a slip of a thing and an optimistic, yet spare, set of essay outlines. From day one, she has told me to trust myself and given me complete freedom to create the book I set out to write. I know that my writing has improved immeasurably under her unconditional encouragement and expert guidance.

To my team at Penguin Random House – Rose Waddilove, Laura O'Donnell and Hope Butler – for their heartfelt enthusiasm and belief in this book.

To my teachers Professor Ankhi Mukherjee and Dr Pelagia Goulimari who gave me the space and confidence to express ideas freely – to seek out new, imaginative ways of thinking.

And finally, to all the incredible voices contained within this book, who inspired me to see that another future is out there, waiting.

# Endnotes

## Introduction

'Disability is not . . .', Neil Marcus quoted in Annabelle Williams, 'Neil Marcus, Whose Art Illuminated Disability, Dies at 67', *New York Times,* 28 December 2021.

'two-thirds of the public . . .', according to Scope research, cited in Frances Ryan, 'Two-thirds of us are uncomfortable talking to disabled people: we need time, money and effort to get over the awkwardness', *New Statesman,* 8 May 2014, https://www.newstatesman.com/politics/2014/05/two-thirds-us-are-uncomfortable-talking-disabled-people-we-need-time-money-and-effort

'millennials are twice . . .', ibid.

'a fifth of . . .', ibid.

'I can walk . . .', Selma Blair's Instagram post quoted in 'Selma Blair Says She "Can Walk" After Photo Shows Sarah Michelle Gellar Pushing Her in a Wheelchair', *Closer Weekly,* 30 March 2019, https://www.closerweekly.com/posts/selma-blair-says-she-can-walk-after-photo-shows-her-in-a-wheelchair/

'Ability and disability . . .', Sara Hendren, *What Can a Body Do? How We Meet the Built World* (New York: Riverhead Books, 2020).

'common-sense nature of ableism . . .', Sami Schalk, 'Disability and Women's Writing' in T*he Cambridge Companion to Literature* *and Disability*, eds Clare Barker and Stuart Murray (Cambridge: University of Cambridge Press, 2018).

'Changing the story…', Rebecca Solnit, *Hope in the Dark: Untold Histories, Wild Possibilities* (Chicago: Haymarket Books 2016).

'twice as likely to be unemployed . . .', figures from the disability charity Scope, https://www.scope.org.uk/media/disability-facts-figures/

'living in food poverty . . .', report by the Equality and Human Rights Commission, 'Being Disabled In Britain', April 2017, https://www.equalityhumanrights.com/sites/default/files/being-disabled-in-britain.pdf

'experiencing domestic abuse…', report by SafeLives, 'Disabled Survivors Too: Disabled people and domestic abuse', March 2017, https://safelives.org.uk/sites/default/files/resources/Disabled_Survivors_Too_Report.pdf

*The Art of Recovery*

'Illness is the . . .', Susan Sontag, *Illness as Metaphor* and *AIDS and Its Metaphors* (London: Penguin Classics, 2009).

'The need to . . .', Cheryl Mattingly, *Healing Dramas and Clinical Plots: The Narrative Structure of Experience* (Cambridge: Cambridge University Press, 1998).

'I like the . . .', Lucia Berlin, *A Manual for Cleaning Women: Selected Stories* (UK: Picador, 2016).

'To become a . . .', Sinéad Gleeson, *Constellations: Reflections from Life* (UK: Picador, 2019).

'It is strictly . . .', Oliver Sacks, *A Leg to Stand On* (UK: Picador, 2012).

'overwhelming embarrassment', Gleeson, op. cit.

'a Golden Globe . . .', David Sedaris, 'Unbuttoned: On Wills, Words, And Wearing My Father's Shirt', *New Yorker*, 2 March 2020.

'Under the spell . . .', Martin Armstrong, *Laughing* (London: Jarrolds Publishers London Ltd, 1958).

'In one study . . .', study cited in May Mccreaddie and Sally Wiggins, 'The purpose and function of humour in health, health care and nursing: A narrative review', *Journal of Advanced Nursing*, April 2008.

'In everything . . .', Immanuel Kant, *Critique of Judgement* (UK: Oxford University Press, 2009).

'a minimalist body', @jil_slander on Twitter, 20 December 2020.

'the sharpest wits . . .', Sophie Kemp, 'This Writer Has No Feet, Loves Shoes, and Is the Funniest Person on Twitter', *Vogue.com*, 10 December 2019.

'The fact that . . .', @jil_slander on Twitter, 15 December 2020.

"It can be . . .', Willem Helf, quoted in Kemp, op. cit.

'i [*sic*] spent . . .', Samantha Irby, 'potty mouth', bitchesgottaeat. blogspot.com, www.blogger.com/blogin.g?blogspotURL= https://bitchesgottaeat.blogspot.com/2010/07/potty-mouth. html&type=blog.

'People find their . . .', Samantha Irby quoted in Rima Parikh, 'Finding Humor When "Shit Is So Terrible": A Conversation With Samantha Irby', *The Nation*, 1/8 June 2020.

'It was going . . .', Adam Kay quoted in Hannah Beckerman, 'Adam Kay: "I thought I was the only doctor who ever cried in the toilet"', *Observer*, 5 October 2019.

'cat piss', Adam Kay, *This is Going to Hurt* (UK: Picador, 2017).

'Illness is an . . .', Gleeson, op. cit.

'No one could . . .', 'The community completely . . .', from an email exchange with Mimi Butlin.

'Living with uncertainty . . .', from an email exchange with Charlotte Amor.

'Self-optimisation challenges . . .', Pandora Sykes, *How Do We Know We Are Doing It Right?* (UK: Penguin Random House, 2020).

'Back into the . . .', Michele Lent Hirsch, *Invisible: How Young Women with Serious Health Issues Navigate Work, Relationships and the Pressure to Seem Just Fine* (Boston: Beacon Press, 2018).

'What if our . . .', Berlin, op. cit.

'We want people . . .', Hirsch, op. cit.

'Life isn't always . . .', Bella Hadid quoted in 'Bella Hadid Shares Photos of Her Life with Lyme Disease: "Finding Time for My IVs"', *People*, 27 February 2021.

'She's spoiled . . .', comments under @bellahadid on Instagram, 26 February 2021.

'It's not something . . .', Selena Gomez quoted in Katherine Langford, 'Selena Gomez's Wild Ride', *Harper's Bazaar*, 7 February 2018.

'lurid', 'punitive', Sontag, op. cit.

'tear[ing] away at . . .', Olivia Laing, *Everybody: A Book About Freedom* (UK: Picador, 2022).

'The metaphors and . . .', Sontag, op. cit.

'seeking attention . . .', Kimhēkim quoted in Kara Nesvig, 'Kimhēkim Is Being Called Out on Instagram for Using IV Bags as an Accessory', *Teen Vogue*, 26 September 2019.

'the surreal life', coverline of *Interview*, December 2015.

'narrative prosthesis', David T. Mitchell and Sharon L. Snyder, *Narrative Prosthesis: Disability and the Dependencies of Discourse* (USA: The University of Michigan Press, 2000).

'crippled America', title of Donald Trump's book, *Crippled America: How to Make America Great Again* (New York: Simon & Schuster, 2015).

'invites you to . . .', Rebecca Solnit, *The Faraway Nearby* (UK: Viking Books, 2013).

### Love, Regardless

'punitive vision', 'date in our twenties . . .', Ayisha Malik quoted in Natasha Lunn, *Conversations on Love* (UK: Penguin Books, 2021).

'For some disabled . . .', Tom Shakespeare, Kath Gillespie-Sells, Dominic Davies, *The Sexual Politics of Disability* (London: Bloomsbury Publishing, 1997).

'It seemed to . . .', Lena Dunham, 'How Lena Dunham Found Her Happily Ever After', *Vogue*, 10 December 2021.

'took time to . . .', Barbara D. Webster, *All of a Piece: A Life with Multiple Sclerosis* (London: Johns Hopkins University Press, 1989).

'It's like we've . . .', the character Rob speaking in 'At the Hospital, an Interlude of Clarity', *Modern Love*, Series 1, Episode 5 (United States: Amazon Studios, 2019).

'Regretfully', Matchmakers Dating quoted in Valentine Low, 'Matchmakers dating service advised wheelchair user not to join', *The Times*, 10 February 2021.

'32 per cent of . . .', according to 'The Future of Dating' report by Imperial College Business School and eHarmony, 2019.

'It weeds out . . .', Sophie Bradbury-Cox interviewed in Lottie Jackson, 'What It's Really Like to Be on the Dating Scene with a Disability', *Sunday Times*, 4 July 2021.

'The right person . . .', Jessica Kellgren-Fozard interviewed in ibid.

'Unsurprisingly, a couple . . .', Meelina Isayas interviewed in ibid.

'*Es un supermarcado . . .*', 'Recién Llegada', *4 Feet High*, Series 1, Episode 1, directed by Maria Belen Poncio (United States: Arte France, 2021).

'fantastic', 'flying all over . . .', Dr Danielle Sheypuk, 'Every Body: Glamour, Dateability, Sexuality and Disability', TEDxBarnard-College, 19 May 2015.

'21 per cent of family . . .', according to data cited by the charity Gingerbread, www.gingerbread.org.uk/information/disability/disabled-single-parents/.

'dateable self-esteem', 'So what?', from an email exchange with Dr Danielle Sheypuk.

'To be desired . . .', John Berger, edited by Tom Overton, *Portraits: John Berger on Artists* (London: Verso Books, 2021).

'a freak', 'a giant', 'King Kong', Damon Beesley, Iain Morris, *The Inbetweeners: The Complete Scripts with Added Extras* (London: Penguin Random House, 2012).

'None of this . . .', Sirin Kale, '"I was worried Lindsay, Paris or Britney would die": why the 00s were so toxic for women', *Guardian*, 6 March 2021.

'Pity or fear . . .', Robert McRuer and Anna Mollow (eds), *Sex and Disability* (USA: Duke University Press, 2012).

'I went to . . .', Nima Misra interviewed in Hannah Witton's podcast, *Doing It!*, Disability, Sex, Relationships & Dating: Roundtable Discussion, 3 October 2018.

'the source of . . .', 'easier to talk . . .', Anne Finger, 'Forbidden Fruit: Why Shouldn't Disabled People Have Sex or Become Parents?', *New Internationalist*, Issue 233, 5 July 1992.

'The real golden . . .', Goop blog post quoted in Christie D'Zurilla, 'Gwyneth Paltrow touts vaginal steaming as "an energetic release"', *Los Angeles Times*, 28 January 2015.

'immediate yen for . . .', 'a wolf's penis . . .', Angus McLaren, *Impotence: A Cultural History* (United States: University of Chicago Press, 2007), citing Albert the Great; James J. Scanlon, M.D. (trans.), *Man and the Beasts: De Animalibus* (Books 22–26), *Medieval & Renaissance Texts & Studies*, Vol. 47, Book 2.

'almost always', 'A sex life . . .', Tobin Siebers, 'Sexual Culture for Disabled People' in McRuer and Mollow, op. cit.

'If you can't . . .', Lotte Berk quoted in Danielle Friedman, 'The Secret Sexual History of the Barre Workout', *The Cut*, 19 January 2018.

'marginalisation or marvelling', McRuer and Mollow, op. cit.

'Sexuality is the . . .', Ellen Stohl quoted in '*Playboy* interview: Hugh Hefner and Playmate Ellen Stohl Talk with Chet Cooper', *Ability Magazine*, 1995.

'bad taste', 'cripple', *Playboy* editorial team quoted in Bob Greene, 'An Uncomfortable Issue for Playboy', *Chicago Tribune*, 17 May 1987.

'real scuzz exploitation', Barbara Nellis quoted in ibid.

'just a sex object', 'I was a . . .', Stohl quoted in *Playboy*, July 1987.

'I wasn't taking . . .', Stohl quoted in *Ability Magazine*, op. cit.

'Disabled Model Defies . . .', *New York Times,* 8 June 1987.

'society's emphasis on . . .', Irving Zola quoted in Lynn Smith, 'The Spirit of Ellen Stohl : Paralysis Doesn't Impair Her Fight for Human, Sexual Rights of Disabled – or Keep Her From Posing for *Playboy* Layout', *Los Angeles Times*, 17 March 1988.

'exploitative kinky type . . .', Hugh Hefner quoted in *Ability Magazine*, op. cit.

'a lily-livered hound . . .', D. H. Lawrence, *Lady Chatterley's Lover* and *A Propos of 'Lady Chatterley's Lover'* (UK: Cambridge University Press, 2002).

'no one is . . .', 'Consider the supreme . . .', Amia Srinivasan, 'Does Anyone Have the Right to Sex?', *London Review of Books*, Vol. 40, No. 6, 22 March 2018.

'Is he cute?', 'I could tell . . .', M. Leona Godin, 'After Losing My Sight, Struggling to Be Seen', *New York Times*, 17 January 2020.

'until one lad . . .', Damien Rose, 'Love at no sight', *BBC Magazine*, 27 May 2009.

'to think that . . .', Srinivasan, op. cit.

'I might have . . .', Tracey Emin interviewed in Mike Wade, 'Tracey Emin: I feel more alive than ever before', *The Times*, 28 May 2022.

'to think expansively . . .', Shakespeare, Gillespie-Sells, Davies, op. cit.

'You wanna know . . .', the character Isaac in *Sex Education*, Series 3, Episode 4 (United Kingdom: Eleven, 2021).

'continuum of sexual practices' . . . Tom Shakespeare, Kath Gillespie-Sells, Dominic Davies, *The Sexual Politics of Disability* (London: Bloomsbury Publishing, 1997).

'What makes that . . .', George Robinson interviewed in Alex Taylor, '*Sex Education*: Isaac actor George Robinson gets intimate about disability', *BBC News*, 21 September 2021.

'more than doubled . . .', according to the UK government's Rape Review, March 2021.

'39 per cent of all . . .', according to data shared by US Department of Health & Human Services, www.cdc.gov/violencepre vention/sexualviolence/svandipv.html.

'not going to court', Disabled Survivors Unite quoted in Charlotte Bateman, 'Sexual violence allegations brought by disabled women "not going to court", campaign group says', *Sky News*, 1 August 2021.

'a different power . . .', Simi Linton, *My Body Politic* (Michigan: University of Michigan Press, 2007).

'national (or international) . . .', quoted in Alison Kafer, 'Desire and Disgust: My Ambivalent Adventures in Devoteeism', in McRuer and Mollow, op. cit.

'Have you always . . .', Venessa Parekh, 'Hot Wheels: The World of Wheelchair Fetishists and Disability Devotees', *VICE*, 18 March 2016.

'a pathological trait . . .', 'How sad that . . . ', Kafer in McRuer and Mollow, op. cit.

'love ethic', 'we see our . . .', bell hooks, *All About Love: New Visions* (New York: Harper Collins, 2000).


*True North*

'I'd mistaken the gas . . .', Margaret Atwood, 'Growing Pains: Driving Lessons', *New Yorker*, 12 & 19 July 2021.

'everything seems accidentally . . .', Virginia Woolf, 'Street Haunting: A London Adventure', 1930, www.bl.uk/collection-items/street-haunting-an-essay-by-virginia-woolf.

'half the distance . . .', according to 2020 statistics from the Department for Transport, 'Transport: Disability and Accessibility Statistics', assets.publishing.service.gov.uk/government/uploads/system/uploads/attachment_data/file/1019477/transport-disability-and-accessibility-statistics-england-2020.pdf.

'always and everywhere . . .', Doreen Massey, 'Thinking radical democracy spatially', *Environment and Planning, Society and Space*, Vol. 13, Issue 3, June 1995.

'Closures', Sara Hendren, *What Can a Body Do? How We Meet the Built World* (New York: Riverhead, 2020).

'They call us . . .', protest chant quoted in Damon Rose, 'The wheelchair warriors: Their rebellious protests to change the law', *BBC News*, www.bbc.co.uk/news/extra/8rvpt6bclh/wheelchair-warriors-disability-discrimination-act.

'To boldly go . . .', DAN slogan quoted in George McKay, *DiY Culture: Party and Protest in Nineties' Britain* (London: Verso, 1998).

'Bodies beyond those . . .', Raquel Velho, '"They're changing the network just by being there": Reconsidering infrastructures through the frame of disability studies', *Disability Studies Quarterly*, Spring 2021.

'Who is the world . . .', Hendren, op. cit.

'I realised then . . .', Barbara Lisicki quoted in Rose, op. cit.

'Some people thought . . .', Barbara Lisicki speaking on the BBC podcast *Ouch Talk Show*, episode 125, November 2015.

'without unreasonable difficulty', according to The Equality Act 2010 legislation, www.legislation.gov.uk/ukpga/2010/15/contents.

'I was left . . .', Alex Taylor, 'I was stranded on a train in a wheelchair', *BBC News*, 1 May 2018.

'too difficult', @ruthmadeley, on Instagram, 14 July 2021.

'regularly', Jack Hunter-Spivey quoted in 'Jack Hunter-Spivey: Paralympian in "think twice" plea to taxi drivers', *BBC News*, 17 September 2021.

'You see I . . .', Lucy Armstrong, 'Life and Anxieties as a Deaf Woman in the Wake of Sarah Everard's Murder', *The Unwritten*, 13 March 2021.

'a country of . . .', Molly McCully Brown, *Places I've Taken My Body: Essays* (New York: Persea Books, 2021).

'over half of . . .', according to research by Kantar TNS and Visit Britain, May 2018, www.visitbritain.org/sites/default/files/vb-corporate/Documents-Library/documents/England-documents/april_2018_accessibility_non_participation_reportv3.pdf.

'takes five trips . . .', according to a survey by AARP Travel, www.aarp.org/research/topics/life/info-2018/2019-travel-trends.html.

'object in the . . .', Joe Hardy, 'My passport application was rejected because of my wheelchair', *Metro*, 16 March 2022.

'eye-opening', Emilie Pine, *Notes to Self: Essays* (Dublin: Tramp Press, 2018).

'a 2021 study . . .', '60 per cent . . .', a survey by AbleMove, disabilityhorizons.com/2021/03/flying-as-a-wheelchair-user-its-time-for-airlines-to-listen-and-make-changes/.

'tedious', 'BBC's Frank Gardner criticises airline over disability access', *BBC News*, 9 January 2017.

'balance between worldly . . .' Elizabeth Gilbert, *Eat, Pray, Love: One Woman's Search for Everything* (London: Bloomsbury, 2007).

'chained', 'The great liberation . . .', Friedrich Nietzsche, *Human, All Too Human: A Book for Free Spirits* (Chicago: Charles H. Kerr & Company, 1908).

'Imagine', Hilton Als, *White Girls* (London: Penguin, 2018).

'There is so . . .', Jean-Dominique Bauby, *The Diving-Bell and the Butterfly* (London: HarperCollins Publishers, 2008).

## Role Call

'Yesterday I overheard . . .', @gendrfuck on Twitter, 17 December 2020.

'I love little . . .', @ProfLCB on Twitter, 17 December 2020.

'one-fifth of . . .', Scope research cited in Frances Ryan, 'Two-thirds of us are uncomfortable talking to disabled people: we need time, money and effort to get over the awkwardness', *New Statesman*, 8 May 2014.

'creators', 'inventors', 'innovators', Jean-Claude Bringuier, *Conversations with Jean Piaget* (Chicago: The University of Chicago Press, 1980).

'concrete development period', Jean Piaget, *The Psychology of Intelligence*, (UK: Routledge, 2001).

'The main reason . . .', Tom Shakespeare, *Disability: The Basics* (London: Routledge, 2017).

'half of people . . .', a 2003 government research project cited in Shakespeare, op. cit.

'45 per cent . . .', according to research by Samsung UK, 2022, https://news.samsung.com/uk/new-research-reveals-nearly-half-of-the-nation-arent-comfortable-talking-about-disabilities-in-the-workplace

'an emotional wallop', Jeannette Catsoulis, 'Review: In the Oscar-Nominated Live Action Shorts, Four Dramas and a Comedy', *New York Times*, 7 February 2018.

'78 per cent', according to the Consortium for Research into Deaf Education report in 2015, a survey on educational provision for deaf children in England, www.ndcs.org.uk/media/6500/cride-2015-england-report-final.pdf.

'National Deaf Children's . . .', according to analysis by National Deaf Children's Society, 9 August 2021, www.ndcs. org.uk/about-us/news-and-media/latest-news/deaf-pupils-achieve-an-entire-gcse-grade-less-for-sixth-year-running/.

'The Anti-Bullying Alliance . . .', according to data compiled by the Anti-Bullying Alliance, anti-bullyingalliance.org.uk/tools-information/all-about-bullying/at-risk-groups/sen-disability/do-children-send-experience-more.

'I feel a . . .', *Amber and Me*, directed by Ian Davies (UK: Amber Doc Films, 2020).

'able to pinpoint . . .', Nancy Eisenberg, *The Caring Child* (London: Harvard University Press, 1992).

'As educators . . .', Dayniah Manderson speaking on the *Disability Visibility Podcast*, Episode 64: 'Disabled Teachers'.

"After a while . . .' Alysha Allen quoted in Yana Trup, 'Deaf Teacher from Brimsdown Primary School Uses Sign Language in Classroom', *Enfield Independent*, 7 January 2020.

'0.5 per cent . . .', according to the government's 2016 census cited in 'Disabled Teachers "Sidelined" and Told "Get On With It"', *TES Magazine*, 29 January 2021.

'We need to . . .', Melissa Blake, 'A Message to TikTok Parents Who Use My Face to Make Their Kids Cry', *Refinery29*, 26 August 2020.

'The United Nations . . .', 'Concluding observations on the initial report of the United Kingdom of Great Britain and Northern

Ireland', United Nations Committee on the Rights of Persons with Disabilities, 3 October 2017.

'Whether or not . . .', Colin Barnes, *Disabled People in Britain and Discrimination: A Case for Anti-discrimination Legislation* (London: C. Hurst & Co, 1992).

'shifts the "problem" . . .', Katherine Runswick-Cole and Nick Hodge, 'Needs Or Rights? A Challenge to the Discourse of Special Education', *British Journal of Special Education*, Vol. 36, Issue 4, 2009.

'My younger self . . .', Michelle Daley, 'Why We Must Discuss the Damage of Segregated Education and the Erasure of "Race" and Intersectional Identity When Addressing "Disability" Inequality', *The Alliance for Inclusive Education Blog*, 29 October 2020.

'Young people need . . .', 'They didn't think . . .', Michelle Daley speaking in '"How Was School?" Interviews with Disabled People about their experience of Education over the last 100 years', *The Alliance for Inclusive Education*, sounds.bl.uk/related-content/TRANSCRIPTS/021T-C1559X0023XX-0000A0.pdf

'It was basically . . .', Zara Todd speaking in '"How Was School?"', op. cit.

'hated', 'One minute . . .', Damian quoted in Liz Pellicano et al., 'My Life at School: Understanding the experiences of children and young people with special educational needs in residential special schools', *Children's Commissioner for England*, December 2014.

'When I was . . .', Jonathan Bryan quoted in Richard Rieser, '"Like a bird released from a cage, I am free to fly in the open fields": An Interview with Jonathan Bryan', *Inclusion Now*, Spring 2021.

'weakens', 'stifles', according to the Centre for Studies on Inclusive Education in 'Reasons against segregated schooling', www.csie.org.uk/resources/reasons-against-seg-04.pdf.

'65 per cent of …', Freddie Whittaker, 'Schools Failing in Legal Duty to Implement "Accessibility Plans"', *Schools Week*, 23 January 2020.

'entirely segregated', 'The Salamanca Statement and Framework for Action on Special Needs Education', UNESCO, 1994.

'I had entered …', Mary Baker quoted in Steve Humphries and Pamela Gordon, *Out of Sight: The Experience of Disability, 1900–1950* (UK: Northcote House Publishers Ltd, 1992).

'A third of …', according to data by UNESCO's Global Education Monitoring, en.unesco.org/gem-report/sites/default/files/GAW2014-Facts-Figures-gmr_0.pdf.

'nine out of ten', according to UNICEF data cited by the Global Partnership for Education, www.globalpartnership.org/blog/children-disabilities-face-longest-road-education.

'The school authorities …', a mother quoted in Anisha Reddy, 'How Children With Special Needs Are Being Left Out of Mainstream Education in India', *The Wire*, 15 July 2022.

'insidious, shadow education …', 'You don't need …', Rachel Aviv, 'The Forgotten Ones', *New Yorker,* 26 March, 2018.

'underpinned by eugenics …', Micha Frazer-Carroll, '"Black kids were written off": the scandal of the children sent to "dustbin schools"', *Guardian*, 19 May 2021.

'That school was …', Noel Gordon interviewed for *Subnormal: A British Scandal,* directed by Lyttanya Shannon. (UK: BBC, 2021).

'Once you're in . . .', 'Education', *Small Axe*, Series 1, directed by Steve McQueen (UK: BBC, 2021).

'When you're in . . .', Steve McQueen interviewed in 'Steve McQueen: We want meaningful change so let's get on with it', *Inclusion Now*, summer 2021.

'58 per cent . . .', according to the Timpson Review of School Exclusion, a report by the Secretary of State for Education, May 2019.

'a devaluation or . . .', Philippe Rochat, 'Five levels of self-awareness as they unfold early in life', *Consciousness and Cognition*, Vol. 12, Issue 4, December 2003.

'a child watching . . .', Flannery O'Connor, 'Good Country People' in *Flannery O'Connor: Complete Stories* (USA: Faber & Faber, 1971).

'clinical gaze', Michel Foucault, *The Birth of the Clinic: An Archaeology of Medical Perception*, translated by A. M. Sheridan (UK: Routledge Classics, 2003).

'We attempt . . .', Jenny Morris, *Pride Against Prejudice: Transforming Attitudes to Disability* (London: The Women's Press Ltd, 1991).

'blinding flash', Judith Heumann with Kristen Joiner, *Being Heumann: An Unrepentant Memoir of a Disability Rights Activist* (London: Penguin Random House, 2021).

'Just as no . . .', Morris, op. cit.

### Varsity Dream

'15 per cent more . . .', according to a report by Stella Chatzitheochari and Lucinda Platt, 'Childhood Disability & Educational Attainment: The Impact of Parental Expectations and Bullying',

April 2018, warwick.ac.uk/fac/soc/impact/policybriefings/
childhood_disability_and_education_chatzitheochari_policy_
briefing_april_2018.pdf.

'when researchers surveyed. . .', Stella Chatzitheochari and
Lucinda Platt, 'Disability Differentials In Educational Attain-
ment In England: Primary And Secondary Effects', *The British
Journal of Sociology*, Vol. 70, Issue 3, April 2018.

'she tweeted a photograph . . .', @SarahMarieDS on Twitter, 10
February 2020.

'I turned and . . .', Da Silva quoted in Greg Barradale, 'Wheel-
chair-using Student Forced to Sit in Stairwells During Lectures',
*The Tab*, February 2020.

'no improvement', Da Silva quoted in '"No Improvement" in
Disabled Access at University, Hull Student Says', *BBC News*,
5 March 2020.

'I was reassured . . .', from an email exchange with Meelina
Isayas.

'I just couldn't . . .', from an email exchange with Rachel Townson.

'It was really . . .', from an email exchange with Lizzie Huxley-Jones.

'It felt overwhelming . . .', Haben Girma speaking on *The BBC
Outlook Podcast*, 'Harvard Law School's First Deafblind Graduate', 12 December 2019.

'concerning', 'It is time . . .', Chris Millward quoted in Eleanor
Busby, 'Disabled Students Dropping Out Amid "Inadequate"
Support, Charities and Unions Warn', *Independent*, 18 October
2019.

'67 per cent of disabled . . .', according to a UCL Disabled

Students' Network report, 'Disability Discrimination Faced by UCL Students & Recommended Measures', January 2020.

'I and many . . .', @Rose_nug on Twitter, 20 May 2020.

'over half of . . .', according to a 2022 report by Disabled Students UK, 'Going Back Is Not a Choice', disabledstudents. co.uk/wp-content/uploads/2022/03/Going-Back-is-Not-a-Choice-Small-Print.pdf.

'left behind', 'alienated', 'forgotten', ibid.

## Fashion-able

'Women often believe . . .', Zadie Smith, *Swing Time* (UK: Penguin Books, 2016).

'vain trifles', Virginia Woolf, *Orlando* (UK: Oxford University Press, 2014).

'breaks the rules . . .', Rosemarie Garland-Thomson, *Staring: How We Look* (New York: Oxford University Press, 2009).

'magic', 'I whip out . . .', 'My final form . . .', Lynn Manning, 'The Magic Wand', *The International Journal of Inclusive Education*, Vol. 9, No. 7, 1 November 2009. Reprinted by permission of the publisher, Taylor and Francis http://www.tandfonline.com

'It's not that . . .', Garland-Thomson, op. cit.

'flawless beauty', 'ugliness', Naomi Wolf, *The Beauty Myth: How Images of Beauty Are Used Against Women* (London: Vintage Books, 2013).

'It would benefit . . .', *New York Times* article quoted in ibid.

'jabs of interest', Jennifer Egan, *Look at Me* (UK: Corsair, 2011).

'permanently deformed', Evangelista quoted in Jason Sheeler, 'Linda Evangelista Shares First Photos of Her Body Since Fat-Freezing Nightmare: "I'm Done Hiding"', *People*, 16 February 2022.

'Since the Middle . . .', Pierpaolo Piccioli quoted in Anders Christian Madsen, '"I Want to Embrace Different Proportions": Pierpaolo Piccioli's Body Diverse Valentino SS22 Haute Couture Show', *Vogue.co.uk*, 26 January 2022.

'big-tent beauty', Robin Givhan, 'The Idea Of Beauty Is Always Shifting. Today, It's More Inclusive Than Ever', *National Geographic*, 7 January 2020.

'only 0.06% . . .', according to survey by Lloyds Banking Group, cited Omar Oakes, 'Less Than 20% of UK Ads Feature Minorities, Says Lloyds Bank Survey', *Campaign*, 6 December 2016.

'the clubbiest realms . . .', Givhan, op. cit.

'Disabled difference . . .', Professor Lennard Davis paraphrased in Stuart Murray, 'The Ambiguities of Inclusion' in *The Cambridge Companion to Literature and Disability*, eds Clare Barker and Stuart Murray (Cambridge: University of Cambridge Press, 2018).

'diseased, maimed . . .', 'unsightly or . . .', Susan M. Schweik, *The Ugly Laws: Disability in Public* (New York: NYU Press, 2009).

There's nothing that . . .', Philip Davidoff quoted in Liam Berkowitz, 'Abercrombie Sued by Former Employee', *ABC News,* 24 June 2009.

'It was the . . .', Riam Dean quoted in Helen Pidd, 'Disabled student sues Abercrombie & Fitch for discrimination', *Guardian*, 24 June 2009.

'so frightened of . . .', parent quoted in Emine Saner, 'TV presenter Cerrie Burnell: "I don't care if you are offended"', *Guardian*, 21 February 2011.

'I'm a mother . . .', Cerrie Burnell speaking in *Silenced: The Hidden Story of Disability in Britain,* BBC Two, 21 March 2021.

'renown for empowering . . .', from fashionscout.com.

'What is that?', 'No, move on', quoted in Simon Murphy, 'Move On – We Don't Do Disabled, Model Hopeful Was Told', *The Times*, 19 June 2021.

'66 per cent of disabled . . .', according to online interviews conducted by the polling company Opinium carried out in August 2016.

'the default assumption . . .', Jia Tolentino, *Trick Mirror: Reflections on Self-delusion* (London: Fourth Estate, 2019).

'a world without . . .', Lottie Jackson, 'Ciascuno Ha La Sua', *Vogue Italia*, November 2020.

'Before I knew . . .' from an email exchange with Aimee Mullins.

'In a world . . .', September 1998 issue of *Dazed & Confused*, guest edited by Alexander McQueen.

'a powerful symbolic . . .', 'a major force . . .', Leslie W. Rabine, 'A Woman's Two Bodies: Fashion Magazines, Consumerism, and Feminism', in *On Fashion*, eds Shari Benstock and Suzanne Ferriss (New Jersey: Rutgers University Press, 1994).

'one of the last bastions . . .', Cayte Williams, 'Fashion breaks the last taboo', *Independent*, 28 August 1998.

'You know, you're . . .' from an email exchange with Aimee Mullins.

'silicone gel', Audre Lorde, *The Cancer Journals: Audre Lorde* (UK: Penguin Classics, 2020).

'stopped you in . . .', Janet Froelich quoted in Pia Peterson, 'The Times Magazine Cover That Beamed a Light on a Movement', *New York Times*, 15 August 2018.

'I am not . . .', Lorde, op. cit.

'a new and . . .', Oliver Rousteing, '"The Flames Completely Engulfed Me": Olivier Rousteing Reflects on the Horrific Accident That Changed His Life Forever', *Vogue*, March 2022.

'Disabled bodies . . .', Tobin Siebers, *Disability Theory* (USA: University of Michigan Press, 2008).

'three in four . . .', according to research by the charity Purple, wearepurple.org.uk/understanding-the-purple-pound-market/.

'I've spent my . . .', Sinéad Burke, 'Designing for Disability', #BoFVOICES 2017, YouTube, 18 December 2017.

'At sixteen years . . .', Matthew Walzer quoted in Sean Fleming, 'Nike's hands-free shoe is a step forward for inclusive clothing', *World Economic Forum*, 10 February 2021.

'According to Stephanie . . .', Brent Crane, 'Adaptive Fashion on the Red Carpet', *New Yorker*, 27 May 2019.

'For the longest . . .', Jillian Mercado quoted in Keah Brown, 'Disabled People Love Clothes Too', *New York Times*, 26 July 2020.

## A Virtual Reality

'exactly the same . . .', Marc Benioff quoted in Göran Wågström, 'Is Social Media Addiction Worse Than Cigarettes?', *Forbes*, 21 November 2018.

'turns us into . . .', Nicholas Carr, *The Shallows: What the Internet Is Doing to Our Brains* (London: Atlantic Books, 2010).

'depressive hedonia', Mark Fisher, *Capitalist Realism: Is There No Alternative?* (UK: Zero Books, 2009).

'the central organ . . .', 'frayed neurons', Jia Tolentino, *Trick Mirror: Reflections on Self-delusion* (London: Fourth Estate, 2019).

'The cross-sectional study . . .', 'they are never . . .', De Nardi L, et al., 'Adolescents with chronic disease and social media: a cross-sectional study', *Archives of Disease in Childhood*, August 2020.

'like an astonishingly . . .', Tolentino, op. cit.

'the future of . . .', 'a consolation prize . . .', Leslie Jamison, *Make It Scream, Make It Burn* (London: Granta, 2019).

'The virtual isn't . . .', Donna Haraway interviewed by Nicholas Gane, 'When We Have Never Been Human, What Is to Be Done? Interview with Donna Haraway', *Theory, Culture & Society*, December 2006.

'In 2018, a documentary . . .' *Our Digital Selves: My Avatar Is Me!,* directed by Bernhard Drax (United States: Draxtor, 2018).

'narcissism epidemic', Jean Twenge, *The Narcissism Epidemic: Living in the Age of Entitlement* (USA: Atria Books, 2009).

'confining', Jia Tolentino, *Trick Mirror: Reflections on Self-delusion* (London: Fourth Estate, 2019).

'Virtual reality is . . .', Josh Glancy, 'Reality+ by David J Chalmers review – how we could all soon be living in the Matrix', *Sunday Times*, 16 January 2022.

'a novelty or a fetish', David J. Chalmers, *Reality+: Virtual Worlds and the Problems of Philosophy* (UK: Penguin Books, 2022).

'In studies, individuals . . .', Patricia Mesa-Gresa, et al., 'Effectiveness of Virtual Reality for Children and Adolescents with Autism Spectrum Disorder: An Evidence-Based Systematic Review', *Sensors*, August 2018.

'As Donna J. Haraway proselytised . . .', 'A Cyborg Manifesto: Science, Technology, And Socialist-Feminism in the Late Twentieth Century', *Socialist Review*, 1985.

'group of schoolgirls . . .', Charles Moloney, 'Sign language app wins St Paul's Girls' schoolgirls £20k', *The Times*, 16 July 2021.

'Be My Eyes . . .', www.bemyeyes.com.

'In Homer's *Iliad* . . .', Homer, *The Iliad* (UK: Penguin Classics, 1992).

'bicycle for the mind', Steve Jobs interviewed for *Memory and Imagination: New Pathways to the Library of Congress*, directed by Julian Krainin, Michael R. Lawrence (1990).

'over 50 million . . .' according to the WebAIM Million 2022 report, webaim.org/projects/million/.

*The Other Glass Ceiling*

'Everyone has the . . .', The Universal Declaration of Human Rights, www.un.org/en/udhrbook/pdf/udhr_booklet_en_web.pdf.

'4.4 million are in work . . .', Scope employment data, www.scope.org.uk/media/disability-facts-figures/.

'inclusive teams are . . .', according to research by Deloitte, www2.deloitte.com/content/dam/Deloitte/au/Documents/human-capital/deloitte-au-hc-diversity-inclusion-soup-0513.pdf.

'costs of £583 . . .', according to research by the charity Scope in 2019, www.scope.org.uk/campaigns/extra-costs/.

'Joseph Rowntree research . . .', according to the Joseph Rowntree report 'Poverty 2019/2020', available at www.jrf.org.uk.

'£2.10 less an hour . . .' according to the Trades Union Congress report 'Disability pay and employment gaps 2020', www.tuc.org.uk/research-analysis/reports/disability-pay-and-employment-gaps-2020.

"FTSE 100 companies . . .', according to a 2021 report from Tortoise Media and The Valuable 500, www.tortoisemedia.com/disability100-report/.

'two in five people . . .', according to The Work Foundation 2015 report, available at www.bl.uk.

'We've created this . . .', Oren Cass quoted in Derek Thompson, 'Workism Is Making Americans Miserable', *The Atlantic*, 24 February 2019.

'The underlying question . . .', Dustin Galer, 'Disabled Capitalists: Exploring the Intersections of Disability and Identity Formation in the World of Work', *Disability Studies Quarterly*, Vol. 32, No. 3, 2012.

'62 per cent . . .', according to research by Deloitte, www2.deloitte.com/content/dam/Deloitte/us/Documents/about-deloitte/us-about-deloitte-uncovering-talent-a-new-model-of-inclusion.pdf.

'almost one in five . . .', according to a report by the charity Leonard Cheshire, 'Reimagining the workplace: disability and inclusive employment', www.leonardcheshire.org/sites/default/files/2020–02/reimagining-the-workplace-disability-inclusive-employment.pdf.

'Financial Times article . . .', Isabelle Jani-Friend, 'Discrimination at work: 'I was shocked when the interviewer ghosted me'', *Financial Times*, 21 July 2021.

'The perception among . . .', James Taylor quoted in Liam Kelly, 'How CEO Steve Ingham is helping to break down the disability barriers', *Sunday Times*, 3 January 2021.

'haven't spent the . . .', Roland Behm quoted in Sheridan Wall and Hilke Schellmann, 'Disability rights advocates are worried about discrimination in AI hiring tools', *MIT Technology Review*, 21 July 2021.

'culture of speed', John Tomlinson, *The Culture of Speed: The Coming of Immediacy* (London: SAGE Publications Ltd, 2007).

'We have never . . .', Robert Hassan, *Empires of Speed: Time and the Acceleration of Politics and Society* (Netherlands: Brill, 2009).

'Research by Charles Duhigg . . .', Charles Duhigg, 'America's Professional Elite: Wealthy, Successful and Miserable', *New York Times*, 21 February 2019.

'A 24/7 world . . .', Jonathan Crary, *24/7: Late Capitalism and the Ends of Sleep* (London: Verso, 2013).

'extract us from . . .', Ellen Samuels, 'Six Ways of Looking at Crip Time', *Disability Studies Quarterly*, Vol. 37, No. 3, 2017.

'not just expanded . . .', Alison Kafer, *Feminist, Queer, Crip* (Indiana: Indiana University Press, 2013).

'It's not limited . . .', Anne Helen Petersen, 'How Millennials Became The Burnout Generation', *Buzzfeed News*, 5 January 2019.

'Right there is . . .', Joan Didion, *The White Album* (London: Fourth Estate, 2017).

'choosing a lifestyle', Emma Gannon, *The Multi-Hyphen Method* (London: Hodder & Stoughton, 2018).

'always filmed from . . .', Ione Gamble, 'My Chronic Illness Makes My Bed a Haven – and a Prison', *VICE*, 1 November 2019.

'over half of . . .', according to a report by the Trades Union Congress, 'Disabled workers' experiences during the pandemic', www.tuc.org.uk/sites/default/files/2021-06/Outline%20Report%20-%20Covid-19%20and%20Disabled%20Workers.pdf.

'33 per cent . . .', according to a report by the charity Leonard Cheshire 'Locked Out of The Labour Market', www.leonardcheshire.org/sites/default/files/2020-10/Locked-out-of-labour-market.pdf.

'half of those . . .', Trades Union Congress, op. cit.

'48 per cent . . .', according to a report by Citizens Advice, 'An Unequal Crisis – Why workers need better enforcement of their rights', 2020.

'unworkable for so . . .', Marsha De Cordova quoted in John Pring, 'Access to Work: 'Scheme's future in jeopardy through cuts and incompetence', *Disability News Service*, 26 October 2017.

'non-disabled colleagues react . . .', Mary E. Mclaughlin, et al., 'Stigma and Acceptance of Persons with Disabilities: Understudied Aspects of Workforce Diversity', *Group & Organization Management*, Vol. 29, No. 3, June 2004.

'We only focus . . .', Diane Cheung quoted in Lucy Abbersteen, 'Inside the Soap Co, the beauty brand with an 80% blind or disabled workforce', *MarieClaire.co.uk*, 19 December 2019.

'9 per cent . . .', according to data from LVMH, https://www.lvmh.com/group/lvmh-commitments/ social-environmental-responsibility/lvmh-disability-inclusion/.

'There is no . . .', Al Etmanski, *The Power of Disability: Ten Lessons for Surviving, Thriving, and Changing the World* (UK: Penguin Random House, 2020).